C000146304

"Corporate Combat provides a rich and fertile array of interesting ideas. Mr Skellon has given us an eminently useful combination of lessons from military history and current business trends. A 'must read' book for modern executives who want to compete effectively."

Donald G. Krause, author of the bestselling
Art of War for Executives

CORPORATE COMBAT

THE ART OF MARKET WARFARE ON THE BUSINESS BATTLEFIELD

NICK SKELLON

NICHOLAS BREALEY
PUBLISHING

LONDON

First published by
Nicholas Brealey Publishing Limited in 1999

36 John Street
London
WC1N 2AT, UK
Tel: +44 (0)171 430 0224
Fax: +44 (0)171 404 8311

1163 E. Ogden Avenue, Suite 705-229
Naperville
IL 60563-8535, USA
Tel: (888) BREALEY
Fax: (630) 428 3442

http://www.nbrealey-books.com

© Nick Skellon 1999
The right of Nick Skellon to be identified as the author of this
work has been asserted in accordance with the Copyright, Designs
and Patents Act 1988.

ISBN 1-85788-251-2

British Library Cataloguing in Publication Data
A catalogue record for this book is available from the
British Library.

Library of Congress Cataloging-in-Publication Data
Skellon, Nick.
  Corporate combat : the art of market warfare on the business
battlefield / Nick Skellon.
      p. cm.
  Includes index.
  ISBN 1-85788-251-2
  1. Industrial management. 2. Competition. 3. Strategic planning.
4. Military art and science.   I. Title.
HD31.S572 2000
658--dc21   99-42548
                                                                CIP

Printed in Finland by WSOY.

CONTENTS

Theory exists so one does not have to start afresh every time sorting out the raw material and ploughing through it, but will find it ready to hand and in good order. It is meant to educate the mind of the future commander, or, more accurately, to guide him in his self-education; not accompany him to the battlefield.

Carl Von Clausewitz

No study is possible on the battlefield; one does there simply what one can in order to apply what one knows. Therefore, in order to do even a little, one has already to know a great deal and know it well.

Field Marshal Ferdinand Foch

*And Caesar's spirit, raging for revenge,
With Ate by his side come hot from hell,
Shall in these confines with a monarch's voice
Cry 'Havoc!' and let slip the dogs of war.*

Julius Caesar, Act 3 Scene 1

War is capitalism with the gloves off.

Tom Stoppard

PREFACE

To find ways of winning on the business battlefield, organizations can do no better than look to military history to see how battles have been fought and won over the past 2500 years. By studying the campaigns of the 'great captains' and understanding the strategies that they pursued, managers can learn not only how to survive the hypercompetition of the twenty-first century, but also how to come out on top. Their shareholders and employees deserve no less.

This book is based on the premise that the three lessons underpinning success in warfare are directly transferable to obtaining competitive advantage, and that a thorough understanding of them will enable a company (large or small) to determine which of the four fundamental strategies that have been used in warfare for millennia is the right one for it to pursue. In expounding this, the book goes beyond theory and uses a unique combination of real military campaigns and commercial case studies to make its point.

A typical dictionary definition of war would be: 'A contest between nations and states, carried on with force, ... for the acquisition of territory, for obtaining and establishing the superiority and dominion of one over the other.'

If we replace the words 'nations and states' with 'companies', and 'territory' with 'customers', then merely by removing the reference to force we get what I feel is as accurate a description of commercial competition as any: 'A contest between companies for the acquisition of customers, for obtaining the superiority and dominion of one over the other.'

However, while war and the military can be great teachers, I would like to make clear that I in no way intend either to glorify war or to encourage companies to put their competition out of business. As a former soldier who spent a large part of his military service preparing to fight a defensive war against the former Soviet Union in the sure knowledge that it could not have been won without resorting to the use of nuclear weapons, I am in a strong position to attest that very few advocates of war are found in the ranks of the military. Professional soldiers know all too well the lethality of modern weapons and the anguish, death and destruction that any war (no matter how small) leaves in its wake. As the famous quotation goes, 'War is hell', and not many soldiers would disagree.

Neither is the book advocating a return to the tradition of a hierarchical command-and-control management style. While companies can learn much from the military in terms of accountability and management by objective, today's competitive environment is far too fast moving to adopt any system that does not encourage flexibility, initiative and empowerment.

A company's competitive strategy should be the cornerstone of everything it does, the foundations on which it builds everything else. Unless it is adding value to its customers better, or faster or cheaper (or all three) than its competitors, many would argue that a company deserves to go out of business. In that way the better companies thrive and the customer benefits.

1

CORPORATE COMBAT, MARKET WARFARE

MOST OF US ALREADY USE THE LANGUAGE OF THE MILITARY. We have all heard of the 'burger war' between McDonald's and Burger King, the 'cola war' between Coke and Pepsi, the 'browser war' between Microsoft and Netscape or even (in the US) the 'book war' between the chains and the independents.

Every company talks from time to time of 'defending its market share', 'going on the offensive', 'attacking the opposition' or 'digging in'. We all have 'war stories' that we love to tell, especially about our time 'in the trenches'.

What this book dares recommend is that companies operating in competitive markets should go one step further, and use not only the language but the *lessons* taught us by a study of warfare over the past 2500 years.

I first became aware of the incredible similarities between military and competitive strategies not long after leaving the British army and joining the world of commerce, and came to the conclusion that the principles underlying both are (or should be) exactly the same.

Nearly 20 years later, I now spend my time as a full-time consultant helping companies in competitive markets with their strategies and observing others around the world, and the relationship between the two is continually reinforced in my mind.

Look in 20 different marketing textbooks and the chances are that you will find 10 different definitions of the subject. Having said that, the differences would probably be fairly minor and most of them would say something like:

Marketing is concerned with the profitable creation, identification and satisfaction of customer needs.

However, just as it would be extremely difficult to find a definition that did not contain the concept of 'satisfying the customer' in some form or other, it would be almost as difficult to find one that made any reference to the *competition*. Over the years I have had dozens (if not scores) of marketing plans presented to me, and the majority of first drafts hardly mentioned this most important of factors.

It is almost as if such plans have stamped on their front cover the main competitor's logo in a red circle with a red diagonal line through it, together with the words: 'This is a competitor-free zone.' Perhaps added to this could have been the rider: 'not because we believe that they have no activity planned of their own, or that they will sit idly by and allow us to steal their market share, but because it is a lot easier to write the plan that way.'

You might think this facetious, but I write it in all seriousness. Plans that talk about brand *x* increasing its share from 14 to 15 percent of the market usually (if not invariably) fail to state from which competitor this extra share is going to come. When questioned, the manager in question will defend such negligence by saying that it is impossible to be that specific, as it is not known what activity is going to take place on individual competitor brands. This is missing the point entirely.

The crime is not in failing to have the competition's plans in that kind of detail, but in failing to acknowledge that such activity will take place. In the real world (i.e. the one outside brand or strategic plans), millions of pounds can be spent by various companies that own competing brands, only for the net share gains of one or two of them to be in the region of 0.5–1 percent.

Obviously, in large markets even a small share gain such as this can be significant in terms of profits, but the fact remains that it is not usually what was written as an objective in the plan at the beginning of the year. Most activity is simply balanced off by similar actions from the competition.

This does not have to be the case, however. There are many examples in this book of organizations that have been incredibly successful in stealing share from their competition. But they are invariably companies that begin their planning with a thorough analysis of what their competitors are likely to do, and then identify how they can stay one step ahead of them.

Not to begin planning in this way is like a professional boxer answering a question about his defensive tactics for a fight by saying: 'I haven't really thought about it; I was sort of hoping he wouldn't hit me back.' It's like the manager of the England soccer team not bothering to watch videos of other international sides before playing them in the World Cup, or the coach of an NFL team not studying a Superbowl opponent before playing them. It wouldn't happen in professional sport, and it wouldn't happen in the armed forces.

Can you imagine a general planning a battle without getting in advance as much intelligence as he possibly could about his enemy's strategy and tactics? Officer cadets at Sandhurst, West Point, St. Cyr and other military academies around the world are taught that when making what they term a 'combat appreciation', the starting point is *always* the enemy.

What is his strength? What is the composition of his troops? How much artillery support does he have? Is he likely to fight defensively or offensively? What is his overall strategy? What are his usual tactics? How has he fought battles in the past? What weapons system does he have that you do not? What are his specific objectives? What are his strengths and weaknesses? And so on.

Carl von Clausewitz, a nineteenth-century Austrian officer who fought in the Napoleonic wars and is regarded by many as the 'father' of western military strategic thought, wrote in his classic book *On War*:

> War ... is not the action of a living force upon a lifeless mass, ... but always the collision of living forces.

And Field Marshal Montgomery said during the Normandy campaign in the Second World War:

> *Battle is not a one-sided affair. It is a case of action and reciprocal action repeated over and over again as contestants seek to gain position and other advantage by which they may inflict the greatest possible damage upon their respective opponents.*

In other words, the enemy fights back! This is the reason that military strategists concentrate on them above all else; because they recognize that while they are planning to defeat the enemy, that same enemy is planning to defeat them.

Field Marshal Helmuth Von Moltke, the German Chief-of-Staff at the time of the Franco-Prussian War of 1870, was of the opinion that 'No battle plan survives contact with the enemy', and Sun Tzu, a Chinese strategist who wrote *The Art of War* several centuries before the birth of Christ, said:

> *Know the enemy and know yourself, and in a hundred battles you will never be defeated; when you are ignorant of the enemy but know yourself, your chances of winning or losing are equal; if you are ignorant of both your enemy and yourself, you are certain to be defeated.*

Competitive strategy should be approached in the same way, but it normally isn't.

Most organizations prefer to spend their time in corporate navel gazing, concentrating on *their* strength, *their* plans and objectives, *their* quality, *their* service levels, *their* salesforce, *their* promotional activity etc., etc. I have even heard directors of major companies say things like: 'I don't intend to worry about the competition; I want them to worry about us.'

I suggest that if you work for an organization whose directors make facile comments like that, you should start preparing a new CV straight away. Companies that operate in an imaginary competitor-free zone are not destined to be around for long.

Readers will be all too familiar with the depressing regularity of articles in the financial press about 'great' companies (Shell, Sainsbury, Marks & Spencer, Boeing, ICI, Nike, British Airways) whose performance has stagnated or started to decline. Some of these companies act as if their financial performance will automatically improve year after year according to some kind of immutable law. No matter how big or established or loved it is, no company has an inviolable right even to existence, never mind to ever-increasing sales and profits.

Most of the companies in question have lost sight of a very basic fundamental, i.e. that they do not operate in a competitor vacuum and that their continued existence (let alone their ability to grow) is conditional on whether they can add value to their customers better or cheaper than can the competition.

It should be noted, however, that while I recommend becoming a keen observer of the competition, I do not mean slavishly imitating them. Smaller companies often fall into the trap of thinking that because the market leader doesn't do something in a certain way, that way must be wrong (or vice versa), as if they had a monopoly on good ideas. In contrast, following its capture of the number one position in the UK grocery market from Sainsbury, Tesco stated that it only did so because it stopped concentrating on its rival and started focusing on the customer instead.

What is important is not to *copy* the competition, but to identify what it is that they do that makes them successful and develop a strategy to do the same thing differently, or better, in a way that adds even greater value for the customer.

THE THREE LESSONS OF WARFARE

Even a cursory study of military history shows that there are certain lessons that have been learned and relearned, war after war. Weapons and the tactics and methods of using them on the battlefield have changed, but these basic lessons have remained constant and apply to battles fought in antiquity as well as to those in the twentieth century.

Before we get on to the lessons, there are two qualifications to this. First, wars can occasionally be won because one side runs out of either financial resources or simply the will to carry on; the best examples of the latter being the French and the Americans in Vietnam. In both the Indochina and Vietnam wars, neither country could be said to have been defeated militarily, but politicians lost the will to continue due to public opposition.

Secondly, there is always the simple matter of incompetence. The military has had as many incompetents as any other profession, and it should not be assumed that just because someone rose to command entire armies that they possessed any measure of ability. On many occasions the 'Peter Principle' has applied, where commanders were promoted to their level of incompetence.

Some military commanders have actually been insane, such as the commander of the Prussians at Waterloo, Field Marshal von Blücher, who was convinced that he had been impregnated with a baby elephant by a French soldier. Likewise, the Confederate general Ricard S Ewell occasionally believed that he was a bird; and the Greek general Hajianestis believed that his legs were made of glass and would sometimes refuse to get of bed in case they shattered.

Others have just been stupid. Ordered in 1916 to defend Fort Douaumont at Verdun to the last man, the French general Chrétien went on leave and forgot to pass the order on to anyone else, with the result that when the fort was attacked it was defended by only 56 men. A lone German sergeant climbed the wall and roamed the interior at will, taking the occupants prisoner as he found them. The official French government line was that it had cost the Germans thousands of lives to take it. In the campaign of 1805, the Austrian planners forgot to take into account that there was a 10-day difference between the Russian calendar and their own, with the result that the Russians were late for the planned rendezvous between the two armies and Napoleon was able to pick them off one at a time.

However, these reservations apply only to a minority of battles or campaigns. History shows that there have been three main reasons that certain armies and generals have been more successful than others, sometimes repeatedly so. They have all tended to possess one or more of the following assets:

❑ a SWAT (superior weapons and tactics system)
❑ a high force:space ratio
❑ a strong defensive position.

Possessing a 'SWAT'

The first and most important lesson is that any strategy (even an incorrect one) stands a far greater chance of success if you possess a superior weapons and tactics system (SWAT), because possession of one can simply outweigh any other advantage that the enemy might have.

An extreme example is the Battle of Omdurman in 1898, where British troops possessing six maxim machine guns avenged the death of General Gordon at Khartoum by massacring an attacking Dervish army. The casualties were 28 British dead versus 11,000 Dervishes. This clearly shows that if a weapons system is superior enough, it can negate virtually any numerical superiority that an enemy may possess.

A SWAT can be weapons based, in that one side in a conflict can have a monopoly of possession, but such monopolies tend to be short lived and do not generally last more than one war. Possession of the atom bomb gave the US an unanswerable advantage in 1945, for example, but its enemies soon developed their own, resulting in the stand-off known as the Cold War.

A SWAT is more usually dominant because of a *combination* of the weapons and the tactics used to deploy them, and/or the organization of the troops involved. Until the introduction of nuclear weapons, it can be argued that no new weapon has had a significant long-term influence on warfare without being accompanied by new tactics that facilitated its use:

❑ The Macedonian *sarissa* was longer and more lethal than any contemporary pike, but only in the hands of the highly trained and incredibly disciplined phalanx of Alexander the Great's foot companions. To any of his enemies, its length would have been a hindrance rather than an advantage.

❏ Likewise, the Roman *gladium*, a short, heavy sword designed for stabbing, was only a superior weapon when used by the organized and flexible Roman legions.

❏ It was not possession of tanks and other mechanized armored vehicles that made the German Army of 1940 unstoppable (a little-known fact is that the combined French and British armies actually had more of them), but the way they were used, i.e. the *blitzkrieg* combination of speed and concentration *en masse* at selected points.

❏ In terms of weapons *per se*, the French army in Indochina (and its American successor in Vietnam) had a vast technological superiority over its Vietminh opponents, but it was eventually defeated because the latter's guerrilla tactics were superior in mountainous jungle terrain.

It can safely be argued that as much as their ability as strategists or tacticians, it was their combination of weapons and tactics in creating a superior SWAT that enabled the 'great captains' to be so repeatedly successful.

Alexander the Great had the world's first combined-arms army, Scipio and Caesar the Roman legion, Frederick the Great the superbly trained and disciplined Prussian army attacking in oblique order and Napoleon the revolutionary French system of highly mobile *corps* acting almost as mini-armies in their own right. All of them defeated more numerous opponents on several occasions due to the fact that the forces they commanded were quite simply better than those of their enemies.

Possession of a SWAT is so crucial that Part II is given over to looking at the subject, explaining not only how three military SWATs (Alexander the Great's combined-arms army, the Roman legion and the English longbow) defeated the others in existence at the time, but also how companies can develop commercial equivalents.

DEVELOPING A COMPETITIVE *SWAT*

There are three main routes to developing a competitive SWAT (often referred to as a competitive advantage), and the choice of one or more of these is essential if a company finds itself fighting a larger competitor or one in a strongly entrenched defensive position (or worse still, both!):

- ❏ low-cost leadership
- ❏ differentiation
- ❏ focus.

Companies that have effectively followed the route of 'low-cost leadership' have succeeded not just by cutting costs, but by structuring their companies so that they simply do not have the costs that their more traditional competitors take for granted. They then pass these savings on to their customers, thereby seriously undercutting the opposition while still remaining very profitable. To use some examples dealt with in more detail elsewhere in the book:

- ❏ Dell Computer has eliminated the need for the resellers that all major PC manufacturers have viewed as essential by selling direct to its customers and cutting out the middleman. In doing this and also making its PCs to order, it has eliminated not only the need for a reseller's margin, but also the huge inventory levels endemic in the industry, enabling it to sell its product at a significant discount. This, backed by uncompromising service levels, has made it the fastest-growing company in its industry.
- ❏ First Direct Bank and Direct Line both introduced a completely new model to the UK banking and insurance industries by dealing with consumers direct over the telephone, to the extent that most of their more traditional competitors have had to imitate them to prevent a significant loss of business.
- ❏ EasyJet, Debonair and a variety of other low-cost, no-frills airlines have offered the public short-haul flights at an incredible

discount compared to existing airlines by stripping out everything but the most essential costs.

The second route, differentiation, concerns being different from the
competition in a way that adds value to the customer and is sustainable. Provided that these two prerequisites are met, virtually anything
can be a source of differentiation. Some examples from later chapters:

❑ Dyson took the UK vacuum-cleaner market by storm with a
product that was quite simply better than that of its competitors
and gained over 50 percent of the market within a few years
(although its product was up to twice as expensive as competitors'). It should be noted, however, that the advantages gained by
having a superior product are usually short lived, and the life of
that advantage is getting shorter and shorter. No matter how
superior you may feel your product is, somewhere one of your
competitors has something better on the drawing board (as I
write, Electrolux has introduced its own 'bagless' cleaner, with
the added advantage of not requiring filters). James Dyson rec-
ognizes this and has also introduced service levels unheard of in
the industry as a defense against the arrival of an even better
competitive product.

❑ Vision Express enjoyed meteoric growth in the optician market
using speed and convenience as a differentiator by offering the
revolutionary service of being able to get a pair of spectacles
made within one hour of a prescription being agreed.

❑ Snap-On Tools has experienced extraordinary success in the US
by producing tools of exceptionally high quality (it is the 'Rolls-
Royce' of its industry) for professional auto mechanics and then
selling directly to them on a weekly basis via a fleet of trucks,
backed up with easy credit terms.

❑ Amazon.com has revolutionized the book trade by selling to consumers via the Internet (avoiding the cost of bricks-and-mortar
shops and duplicated inventories) and has become the biggest
bookshop in the world by doing so.

The third route is focus, where a company chooses to specialize in one particular sector of a market and in doing so satisfy customer needs better or cheaper than its mass-market competitors. Some more examples discussed elsewhere:

❑ Jan Carlzon turned Scandinavian Air Services (SAS) around by concentrating on business travelers above everything else, and structuring the company's services around their needs rather than any other type of passenger.

❑ Enterprise Rent-A-Car chose to deal only in the auto replacement market, and was able to meet the insurance companies' demands for very low prices, and still make a profit because its cost structure was so much lower than the likes of Hertz or Avis.

❑ Holiday Autos has specialized in providing rental cars to tourists traveling abroad and, like Enterprise, has avoided the bigger, more lucrative business rental market.

❑ Snap-On Tools has consciously chosen only to deal with professional auto repairers and body shops, and has deliberately avoided being side-tracked into the massive (and potentially very profitable) home DIY market.

POSSESSING A HIGH FORCE:SPACE RATIO

So the importance of a SWAT is the first lesson of warfare. But in many military campaigns neither army has possessed a SWAT, either because the introduction of new weapons and tactics was quickly imitated by an army's opponents, or because the military commanders of the time lacked either the creativity or the technological innovation to create one.

When this has been the case, victory has usually been due to the possession of one of two other assets. The first of these is a high force:space ratio. All of the great theorists on military strategy have agreed that numerical superiority is critically important. Clausewitz even thought that it was the most important factor in determining success or failure, writing that:

Superiority of numbers is in tactics, as well as strategy, the most essential principle of victory.

He even stated (in the mid-nineteenth century) that he had studied all the battles of recorded military history and that in only three had a force outnumbered by more than two to one been victorious.

However, what is crucial is not just numbers *per se*, but the *concentration* of force to dominate a particular area and produce what I call a high force:space ratio. Many smaller armies have been successful because their commanders have concentrated their force so that while they were numerically inferior overall, they were numerically superior at one important part of the battlefield.

Much of strategy is therefore concerned with forcing the enemy to give battle at a time and place when he is inferior in numbers, and tactics with the concentration of force on the battlefield so as to obtain a local superiority at one specific point.

The same is true in commerce. All things being equal, the biggest company or brand will win, for four main reasons.

First, there is an overwhelming tendency on the part of both customers and consumers to believe that the biggest must automatically be the best, and that size itself is an indicator of quality and value. Being the biggest normally translates into greater brand awareness, and people tend to think that if the company weren't the best, it wouldn't have become the biggest in the first place, would it? This is why people automatically choose brand leaders if they are ignorant about a particular product or service.

The second and often most important reason from a competitive strategy point of view is that bigger companies tend to have deeper pockets than small ones. Possessing greater resources does not automatically go hand in hand with a willingness to use them, but it does mean that the ammunition exists if the larger company does have the will.

While it is a simple matter to think of examples of large companies that have been usurped/decimated by smaller ones (the most commonly used ones being IBM or the 'Big Three' auto manufacturers in the US), they are usually organizations that did not start to fight back until it was too late. IBM could probably have strangled any of the small PC manufacturers at birth if it had wanted to, by pouring more resources into PCs itself (it is generally not realized that IBM launched the first PC, in 1971), but it held back because it saw the PC as a threat to its profitable mainframe business.

When a large company decides that 'enough is enough' and that it is going to defend itself against attack from a smaller competitor, watch out! The study of how Microsoft trampled on Netscape once it regarded it as a real threat demonstrates the dangers of taking on an industry giant 'head on', even if the attacking company itself is a significant player in the market.

The third reason is the 'law of increasing returns', in which size in some industries generates an unstoppable momentum where the big simply get bigger. This is most prevalent in the software industry, the best example being Microsoft's Windows operating system that has become an industry standard, virtually making it impossible for anyone else to get a foot in the door.

The fourth reason, and why most companies have traditionally aimed for significant market share as a key objective, is economies of scale – the main key to profitability in some industries.

An important point to note, however, is that companies do not need to be bigger than their competitors in order to take advantage of the above. Whereas most organizations spread themselves thinly across a whole market or series of markets, many of the most successful concentrate their resources on one particular segment of the market and dominate it with a high force:space ratio. In this way they can be the biggest player in their chosen part of the market, even if they are not the biggest overall.

POSSESSING A STRONG DEFENSIVE POSITION

The third lesson of warfare is that all other things being equal, the force fighting defensively will win.

However, it should be noted that this applies to battles rather than wars. While Clausewitz wrote: 'The defensive form of warfare is in itself stronger than the offensive', he was also of the view that:

> *A mere parrying of a blow is something quite contradictory to the con-*
> *cept of war. A swift and vigorous assumption of the offensive – the*
> *flashing sword of vengeance – is the most brilliant point in the*
> *defensive.*

Sun Tzu was of the same mind when he wrote: 'Invincibility lies in the defense; the possibility of victory in the attack.' What both were saying was that defense could win you a battle, but very rarely a war. To win a war, armies invariably need to act offensively.

For example, the Soviet Red Army did not stop at chasing the Nazis from Russian soil, but continued until they were in the heart of Berlin. And the British 8th Army (the 'Desert Rats') could never have defeated the Afrika Korps under General Rommel purely by fighting defensively at Tobruk. It needed the offensive victory at El Alamein (and several others) to do that.

It is generally accepted in military circles around the globe that where an attacking force does not have a SWAT, it needs a superiority of about 3:1 in order to cancel out the automatic advantage that being on the defensive gives.

If the two sides are similarly trained and equipped, then without a significant numerical advantage attacking armies can throw themselves against prepared defenses again and again, without success, until they eventually run out of steam. The reasons for this are threefold:

❏ The defense has usually chosen the battleground.
❏ The defense can strengthen its position with fortifications.
❏ The defense usually only has to concentrate on firing, as opposed to moving and firing, giving it a faster and more effective rate of fire.

Anyone who doubts the truth of this principle need only look at the First World War, when the mass introduction of the machine gun led to the power of the defense reaching its zenith at such battles as Mons, Ypres, the Somme and Passchendale.

The tactical power of the defense has meant that numerically inferior armies have usually sought to assume the defensive, and have often refused battle unless this could be assured. Whole wars and even periods (such as fifteenth-century Italy) have been characterized by the avoidance of battle unless it could be fought on acceptable terms, with armies simply refusing to fight unless they could do so defensively. This is not always the case, however; remember that possession of a SWAT can make numerical inferiority irrelevant.

The power of a strong defensive position also applies to commerce. Companies and brands that are well established in their respective markets are incredibly difficult to dislodge. If we ignore high-tech industries (such as the computer industry) that have not been around for very long, and study those in which a comparison can be made (such as consumer goods) between now and 20 or even 50 years ago, it is immediately obvious how little has changed.

Thousands upon thousands of new consumer products are launched each year, many with marketing spends behind them of tens of millions, and about 90 percent of them fail. They are either taken off the market after a few years or end up among the plethora of 'me-too' brands littering most markets, with a brand share and volume that make it worthwhile to keep producing them but that are far, far below the ambitious objectives set for them at launch.

If we look at the UK's top 50 brands through grocers, as measured by AC Nielsen, the point is made even more strongly. Four of them were launched when Queen Victoria was still on the throne, 16 between 1905 and 1950, 21 between 1950 and 1975, and 9 since 1975. Yet all operate in competitive markets, all have faced severe competitive pressure, and all are still around!

Attacking a larger company that is also well established in a particular market sector without a SWAT is tantamount to commercial suicide, but the financial press is full of examples of small companies that proudly trumpet their intention to try.

APPLYING THE THREE LESSONS TO YOUR STRATEGY

Every military campaign in history (whether we take Alexander the Great's invasion of Persia, Hannibal's invasion of Italy, Edward III's 'invasions' of France during the Hundred Years' War, Napoleon's various conquests of Europe, the stalemate on the Western Front in the First World War, the German invasion of France in 1940, the U-Boat campaign in the Atlantic, the recent NATO bombing of Kosovo or any other) can be categorized as following one of four basic strategies, which are further explained in depth in Part III. Each of these is more applicable and 'correct' than the other three, depending on different circumstances.

These same four strategies are equally applicable to commerce, and the decision on which of them to pursue is the most important choice a company can make.

Before going any further, however, I need to explain the difference between strategy and tactics, as the two are often confused. 'Strategy' determines the broad plan for the conduct of the war, integrating military means with the state's overall political objectives, and is concerned with the concentration and maneuver of military forces, usually to create the conditions for battle. 'Tactics' are concerned with maneuver, movement and combat on the battlefield itself.

William Seymour, in *Decisive Factors in Twenty Great Battles of the World*, sums it up as follows:

> ... strategy [is] the art of bringing the enemy to battle on the most advantageous terms; it decides the time, the place and the numbers with which the battle will be fought. Having committed the enemy to the fight, tactics have been the ways and means of defeating him.

Understanding the difference between the two is crucial. When most companies talk about 'strategy' they are really speaking either of tactical issues (such as advertising or sales campaigns, or individual features of their products or service) or vague 'aims' (e.g. 'to be the number one in the market'), unaccompanied by any clear vision of how to achieve them.

These tactical issues are merely the 'icing on the cake'. The cake itself (i.e. the strategy) is a carefully considered vision of where the company wants to go and how it is going to get there, based on a

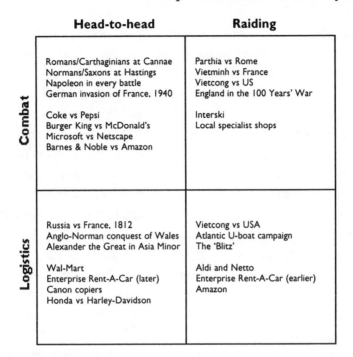

	Head-to-head	Raiding
Combat	Romans/Carthaginians at Cannae Normans/Saxons at Hastings Napoleon in every battle German invasion of France, 1940 Coke vs Pepsi Burger King vs McDonald's Microsoft vs Netscape Barnes & Noble vs Amazon	Parthia vs Rome Vietminh vs France Vietcong vs US England in the 100 Years' War Interski Local specialist shops
Logistics	Russia vs France, 1812 Anglo-Norman conquest of Wales Alexander the Great in Asia Minor Wal-Mart Enterprise Rent-A-Car (later) Canon copiers Honda vs Harley-Davidson	Vietcong vs USA Atlantic U-boat campaign The 'Blitz' Aldi and Netto Enterprise Rent-A-Car (earlier) Amazon

Figure 1 The market warfare matrix

thorough understanding of its objectives and the most efficient and practical way of achieving them. This in turn will depend to a great extent on the competition's objectives and the company's strength and size relative to competitors.

Relative strength and size are probably the most important factors, in that the amount of force a company has and its relationship to the size of the area it is operating in (the force:space ratio) may immediately make certain of its options impractical.

The main choice lies between following a **head-to-head** or **raiding** strategy, i.e. whether to attack the enemy straight on or do so indirectly. The second choice that then needs to be made is whether it is to be a **combat** or **logistics** strategy, i.e. whether you will attack the enemy's forces or its resources. These four basic choices are shown in Figure 1, together with military and business examples discussed in detail elsewhere in the book.

Occasionally someone will criticize a comparison of military and competitive strategies as inappropriate because warfare aims at the complete defeat or even destruction of the enemy, and this rarely happens in competitive strategy; most commercial 'victories' are short term and tactical in nature.

Such critics display an ignorance of military history. This is understandable, as most people's knowledge is based on famous battles that were decisive in that one side achieved a crushing defeat of the other (such as Hastings, Agincourt, Gettysburg or Waterloo). The reality is that most battles have been *indecisive* in nature, in that although there might have been a clearly identifiable victory, either the defeated forces were allowed to escape to fight another day or it did little to hasten the end of the war.

In most wars victory is achieved via an accumulation of tactical successes and a gradual attrition of one side's manpower, military equipment, food and financial resources, rather than by the delivery of a decisive 'knock-out blow' aimed at the destruction or annihilation of the enemy.

Another reason that wars have often appeared to be inconclusive is that not all are fought with the objective of fighting 'decisive' battles. The military commander has always had a variety of strategies available, and an examination of these shows strong similarities with the choices available to the commercial strategist. These basic strategies are examined in detail in Chapters 8 to 10, with both military and commercial examples, but it is worth looking at each in outline here.

HEAD-TO-HEAD STRATEGIES

A head-to-head combat strategy aims at the decisive defeat of the enemy forces, and the precipitation of a major battle (or battles) in which this can be achieved therefore becomes a significant objective.

The most famous battles of history have usually occurred when both sides have followed this type of strategy and have been determined to fight a decisive military encounter. To give a few well-known examples, Napoleon adopted this strategy in virtually every campaign, which resulted in most of the great battles of the Napoleonic era, such as Austerlitz, Jena and Waterloo. Likewise, both Normans and Saxons wanted battle in 1066, the result being

Hastings; the majority of the battles of the American Civil War would also fall into this category.

The commercial equivalent of a **head-to-head combat** strategy occurs when two or more companies decide to 'slug it out' in the marketplace like two boxers.

Usually these are 'wars' between the number one in the marketplace and a strong number two, where each basically offers the same product or service but attempts to do it better than the competition. It is also the most common strategy because it is the simplest to adopt. However, unless a company is a strong number two (or perhaps three) or has a demonstrably better SWAT than its larger competitors, it is usually commercial suicide. Unless one of these two preconditions exists, a strategy based on taking on a much larger competitor 'at its own game' is virtually doomed to failure.

It should not be assumed, however, that military commanders always have as their objective the destruction of the enemy's army; very often the main objective of a war has been a bloodless seizure of territory or the forcing of the enemy to the negotiating table without having to fight a major battle. A **head-to-head logistics** strategy is aimed at the wholesale destruction or capture of enemy resources, thus preventing them from being available to the enemy and hastening the end of hostilities.

Defensively, it involves a 'scorched earth' policy where the defensive army retreats, burning and destroying anything that might be of use to the invaders, leaving a wasteland behind them. For most of history invading armies have had to live off the land, and this strategy has at times been devastatingly successful. Although the Russian army fought three major battles with the French invaders in 1812 at Smolensk, Borodino and Maloyaroslavets, it was a lack of supplies caused by the Russians' **head-to-head logistics** strategy rather than defeat on the battlefield that eventually forced Napoleon to retreat to France.

Offensively, this strategy involves the piecemeal conquest of territory area by area, gradually capturing land, food, population, troops, tax revenue and other supplies and thus diminishing the enemy's resources and capacity to fight. It is usually adopted by an army that is failing to succeed with a **head-to-head combat** strategy because its enemy adopts a **raiding** one and refuses to accommodate its wishes by meeting it on the field of battle.

A perfect example of this is the Anglo-Norman conquest of Wales, where the Welsh refused to give battle and instead fought an early form of guerrilla warfare based on raids and harassment. The response was to take the country valley by valley, never moving on to the next until the previous one had been garrisoned and pacified. As this involved the building of numerous castles, it was a slow process and took several centuries to complete.

Just as an army cannot survive without food, companies cannot survive without customers. They are the biggest and most important resource, and the commercial equivalent of a **head-to-head logistics** strategy is the conquest of a market or market sector region by region. Adopting this strategy, companies concentrate on one geographic region at a time and wait until its domination has been achieved before moving on to another.

In the late 1970s and early 1980s, Canon adopted this strategy against Rank Xerox. Rather than enter the UK 'across the board', it concentrated all of its resources in Scotland, achieving local superiority, and waited until it had achieved about 40 percent of the Scottish market before it moved on to attack tightly defined regions in England. Its market share grew steadily until it eventually 'attacked' London with a (by now) much bigger salesforce than Rank Xerox could muster.

The strategy was also adopted initially by Wal-Mart in its expansion across the US. Aiming solely at rural towns that were ignored by its larger competitors (which preferred larger catchment areas), it picked areas that were small enough for it to dominate. This domination created a barrier to entry by preventing the later arrival of competition, as the populations were not large enough to sustain two large stores. The company then expanded rapidly but in tightly defined geographic areas, which allowed it to link its branches in the famous Wal-Mart 'hub-and-spoke' distribution network. This in turn enabled it to achieve economies of scale, which enabled it to reduce prices, thus further cementing its hold on the market.

RAIDING STRATEGIES

Raiding strategies are normally pursued by armies that are at a numerical disadvantage and would stand little chance of fighting an open battle, or that lack a sufficient force:space ratio to be able to capitalize on a battlefield victory if one were achieved.

A raiding combat strategy is aimed at the enemy's forces, but is confined to raids, harassment, minor encounters and the specific avoidance of a pitched battle. It is more often than not a defensive strategy, adopted by a small defending army against a larger attacking one, such as the Persians against the Roman invasion in 359. For much of this campaign the Persians simply refused to give battle and avoided the Roman army, while continually harassing it on the march. Even when it was forced into battle the Persian army was not destroyed, and the Romans found themselves far from home in a desolate foreign land without any supplies; much like the French in Russia in 1812. Eventually the Romans were forced to negotiate a humiliating settlement with the Persians and return home with their tails between their legs.

However, this strategy can also be offensive in nature, one of the best examples being the English strategy during the Hundred Years' War. During this war, the Plantagenet kings' stated aim was the throne of France (to which they felt they had a legitimate claim) and they repeatedly invaded France with forces that were never large enough to conquer the country, given the huge geography involved. Although pitched battles were fought when the French reacted, at Sluys, Crecy, Poitiers and Agincourt, this low force:space ratio meant that each 'invasion' was really nothing more than a large-scale raid, resulting in great devastation of French territory and resources, the capture of booty and the gain of minor temporary territorial concessions.

Guerrilla warfare is another perfect offensive example, where small forces adopt 'hit-and-run' tactics, attacking wherever they sense weakness but withdrawing whenever they encounter strength. It is for this reason that I do not treat guerrilla warfare as a separate strategy in this book. Although there are a plethora of books on the market about 'guerrilla marketing' for small businesses, this is simply a raiding strategy implemented on a micro scale.

The fourth option is a raiding logistics strategy. Like raiding combat this involves raids and harassment, but this time aimed at the enemy's resources rather than its troops.

In the various wars between the city-states of ancient Greece, the objective of the attacking force was often to destroy its enemy's crops to force it to the negotiating table, rather than the defeat of its military forces. More modern examples would be the German U-Boat campaign in the Second World War, aimed at the destruction of Britain's Atlantic lifeline in an attempt to starve it into surrender, and the 'Blitz', focused on the destruction of the country's industrial capacity and morale.

Commercial raiding strategies are also usually adopted by companies that are inferior to their major competitors in size and that appreciate that they would stand little chance 'slugging it out' with them in a head-to-head strategy. The difference between the combat and logistics variants is in approach.

A commercial head-to-head combat strategy brings a company into direct competition with other companies in the marketplace for the same customers and business (such as Coke vs Pepsi or Burger King vs McDonald's). Those adopting a raiding combat strategy also compete directly with larger competitors, but do so within specific customers rather than 'across the board'.

Too small to take larger competitors on head to head, the combat raider carefully picks individual customers where it feels their position is weak, and concentrates all of its resources on attacking there. This concentration could be in the form of price reduction, or personalization of its services to suit the customer's individual needs in a way that the competition could not emulate. If the competition subsequently decides to 'retake' the customer by redeploying its own massive resources, the combat raider has to be ready to withdraw in order to fight elsewhere.

A raiding logistics strategy aims to deprive the competition of access to a customer completely by 'removing' it from the marketplace. A company does this by identifying and concentrating on a group of customers with a particular specialized need that it can satisfy better than the competition. Whereas a **head-to-head logistics** strategy aims at the piecemeal (normally region by region) 'conquest' of a large market, a **raiding logistics** strategy aims at the complete conquest of a sector of that market.

Many sectors of a marketplace are unattractive to larger companies for a variety of reasons, such as low volume, low profitability or high service level requirements. These same sectors can be extremely profitable to smaller companies, which can often have them almost to themselves and which they can eventually dominate.

Aldi and Netto have both followed this strategy in the grocery market across Europe and in the US by concentrating on extremely price-conscious customers with low levels of disposable income. These customers are 'unattractive' to the larger, more upmarket players (e.g. Tesco and Sainsbury in the UK), yet provide a profitable niche for Aldi and Netto because of their much lower cost base and willingness to accept lower margins.

WHICH STRATEGY IS RIGHT FOR YOU?

The three routes to developing a competitive SWAT have already been outlined in brief on page 9. When many companies (and academics) talk about strategic options, they refer to which of the three they have chosen to follow, i.e. whether to concentrate on differentiation, low-cost leadership or focus.

In my view such an approach is seriously flawed. While possession of a SWAT may significantly enhance a general's ability to pursue his chosen strategy, how he chooses to arm and equip his troops and use them tactically on the battlefield is not a strategy in itself.

The same is applicable to business. Possession of a competitive SWAT very often represents the difference between success and failure in the implementation of one of the four strategic options already outlined, but choosing between low-cost leadership, differentiation or focus as a route to achieving it is not a strategy *per se*.

The key choice has to be whether to adopt a **head-to-head combat, head-to-head logistics, raiding combat** or **raiding logistics** strategy, and in this choice the company's overall objectives (both long and medium term), its objectives and strategy and especially its size and force:space ratio (i.e. its size in relation to the size of the market) will be the key deciding factors.

Just as it would be foolish for any army lacking (a) a numerical superiority, (b) a SWAT that balanced this lack or (c) a strong defensive position to choose a **head-to-head combat** strategy, the same is true commercially. Only companies that (a) are market leaders or strong number twos or threes, (b) possess a competitive SWAT or (c) are defending a well-established market position should choose to pursue such a strategy.

Any company that does not possess at least one (but preferably more) of these three prerequisites is almost guaranteed to fail. Unfortunately, however, **head-to-head combat** strategies are the most common choice, regardless of the above. Sometimes this is because it is seen as the most macho thing to do, but generally it is because it is the most obvious and simplest strategy to pursue.

The lessons of numerical superiority and the tactical power of the defense are both timeless and accurate in business as well as in warfare. Big companies and those defending well-established positions have everything on their side.

While possession of a competitive SWAT alone can enable a small company to adopt a **head-to-head combat** strategy and be victorious against a larger competitor (as James Dyson's amazing success in the vacuum cleaner market demonstrates), a strategy more likely to be successful for such a company would be **head-to-head logistics**, as such an approach would enable it to focus its resources on one region at a time, thus achieving local superiority where it counts.

However, 95 out of 100 companies should pursue **raiding** strategies, because only a handful can (by definition) be market leaders or strong number twos or threes. Companies with expansionist plans or long-term dreams of market leadership may find this advice unwelcome, as they may feel it would condemn them to permanent niche status, but it need not remain their strategy forever.

Just as a military commander will change his strategy when circumstances demand or permit, so business strategists can change theirs as they grow and strengthen their market position and force:space ratio. The discussion of the various strategies of Alexander the Great in Part III clearly demonstrates this. Although his preferred strategy was head-to-head combat, he regularly switched between this and head-to-head logistics, depending on which would suit his long-term objectives best.

Likewise, the discussion of how the Vietminh defeated the French in Indochina shows how a raiding strategy of either type can be superseded by strategies of raiding logistics and finally head-to-head combat when circumstances allow.

The success of Enterprise Rent-A-Car shows how an initial raiding logistics strategy developed over time into a head-to-head one as the company gradually assumed market leadership; and that of Dell Computer in Chapter 11 shows how the company 'matured' from a strategy of raiding logistics via raiding combat to head-to-head combat.

In practice, many company 'strategies' are merely lists of aims and objectives and a series of action points, without any mention of the competition or what type of competitive advantage the company possesses. They are also based on a myriad of assumptions about the future in terms of inflation, exchange rates, price increases, costs and market growth that invariably prove to be inaccurate, and that are later used as justifications for the strategy's failure.

This approach, however common, is seriously flawed. A fundamental understanding of the competitive forces operating in a market, leading to the correct choice of one of the four options, will determine a company's success no matter what the economic variables turn out to be.

This book will give you advice on how to choose the strategy that is appropriate for your company at a particular point in time and how to develop a competitive SWAT that will facilitate its implementation, by learning from the great military commanders of the past 2500 years. The lessons are there to be learnt from history, and those who choose to ignore them are unnecessarily 'reinventing the wheel'.

It is my belief that a study of military strategy throughout the ages should be compulsory in all business schools and part of any

MBA, and that managers and aspiring managers would benefit immeasurably from this. The process of choosing how best to marshall the troops under one's control in order to defeat an enemy is exactly the same as that of deciding how to allocate commercial resources to defeat a competitor.

Napoleon made it clear that his own success was a direct result of the study of the great generals who had preceded him:

Read and reread the campaigns of Alexander, Hannibal, Caesar, Gustavus, Turenne, Eugene and Frederick. Make them your models. This is the only way to become a great general and to master the secrets of the art of war.

PART I

THE THREE MOST IMPORTANT LESSONS OF WARFARE

Part I outlines details of the three main lessons of warfare: a high force:space ratio; a strong defensive position; and a SWAT (superior weapons and tactics system).

Possession of a SWAT is undeniably the most important asset that an army or business can have, and Part II is therefore devoted to discussing SWATs in detail. Its significance is discussed in outline in Part I.

2

THE FORCE:SPACE RATIO

MAO TSE TUNG REGARDED NUMERICAL SUPERIORITY AS 'THE first and most essential condition' of battle, while Sun Tzu advised that 'if in all respects unequal, elude (the enemy), for a small force is but booty for one more powerful'. One of Napoleon's maxims was 'when an army is inferior in numbers, it is essential to avoid a general action'.

Clausewitz wrote:

> *If we ... strip the engagement of all the variables arising from its purpose and circumstances, and disregard the fighting value of the troops involved, we are left with the bare concept of the engagement ... in which the only distinguishing factor is the number of troops on either side. ... These numbers, therefore, will determine victory ... superiority of numbers in a given engagement is only one of the factors that determines victory [but] is the most important factor in the outcome ... so long as it is great enough to counterbalance all other contributing circumstances. This ... would hold true for Greeks and Persians, for Englishmen and Mahrattas, for Frenchmen and Germans.*

In other words, if two forces are equal in other respects, i.e. their skill and morale are equal, and neither has a SWAT, then nine times out of ten the one that is the largest will win!

BATTERING THE ENEMY INTO SUBMISSION: EL ALAMEIN, 1942

By 1942 the 'Desert War' had reached a stalemate. The German victories of 1941, including the taking of Tobruk, had been checked and Field Marshal Rommel's advance on Egypt had been halted. Rommel now faced a desperate supply situation, with his main supply base and port over 1000 miles away, and the British aimed a final knockout blow to destroy Axis hopes of victory for good.

The 38 miles of front at Alamein, where the two armies now faced each other, were anchored on natural obstacles on both sides, i.e. the Mediterranean to the north and the Qattara Depression to the south. Flanking attacks were therefore impractical and Lt General Montgomery planned to launch a frontal attack on the German positions, using his massive numerical superiority to break through in the north. He had almost complete control of the air, 1000 guns, outnumbered Rommel by two to one in men and tanks, and had more supplies.

However, the Germans and Italians had prepared formidable defenses with mines and booby traps up to five miles deep, and such an attack was bound to be costly. Montgomery planned to use massive artillery bombardment and a full-frontal infantry attack to clear these defenses, followed by an armored thrust to destroy what was left of the Axis armor.

Rommel could neither advance nor retreat for lack of fuel, and planned to 'soak up' the Allied attack until stalemate set in once again. He had his armor in reserve to be used as he saw fit, but only had enough fuel for it to be brought up from the south once. He did not have enough to send these men back, so he had to be sure where the main attack was intended before committing them. Not knowing where to expect the attack, Rommel had to defend the entire front, while Montgomery could concentrate his forces to achieve even greater superiority at specific points than he possessed across the battlefield as a whole.

The attack began on the night of 23 October with the biggest artillery bombardment since the First World War, but although some initial gains were made immediately, the Allies failed to achieve all of their objectives due to a spirited defense and the fact that the minefields were deeper than had been thought.

On 25 October feinted attacks were made in the south and, although the British suffered heavy casualties for little gain, they did their job; unsure of the direction of the main thrust, the Axis armor was held in the south, away from the main battle.

Over the next few days, Montgomery persisted with his ruthless application of numerical superiority at several points and succeeded in pinning down Rommel's forces and gradually eroding their strength. One attack penetrated right through the German positions and, although it was eventually forced to withdraw, it succeeded in knocking out over 34 Axis tanks, a significant proportion of Rommel's armor.

On 30 October, the Australians managed to advance along the coast road and thus threaten the Germans' left flank, and Rommel threw everything he had into a counterattack to stabilize the situation. While he was doing this, Montgomery recognized his opportunity and changed the planned thrust of his attack via 'Operation Supercharge'. This was an attack slightly to the south of the Australian position, and was to consist of another massive bombardment followed by an infantry attack to secure a breach of the defenses through which the armor could then pour and envelop the Germans from behind.

Montgomery was determined to succeed regardless of casualties and had even told the commander of the 9th Armoured Brigade that he was willing to accept '100 percent casualties' from his unit if necessary. The infantry attack went like clockwork and achieved its objectives deep within Axis territory without too much difficulty. However, a delay of only 30 minutes meant that an intended armored attack before dawn took place just as first light silhouetted the tanks and in minutes the brigade was eliminated, losing 75 tanks out of 94. Montgomery's words had proved strangely prophetic.

Desperate German and Italian counterattacks took place all the next day, the Germans losing 117 tanks in a single day. The British breakthrough was eventually held, but at enormous cost. By 3 November the Axis forces had been reduced to one-third of their initial strength and they had only 35 functioning tanks.

Despite direct orders from Hitler not to give a yard, Field Marshal Kesselring, Rommel's commander, ordered him to withdraw. However, he was unable to do so effectively, as the British forces broke through his lines and captured large numbers of prisoners. After a 12-day battle, Montgomery had 13,650 casualties and had lost 500 tanks, but had completely smashed the Axis 'Panzerarmee Afrika', taking more than 35,000 prisoners.

The battle was won not because Montgomery displayed superior generalship or had better troops at his disposal, but because he had more of them. He literally battered the enemy into submission, focusing his troops at specific points of attack to achieve massive superiority. The question was not whether he would win, but how long it would take.

NUMERICAL SUPERIORITY: LANCHESTER'S N-SQUARE LAW

The reasons for the massive advantage that numerical superiority brings, either on the battlefield as a whole or at one specific point, are best explained by FW Lanchester's N-Square Law, which states that 'the fighting strength of forces is in proportion to the square of their strength', i.e. that a force of 2000 men is *four* times (not twice) as powerful as one of 1000. Let's look at this in a little more detail.

Prior to the development of firearms, if both forces engaged in a battle secured their flanks on natural obstacles, then only the front ranks could engage each other. Therefore skill played a greater role than numbers, as it was only if both sides fought to the finish that numbers would count. If force A of 2000 men met force B of 1000 and the fighting skill of both was equal, then A would have 1000 left after wounding or killing all of its opponents. Of course, armies don't usually fight to the finish; unless surrender will mean death, the defeated force will usually capitulate once it is obvious that it is going to lose.

The development of gunpowder and the gradual enlargement of the size of the battlefield, however, meant that more men than the front rank alone could take part at the same time. If all troops could participate (an important proviso of Lanchester's law), then numerical superiority could start to give an advantage out of proportion to the actual numbers involved.

Now, at every exchange of fire, B would lose two men to A's one. Let's assume that A's 2000 men meet B's 1000 and that they attack each other armed with similar weapons. If we also assume a success rate of one shot in five hitting a target, after round one of an engagement force A would be reduced to 1800 (i.e. B's 1000 shots would have incapacitated 200 men) and force B to 600 men (force A's 2000 shots having incapacitated 400). The ratio of A:B would now be 1,800:600, or 3:1.

After round two, A would have 1700 men left (B's 500 shots having hit 100 men) but B would be reduced to 140 as A's 1800 shots hit 360. The ratio would now be *10:1*!

After round three, A would be reduced to 1684, but B would have been annihilated.

Awareness of the disproportionate advantage created by having larger forces has prompted commanders over the ages to try to achieve numerical superiority on the battlefield wherever possible. The Germans fighting in the Second World War had *Gott ist mit uns* (God is with us) inscribed on their belt buckles, but Napoleon was probably more accurate when he said: 'God is on the side of the big battalions.' Stalin had a similar view – when someone asked him what he thought the Vatican's reaction to a particular course of action might be, he responded: 'How many divisions has the Pope?'

MY WALLET'S BIGGER THAN YOUR WALLET

Numerical superiority also applies in business. Perhaps the biggest advantage that a larger company or brand has is more resources at its disposal, and therefore the ability to suffer short-term financial loss in a marketing struggle. Once a big company decides that enough is enough and it is going to fight back against the 'upstart' that is attacking it, watch out! While a small company will rarely win fighting a big one at its own game, the same is not true in reverse. If the bigger one decides to imitate whatever it is that has been making the smaller one successful, it can usually win.

This is true for all companies, not just small ones. A company with sales of hundreds of millions of pounds is just as vulnerable if its competitors are even larger. This is illustrated by the example of Microsoft vs Netscape.

NUMERICAL SUPERIORITY: MICROSOFT VS NETSCAPE

In 1994 a company that was destined to become the fastest growing in history was created to develop what was to become the most popular Internet browser (software that makes the job of navigating around the Internet easier). Recognizing what Microsoft had achieved with MS-DOS and Windows, Netscape Communications came up with the brainwave of giving away its software (called Navigator) in a deliberate attempt to build fast market share, which could then be exploited to make profit at a later date, in order to capitalize on the law of increasing returns.

The plan worked brilliantly, and the company was suddenly thrust into the spotlight as the Internet began to really take off and spread in popularity beyond the narrow band of academics who had been using it until then. Within five months Netscape had grabbed 70 percent of the growing browser market.

Revenues from its other products started to roll in and by the end of its first quarter it had sales of $4.9 million. Quarter two saw $11 million, and by the end of 1995 the company had revenues of $80.7 million.

Although not in direct competition with Microsoft at this point, comparisons between the two were unavoidable. Would Netscape be the next Microsoft? Had Bill Gates neglected the Internet to the point where this brash young upstart could overtake it as the number one software and operating systems company in the industry? Netscape was portrayed as a Silicon Valley David taking on the Microsoft Goliath, and investors queued up to invest in what was *the* hot stock in the IT industry.

Although Netscape had not yet made a profit, Wall Street went crazy when it was floated on the stock market in August 1995. The flotation had intended to offer 3.5 million shares at $14 per share, but demand was so high that it was decided to change this to 5 million at $45 per share. The opening of trading saw the price of the shares rise to $71, valuing the fledgling company at $2.7 billion, though they later stabilised at $58.25.

However, now that it answered to shareholders the company needed to make a profit. It started to charge $30 for its software (it could still be downloaded free from the Internet, but the company thought that corporations would prefer to pay for it and benefit from after-sales service) and this, together with license revenue from online information service providers such as AOL and Compuserve, pushed the company into the black.

By now Netscape had identified intranets as the big opportunity for the future (the equivalents of the Internet, only inside companies) and began developing business software that would enable these to develop, but for the first time it was competing directly with the giants of the industry, IBM and Microsoft. However, with 85 percent of the browser market, Netscape was nonplussed. Until now, it had pursued what could best be described as a **raiding combat** strategy, competing with Microsoft, IBM and other giants for a share of customer spend. The strategy effectively changed to **head-to-head combat**, when it began to compete directly with them for the same business.

With the typical arrogance of a barbarian invader, the company's vice-president for marketing said in mid-1996:

> *Microsoft is following us in this market, they are doing all the things we did six months ago. We have the lead in the world's fastest-growing market; it's an area where Microsoft has certain weaknesses, and we have the biggest resource pool that is totally dedicated to business. So while I respect Microsoft as a competitor the only way they would catch up is if we screw up.*

If Netscape's management team had been students of military history, they would of course have known about the importance of numerical superiority and avoided such complacency; but apparently they were not.

Stung by criticism that Microsoft had been caught napping (and aware that much of it was true), as well as by a drop in his company's share price, Bill Gates turned his company through 180 degrees in a phenomenal bout of corporate reengineering to focus almost exclusively on the Internet market.

Microsoft saw the threat as a serious one. Netscape's browser was designed to run on any operating system, and if other software companies began to write applications that were compatible with it instead of the system (such as Windows), Navigator might ultimately make those systems irrelevant, leaving Windows a mere commodity. This threat appeared just as Windows 95 was about to be launched.

In December 1995, Gates announced that he was putting 2000 of his best programmers into developing a rival browser and the stock price of Netscape fell by $30 in a single day.

The first Microsoft browser, called Internet Explorer, was inferior to Navigator, and even when given away free, it was adopted by only 5 percent of browser users. But Microsoft had no debt and $8 billion in cash reserves, and quietly poured millions of dollars into developing improved products, leading to Explorer 3.

Most individual users of the Internet connected to the Web via a service provider that gave them an e-mail address, a browser and a local telephone number for access. In early 1996, most provided them with Navigator. The exception was the biggest Internet service provider, AOL, which used its own browser. The company recognized that this was inferior and was looking to replace it with either Navigator or Explorer. While Netscape took a hard negotiating stance, wanting to charge a license fee for every copy and resisting pressure to make any changes, Microsoft offered to supply Explorer for free and bent over backwards to be flexible.

Eventually, Gates offered AOL space on the all-important Windows desktop (not an icon, but a folder only a few clicks away that enabled users to sign up with AOL very easily and automatically downloaded its software) and the service provider chose Explorer, much to Netscape's dismay.

A selling blitz quickly persuaded nearly all the other commercial online service and Internet access providers to make Explorer the standard tool for their customers to find their way around the Web.

Before the browser 'war' began, Netscape had license agreements with more than 1000 Internet service providers. Two years later it had none.

Explorer 3 was bundled into the Windows 95 operating system to provide easy Net access. Over the next year a further $2 billion was spent, increasing market share from a measly (by Microsoft standards) 8 percent to 30 percent, more or less all taken from Netscape. Over the last three months of 1997, Netscape's sales fell by almost two-thirds and for the first time Microsoft took over 50 percent of the market.

Suddenly, Netscape found itself backpedaling. David had to drop his slingshot and fight Goliath with sword and shield, and the conflict began to look one sided. Its management's tune changed. Now they were saying:

> *Microsoft doesn't have to lose for us to win ... people who focus on the browser wars don't get the point. The real money is in intranet software – that's where 80% of our revenue comes from and we have always said that this was going to be our main market. There isn't going to be any one winner in the browser wars.*

Admitting that Netscape might not dominate the market was a long way from the combative language of earlier days.

Microsoft's *coup de grace* was a plan to integrate totally its new Explorer 4 into the Windows 98 operating system so that the two became seamless.

Its share price having plummeted, Netscape resorted to complaints to the US Justice Department in a perfect case of the pot calling the kettle black. Forgetting (or ignoring) the fact that Netscape chose to give its products away free in its early days in an attempt to dominate the market, it asked: 'How can Microsoft give away its product that is taking 2000 people at a cost of $2 billion per year to develop?' The only way in which the company was able to fight back was to recruit the assistance of someone even bigger than Microsoft (i.e. the US government) by claiming that Microsoft abused its 'monopoly' position and, at the time of writing, the outcome of the case is still undecided.

In the last quarter of 1998 Netscape posted a loss of $85 million and during that period its stock price fell by 50 percent, to the point where AOL could afford to purchase it (though $4.2 billion for a loss-making company would still appear a hefty premium to most), something that would have been inconceivable only 12 months previously.

THE POWER OF ECONOMIES OF SCALE: INTEL

Another reason that large companies have an inherent advantage over smaller ones is that in some markets and industries economies of scale are vital to profitability.

One example is the microprocessor industry, dominated by Intel, whose product can be found in about 80–90 percent of new PCs around the world.

In the 10 years from 1987 to 1997 when Andy Grove was at the helm of the company, sales grew tenfold to $25 billion. Over the same period, the average annual return to shareholders was a staggering 44 percent! In 1998 Intel was the sixth most profitable company in the US (despite being ranked number 40 in sales), with almost 40 percent more profits than Microsoft. This is in an industry where many competitors struggle to earn any profit at all.

Intel has achieved this position of dominance with a strategy that comprises four main elements. First, it has consistently delivered on what is known as 'Moore's law' (Gordon Moore, one of the founders of Intel, predicted in 1975 that computers would double in power and halve in price every 18 months). Microprocessing power is today about 500 times faster than when IBM launched the first PC in 1981.

The 'law' has been sustained over the years by a predictable series of events. Computer manufacturers and software developers such as Microsoft have developed new power-hungry features and applications, and have needed a chip supplier that could keep pace.

Intel has consistently supplied the computer industry with ever more powerful chips to power each successive generation of new PCs. The 486, introduced in 1989, was succeeded by the Pentium

(1993), which in turn was made obsolete by the Pentium Pro (1995) and the MMX (1997), which are about to be replaced by the Merced (due for launch 1999). Intel has been the only supplier that could do this, which has enabled it to charge prices nearly five times greater than its nearest competitor's.

Second, the company has become the most efficient manufacturer in the industry. In 1985 it abandoned the memory chip market as a result of not being able to compete with Japanese manufacturers, who were thought to be 'dumping' their surplus capacity in the US at prices that were 10 percent cheaper than those of US companies.

Intel decided to concentrate on microprocessors, but also realized that the main reason for Japanese competitiveness was their superior manufacturing techniques. The following two years were characterized by cost cutting, factory closures and redundancies for almost one-third of its employees, as Intel reengineered itself and introduced new manufacturing techniques in all of its plants.

Its strategy also called for the company to be able to satisfy customer demand so that they would not look elsewhere. This in turn required investment on a grand scale, in advance of requirements.

Intel builds a new plant about every nine months to prepare itself for the next stage of the cycle. Each time it does so is a $2 billion bet on the future, as the company is gambling that demand will exist in order to fill that extra capacity. Craig Barrett, who replaced Grove as President in 1997, says:

> *We build our factories two years in advance of needing them, before we have the products to run in them, and before we know the industry's going to grow. ... We build them and hope people will come.*

Third, Intel has made sure that customers do come. Grove embarked on a radical approach to stimulate demand by creating more and more uses for his company's microprocessors. The company now spends about $500 million per annum on projects that have nothing directly to do with microprocessors but that develop the market.

For example, in the early 1990s Intel reengineered the basic structure of the PC to enable it to handle data as fast as the microprocessor could handle it. Today, the Intel 'bus' (i.e. the internal network that directs electrons around the PC) is an industry standard.

Intel is also spending huge amounts developing programs that will advance digital photography, videoconferencing and Internet telephony. Confident that its SWAT will enable it to maintain its market share, it is determined to try to grow the market itself.

Fourth, the company has built a brand name for itself outside the rarified world of computer manufacture. By insisting that all PCs with an Intel microprocessor have an 'Intel inside' sticker, the company has created brand awareness among the public so that people actually expect to get one, and think that the PC is inferior if they don't.

The overall result of this strategy is that Intel's competitors have quite simply never been able to catch up. When it launches a new product, the initial wave sells for about $1000 and is destined for technophiles and early adopters who just can't wait to get their hands on the new product. As production increases, the price gradually falls to around the $200 mark, which is then low enough to produce mass-market sales but still high enough to make huge margins. At about this time the competition (who have been working hard to replicate the technology without infringing Intel's patents) bring out their own variant of the chip, which forces prices still lower. However, by then Intel has the next generation of microprocessors ready for launch, and the cycle starts over again.

The combination of Intel's size, profitability (it is as profitable as the top ten PC manufacturers combined!) and the fact that it is so established make it almost impossible to dislodge.

THE BIG GET BIGGER WHILE THE SMALL...

One of the main reasons that the big not only stay big but actually get bigger in some industries is the law of increasing returns. This is the opposite of the concept learnt by every student of economics, the law of diminishing returns. Traditional economic theory states that the more you make and sell, the harder it gets. If you are in the widget business, for example, and are market leader, then eventually the easy share gains will all have been achieved and each share point will become harder and harder to obtain. Each pound or dollar invested in growth will bring a steadily diminishing return.

In most markets this is exactly what happens. But sometimes a market defies the laws of economics and does exactly the opposite. The big keep getting bigger and it keeps getting easier for them to do so. This explains why some products have completely dominated a market to the point that all others have had to use them as a standard.

Take the QWERTY design of a keyboard, for example. This did not become the standard because it was a better layout than others. It was actually designed to slow typists down, as early typewriters tended to jam if typists used them too quickly. However, the Remington Sewing Machine Co. decided to manufacture its typewriters in this format, and as it was the brand leader of its day, most machines on people's desks tended to have the QWERTY configuration. The more this happened, the more typists got used to the layout and became reluctant to switch to an alternative, and the larger the pool of skilled QWERTY typists, the more aspiring typists wanted to learn how to use it. Eventually it became the standard, and now virtually all typewriters, wordprocessors and computers use it.

THE LAW OF INCREASING RETURNS AND COMPUTER SOFTWARE

The most extreme examples of the law of increasing returns are evident in the computer software business, where the key to success is the size of the user base. No other industry has ever had the benefits that derive from economies of scale to the same extent as the software industry, because software costs almost nothing to produce, its main costs being incurred in research and development. The unit cost therefore decreases substantially as volume increases. The more you sell, the higher the margin you make.

Take two software companies, each selling a similar application for $200. Each has spent $200 million on R&D, and variable costs such as packaging, distribution, manuals etc. are $25 per unit. Software company A sells 10 million copies, while company B sells 2 million. Look at the difference between the margins earned.

Company A's pre-tax profit is £1.55 billion, compared with B's £150 million. A fivefold difference in sales generates a tenfold difference in profit. The economics of this give the volume leader an incredible advantage in that it can use price as a powerful weapon. It can virtually kill off the competition if it lowers the price of the product enough.

In our hypothetical example, if A reduces the price of its software to $150, it would still earn just over $1 billion. Assuming B is forced to follow suit, it would earn only $50 million. If A reduced the cost to $125 per unit, B would make nothing while A would still make $800 million. As many of these sales will be upgrades, it is essential to success that as many people as possible buy the original application, which has led to the phenomenon of software actually being given away free of charge (for example the Netscape browser).

A perfect example of this is id Software, a 14-employee company that created one of the all-time computer game hits with Doom, a violent 'shoot-'em-up' that pits the player against all manner of bad guys. Apart from the quality of the game itself, the reason for its runaway success was id Software's strategy, which it has since repeated with the game's successors.

Having spent a couple of million dollars developing a game, it distributes an abbreviated version of it on the Internet, where it can be downloaded for free by game players all over the world. Once they have learnt how to play and are 'hooked' after the first few levels, these 'game slaves' then pay out for the full version, from a retail outlet or direct from id via a freephone number. The result of this strategy is that this tiny 12-employee company made $20 million at the end of 1997.

INCREASING RETURNS: MICROSOFT'S MS-DOS AND IBM

A similar strategy is the reason that Microsoft wins virtually every market-share battle it enters, even when it can be argued that its product isn't necessarily any better. Microsoft's MS-DOS and Windows operating systems have both become *de facto* industry standards. They are licensed to nearly 1000 different hardware manufacturers, who have to agree not to introduce modifications that will cause incompatibility problems, and the result is that the hundreds of thousands of software manufacturers don't have to worry about on which PCs their software will run and on which PCs it won't.

Anyone can develop application software that runs on Windows without having to get permission from Microsoft or even notifying it. Microsoft doesn't earn money from these software developers, but from the fact that about 80 percent of the world's PCs use its systems.

Back in the late 1970s, IBM recognized that as its expertise and focus were in the design and manufacture of mainframes, it would need to break its normal *modus operandi* and use the help of outsiders if it were to bring a small personal computer to the market quickly. Thus for the first time it abandoned its traditional course of designing all the software itself. One of the small companies that benefited from this was Microsoft, which worked with IBM to design an operating system for PCs that eventually became MS-DOS (Microsoft Disk Operating System).

IBM launched its first PC in 1981 with a choice of three operating systems: PC-DOS (IBM's name for MS-DOS) and two others. Bill Gates and his partner Paul Allen realized that any one of the three systems could eventually become the industry standard, and saw three ways to safeguard MS-DOS as the winner: make it the best product, ensure it was inexpensive, and help other software companies write MS-DOS-based software.

They gave IBM a very advantageous deal – a low, one-off fee that gave it the right to use their system on as many PCs as it wanted. This gave IBM the incentive to use MS-DOS and to sell it inexpensively, which it did. While the other two systems on offer sold for $450 and $175, MS-DOS sold for only $60! Eventually IBM dropped the other two systems and concentrated exclusively on MS-DOS.

Microsoft's objective was not to make money from IBM, but from licensing its system to other companies that wanted to make IBM-compatible computers. While IBM could use MS-DOS virtually for nothing, it did not have an exclusive license to it. The IBM PC sold well and for a few years accounted for more than half the personal computers sold. Software developers began to write software for it and lots of companies began to manufacture 'add-ons' such as accessory cards; each new customer, software application and add-on enhanced IBM's position as the industry standard.

Within a few years almost all competing standards for personal computers had gone by the wayside, with the exception of Apple Macintosh. HP, DEC, Texas Instruments and Xerox all failed because their machines were not compatible with IBM's, even though it can be argued that their products were in some ways superior. By the mid-1980s there were literally dozens of companies manufacturing IBM-compatible computers. As Gates says:

Although buyers of a PC might not have articulated it this way, what they were looking for was the hardware that ran the most software, and they wanted the same system the people they knew and worked with had.

THE IMPORTANCE OF THE FORCE:SPACE RATIO

Dominance of a particular battlefield or market is not always as simple as mere strength of numbers, however. In warfare and in business, numbers must always be looked at in relation to the area in which they are operating, and this is true both strategically and tactically. This is called the force:space ratio.

Strategically, an attacking army usually finds it difficult (if not impossible) to compel its opponents to fight except under conditions of its own choosing, unless it has a force large enough to dominate the area in which it is operating. After his initial victories, Hannibal wandered around Italy frustratedly for years without being able to force the Romans to give battle, because they had a country and population too large for him to dominate with an army of only 50,000 men.

Likewise, although they won a series of brilliant victories, successive English kings were unable to do anything but mount a series of raids on France during the Hundred Years' War, as their armies were simply too tiny to do anything else. In the sixteenth century, Marshal de Montluc wrote of the English strategy:

> *France if united cannot be conquered even by a dozen battles ... There are so many ... cities and fortresses in this realm, that it would take thirty armies to capture and garrison them all. To hold down what he had won, the conqueror would have to unpeople his whole kingdom, which is obviously impossible. While the invader was taking one place, he would be losing another, for want of garrisons he could not provide.*

It did not matter that Napoleon gathered his largest ever army to invade Russia; the ground he needed to cover was just too large for him to be able force battle on the Russians except at their choosing. This was a lesson that had to be relearned by the Germans in their own invasion. No matter how many troops they poured into the Eastern Front, they never managed to achieve a sufficiently high force:space ratio to achieve their objectives.

THE FORCE:SPACE RATIO: NAPOLEON AND THE FRENCH SYSTEM OF CORPS

Despite the fact that he was unsuccessful in his invasion of Russia, it was Napoleon and the wars of the French Revolution that first introduced armies large and mobile enough to dominate the territory in which they were fighting. By separating the French armies into divisions and uniting them in self-contained *corps* similar to a small army, Napoleon could keep his forces widely dispersed and thereby dominate the theater of war, yet also quickly bring them together when needed. No longer could defending armies avoid battle just by moving out of reach of their opponent.

Prior to this, the traditional method was for the entire army to march together, a throwback to the late middle ages when this was necessary for protection against either an 'encounter' battle (i.e. where two armies literally 'bump into' each other and a battle ensues) or attack and harassment from enemy cavalry. This was now an anachronism for two reasons.

First, the mutual consent aspect of eighteenth-century warfare and the length of time it took to array into battle formation meant that it had been a long, long time since an encounter battle had taken place (one Prussian general, finding himself suddenly facing the undefended flank of his enemy, made a large detour in order to facilitate the traditional face-to-face battle!).

Second, the introduction of the bayonet meant that infantry were now far more capable of defending themselves against cavalry attack. Even infantry marching in column that had not had time to deploy into square still presented a formidable target. In any case, the likelihood of either of these things happening could be significantly reduced by the deployment of a wide light cavalry reconnaissance screen.

The advance of the army in widely spread columns rather than one dense mass made living off the countryside much easier and also spread the load over a number of roads, each division or *corps* having its own separate line of advance. This greatly increased rapidity of movement during the advance to contact, after which the army rapidly reconcentrated. One of Napoleon's favorite sayings was: 'We must separate to eat, and concentrate to fight.'

The benefits of this system were demonstrated at Ulm in 1805. Napoleon faced the armies of Austria and Russia in south Germany and Italy, but had no opposition elsewhere in Germany, Bavaria even being his ally. Knowing that a campaign against Austria was inevitable, he embarked on extensive planning and preparation for the advance south through largely friendly territory. The supply method used was called requisitions, whereby receipts were given to civilians in return for supply. In friendly territory, these were honored by the French government; in hostile territory, suppliers had to try to get their own government to pay.

The Austrians under Archduke Ferdinand (in name only; command in reality belonged to General Mack) marched into Bavaria in September with 45,000 men, the Bavarian army avoiding him and marching north to meet the French. The advance was intended to block the roads through the Black Forest, through which the French must emerge on their way to the Danube.

At Ulm they halted to await the arrival of their Russian ally, General Kutusov, not realizing that the Russians were still using the Julian calendar and would therefore be 10 days later than any date on which they had promised to arrive!

By 24 September, the whole of Napoleon's army was in its designated positions on the Rhine, the move being one of the most amazing feats in military history. Soult's Corps of 40,000 men marched more than 640 kilometers with the loss of only 30 sick and stragglers, and Davout's III Corps claimed to have marched from Bruges to Mannheim without losing a man.

On 25 September, seven French army corps crossed the Rhine on a 100-mile front, aiming not for Ulm itself but a stretch of the Danube to the northeast in order to separate the Austrians from their slowly advancing Russian allies. Two weeks later they were approaching their objective, and when they eventually crossed the Danube and swung southwards, Mack finally realized his predicament and planned to retreat to the northeast. An opportunity existed to do so, for Napoleon anticipated that he would head due east and placed virtually all of his forces there, ready for battle.

However, Mack missed his chance. The Austrian army delayed and prevaricated, and only managed to extricate one small detachment before Napoleon realized what was happening and blocked off the escape route. On 20 October, Mack surrendered his entire force. The French army's official pronouncement claimed 60,000 prisoners for the campaign in total, and concluded: 'Never have victories been so complete and less costly.'

Napoleon had won his victory almost without having to fire a shot, due to his numerical superiority of two to one and a very high force:space ratio. When the generals Turenne and Montecuccoli campaigned in the same area in 1673, they each had about 30,000 men, hardly more than pinpricks in the huge geography covered. Even Marlborough and Talleyrand, fighting in 1704, had only 60,000 men each. Each of Napoleon's seven corps was comparable in size to Turenne's entire army, and it was his ability to dominate the area completely that enabled him to win an almost bloodless victory.

ACHIEVING LOCAL SUPERIORITY

The force:space ratio is also important tactically. During the 1812 invasion of Russia, Napoleon is reported to have remarked:

What is war? A barbaric profession, of which the only art is to be stronger at a given place.

The last four words are the most important, as while a larger army automatically starts with a major advantage, on many occasions the opposing military commander has managed to negate this advantage by achieving local superiority.

This was the main thrust of Napoleon's battlefield tactics, and is what Clausewitz meant when he wrote:

The greatest possible number of troops should be brought into action at the decisive point.

If Napoleon's opponents were numerically superior, he would employ both the tactical power of the defense and superiority of numbers. First, he would divide his own force into an advance guard, two wings and a reserve, and then advance to seize a central position that divided the enemy into two parts. By using the lesson of the tactical power of the defense, he would then tie one part of the enemy down using a small force to fight a delaying action, while he maneuvered the rest of his forces to fight a series of small battles in which he possessed *local* numerical superiority.

This was the basis, for example, of the Waterloo campaign, when Napoleon divided the British and Prussian armies and planned to defeat them each in turn. He calculated that a division on its own could hold out for a number of hours, a *corps* for up to a day.

His battle tactics were a smaller version of his envelopment strategy. First he would attack frontally to attract the enemy's reserves. Then a hidden force would attack one flank, causing the enemy to weaken its line somewhere else in order to face this new threat. Finally, the reserve would attack this weakened spot and create a *masse de rupture* through which the cavalry would swarm, turning the defeat into a rout. A non-Napoleonic battle from the eighteenth century, Blenheim, as well as the Arab-Israeli war of 1973, illustrate perfectly the power of achieving local superiority.

ACHIEVING LOCAL SUPERIORITY: THE BATTLE OF BLENHEIM, 1704

During the War of the Spanish Succession, the English general the Duke of Marlborough marched from the Netherlands to Bavaria, with the objective of driving the latter from the war. With 52,000 men and 60 guns, the Duke ravaged Bavaria and burned 300 villages, but found himself cut off from his retreat northwards by a combined French/Bavarian force totalling 56,000 men and 90 guns under Marshal Tallard.

This force took up a strong defensive position, with the flanks secured by woods on the left and the village of Blenheim on the right, and a marshy stream to the front. On the right the French placed 27 battalions of infantry, 11 of which were in Blenheim itself.

A further 15 held the village of Oberglau in the center and the space between the two villages was filled by the French cavalry and another nine battalions of infantry. On the left, the Elector of Bavaria drew up an almost independent position, anchored on the village of Lutzingen.

In military terms, the eighteenth century was a period of general mediocrity, with the various armies in Europe almost identical in terms of weapons and tactics. As a result, success normally came as a result of numerical superiority and Tallard was therefore confident

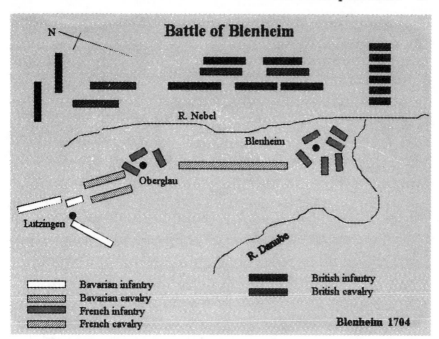

that Marlborough would never attack him with fewer forces, expecting him to retreat southwards. However, all that lay south was the devastated Bavaria, now devoid of rations for men or horses, and the Duke (supported by Prince Eugene of Savoy) had no real option but to attack and try to break free.

At about 1 pm on 13 August, the Duke sent 15 battalions of his own infantry against Blenheim. As they approached, 2400 Englishmen received a volley from 4000 Frenchmen at a distance of only 40 yards, immediately losing 800 killed or wounded, but they carried on with the attack. The French officer defending the village panicked and put his entire reserve into it. Some 18,000 men were crammed into the tiny village, an observer saying:

> ...*the men were so crowded in among one another that they couldn't even fire, let alone carry out orders. Not a single shot of the enemy missed its mark, whilst only those few out front could return the fire.*

Marlborough had trapped 27 battalions using only 15 of his own!

At the same time, Prince Eugene pinned down enemy forces twice as large as his own on the right wing, enabling Marlborough

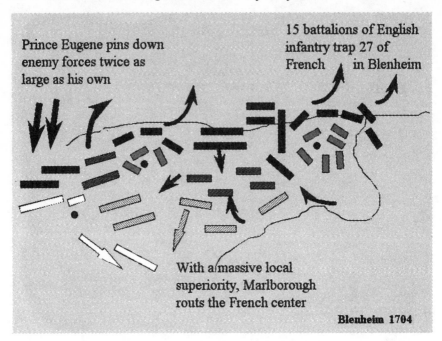

Prince Eugene pins down enemy forces twice as large as his own

15 battalions of English infantry trap 27 of French   in Blenheim

With a massive local superiority, Marlborough routs the French center

Blenheim 1704

to achieve a massive numerical superiority in the center. Here he had a 50 percent advantage in cavalry and 27 battalions to Tallard's nine.

With no reserves available from the right, the French had to rely on cavalry, whose only defense capability lay in the countercharge. They repulsed the first British cavalry attack, but were too exhausted to fight off the second, and the nine infantry battalions died where they stood, with over 3000 cavalry drowning while trying to swim the Danube.

By seven in the evening, the virtually unused garrison of Blenheim, which had been trapped there all day, was forced to surrender. By nightfall, the French had lost 26,000 casualties and 14,000 prisoners (including Tallard himself). Allied casualties were 12,500. The French had lost 70 percent of their force, the Allies 23 percent.

ACHIEVING LOCAL SUPERIORITY: THE ARAB–ISRAELI WAR, 1973

On 6 October 1973, Egypt and Syria invaded Israel from the south and north respectively, at a time when the latter was without its reserves on the Jewish holiday of Yom Kippur. Some 8000 Egyptians crossed the Suez Canal in a well-planned operation, using small boats on a 50-mile front. Armed with bazookas and wire-guided anti-tank missiles, they were supported in the attack by 4000 guns that fired over 10,000 shells in the first minute of the attack. As long as they remained near the canal bank, they were also protected by sophisticated anti-aircraft missiles.

This development of portable anti-tank missiles had restored to infantry the capacity they had possessed for centuries to defend themselves successfully against heavy cavalry. Just as the English archers at Crecy could resist attack from heavily armored French knights, the Egyptians could successfully resist Israeli armor.

In the first Israeli counterattacks the Israelis lost almost all of their tanks, on one occasion losing 90 percent of the attacking tanks within 10 minutes. The following day they lost as many as 250 tanks, as the Egyptians reinforced their troops with recoilless rifles and 85- and 100-millimeter anti-tank guns, together with small, lightly armored vehicles with missiles.

Following this the Israelis adopted a defensive stance, and the Egyptians made no attempt to exploit their initial success, being content to fortify their positions and reinforce them with 800 tanks and nine full divisions. They were loath to take on the Israelis in the open armored warfare in which the latter exceled.

One the one occasion they did so, in a half-hearted attack right across the front, the Egyptians lost 260 of the 1000 tanks involved. The Israeli tanks adopted previously prepared defensive positions excavated for the purpose where only the turrets of their tanks were exposed, and the fully visible advancing Egyptian tanks were sitting ducks. All of the Egyptian forces fell back to their original starting points. The Egyptian objectives were to establish an impregnable defensive position against which the Israelis would batter themselves until they were forced to negotiate a peace on Arab terms.

The Israelis were determined to oust the Egyptians, but without a massive numerical superiority could make no progress against the Egyptian positions. One result of the abortive Egyptian attack was that part of the western bank of the canal had been almost denuded

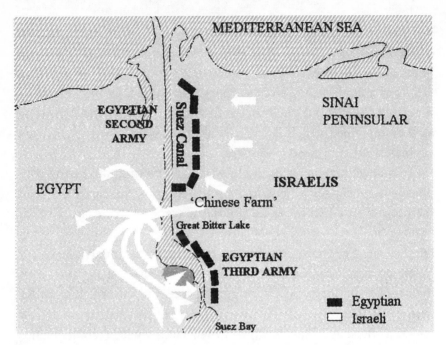

of troops. The Israelis decided to concentrate their forces so as to achieve superiority at that one point and break through and over the canal, from where they could envelop the Egyptians and turn their position. Having identified a weak spot roughly in the center of the Egyptian defenses, they attacked there and a struggle ensued for several days, with the Egyptian forces north of the spot counterattacking and the Israelis also attacking north to protect their flank.

The Egyptians thought that the Israeli intention was to assault the flank of their northern forces, and didn't realize that their true objective was to cross the canal and attack them from behind. By the night of 17 October the canal was bridged and the Israelis had three divisions on the west side.

The following day the Israelis drove due west, meeting heavy opposition, and the day after that headed due south. The anti-aircraft missiles stationed on the west bank were defenseless against Israeli tanks and artillery, and after several were destroyed the Egyptians moved them. As the low-level anti-aircraft defenses were all on the east bank, the airforce could now give close support to the advance. Bypassing Egyptian strongpoints, the lead division pushed on and left them to the one following behind.

By 23 October the lead Israeli division had reached the Gulf of Suez, a point south of the southern tip of the Egyptian Third army on the eastern bank of the canal. The following division then pushed out to the west, preventing Egyptian reinforcement, the result being the entrapment of about 40,000 men. Capitalizing on this situation would have been difficult for the Israelis because the Egyptians possessed a strong defensive position and were protected by the canal itself to their rear, but further developments were halted by a hastily arranged ceasefire.

Completely outnumbered on this part of the battlefield, the Israelis managed to achieve local superiority at one specific point and then concentrate all their available forces there. The resultant breakthrough was sufficient to turn the situation around, and was one of the key factors behind the arrangement of the ceasefire.

THE FORCE:SPACE RATIO IN BUSINESS: THE DOWNSIDE OF SIZE

It should not be assumed that size *per se* is automatically a good thing. It is only beneficial when it generates a genuine advantage. Remember the force:space ratio – it is the size in relation to the area covered that is significant. The huge size of the US armed forces in Vietnam, for example, gave them no advantages in terms of speed and flexibility, both absolutely essential when fighting an enemy following a raiding (read guerrilla) strategy.

When companies reach a certain size, they tend to become slow, bureaucratic and myopic. 'Their' way becomes best, and the 'not invented here' syndrome often takes over. They become staffed by managers who are indoctrinated in the company way of doing things and who have a vested interest in not rocking the boat. Viewing the world through the windows of their plush executive offices, they suffer from 'analysis paralysis', with anything major being discussed endlessly in committee.

When Ross Perot and General Motors parted company after a brief but unhappy cohabitation following the latter's purchase of his company EDS, he said:

> *If there was a meeting at GM and a poisonous snake entered the room, they would set up a committee to investigate how to kill snakes. At EDS we would have just stood on it.*

With factories that are always busy, a complete reengineering of the production process becomes impractical, if not impossible, which is the main problem behind Boeing's recent fall from grace. Despite (or perhaps because of?) being the world's largest aircraft manufacturer, Boeing found itself saddled with an outdated (but busy) production line based on outdated technology, selling many of its aircraft at prices that were unprofitable. Regarding any customers 'stolen' by Airbus as having been lured away by an artificial competitor kept alive on the back of European government subsidies, it failed to see that it had problems. It now faces years of reengineering and investment, while at the same time having to fill an unwanted backlog of unprofitable orders.

An e-mail was reproduced in the *Sunday Times* recently which is doing the rounds in a very large and well-known UK company currently competing with a smaller, fast-moving competitor. It illustrates the problem perfectly (I have changed the names of the two companies concerned):

> *Once upon a time companies X and Y decided to have a boat race on the Thames. Both teams practised long and hard to reach their peak performance. On the big day they were as ready as they could be and company Y won by a length. Company X became discouraged and senior management set up a project team to investigate the problem.*
>
> *Its conclusion was that the company Y team had eight people rowing and one person steering. The company X team had one person rowing and eight people steering. Senior management immediately hired consultants to study team structure. Millions of pounds were spent and several months later they concluded that too many people were steering and not enough were rowing.*
>
> *The next year the team structure was changed to four steering managers, three senior steering managers and one executive steering manager.*

> *A performance and appraisal system was set up to give the person rowing more incentive to work harder and become a key performer. 'We must give him empowerment and enrichment – that ought to do it', they concluded.*
>
> *... The big day arrived and company Y still won. Company X laid off the rower for poor performance, sold off the paddles, cancelled capital investment and halted development of the new boat. Then they gave high performance awards to the consultants and distributed the money saved among senior management.*

One of the main reasons behind Levi Strauss's failure to react to changing market trends and a main cause of its market share loss is its slow group decision-making processes. The company's CEO Bob Haas has seemed at times more interested in making Levi's 'the most enlightened work environment in the world' than in innovating. Part of the company's core culture was consensus, and if managers did not have the ability to convince everybody about an idea, they did not have the authority to proceed with its implementation. While this degenerated into endless meetings, taskforces and memos, the market simply moved on without it noticing.

In a chapter on Levi Strauss in *Brand Warriors*, the company's VP for global marketing actually *boasts* that 'With minor variations such as the addition of belt loops..., Levi's 501® jeans today are the product that has been worn by miners, cowboys and California farm-workers since the late 1800s.' This in a fashion industry where purchases are dominated by teenagers!

Without any sense of irony, he goes on to write:

> *History is only one element of the brand-building equation. ... A classic mistake brand managers frequently make is to become too interested with their own culture, ... preaching history. Customers don't like it ... as marketeers, we need to be sure we're talking to consumers, not just to ourselves.*

The company knew as far back as 1993 that teenagers were telling retailers that the legs on Levi's jeans were too narrow, but the company refused either to listen or respond, secure in its conceit that 'the design is so right it need never alter, a timeless classic of clothes'.

Similar criticisms can be aimed at the IBM of the 1980s and early 1990s. It was unable to see that what had made it great in the past would not continue to do so in the future, and it never really tuned in to the PC market because its approach was handcuffed by its legacy of success in mainframes. For example, because mainframes took 15 minutes to reboot, it thought that its OS/2 operating system was fast when it 'only' took three minutes to do the same. Writing in *The Road Ahead* about Microsoft's joint development of an operating system for PCs with the company, Bill Gates says:

> *IBM, with more than 30,000 employees, was ... stymied by its commitment to company-wide consensus. Every part of IBM was invited to submit Design Change Requests, which usually turned out to be demands that the personal-computer-system software be changed to fit the needs of mainframe products better. We got more than 10,000 such requests, and talented people from IBM and Microsoft would sit and discuss them for days.*

All companies need to ensure that as they grow they do not lose the flexibility and agility they once possessed when they were small. In virtually every case where giants have lost their market dominance, a slow-moving, over-bureaucratic, top-heavy management system that distanced the decision makers from what was happening in the marketplace bears a significant part of the blame.

3

THE TACTICAL PRIMACY
OF THE DEFENSE

I F AN ARMY DOES NOT POSSESS A SWAT, THE MOST COMMON RESPONSE
of a commander facing a larger opponent is to fight defensively, as
this in itself will give it an advantage. In the vast majority of battles fought between similarly armed and equipped troops where one
side did not possess numerical superiority, the side fighting defensively
has won, for the reasons already outlined in Chapter 1.

Likewise, in any commercial contest where an established company or brand and a new one without a competitive SWAT come up
against each other head to head, the former will invariably win. This
doesn't mean that a new company can never beat an established
one; it means that it can't beat it fighting head to head.

If we take this into account, and revisit our hypothetical engagement between A and B (page 31) in light of the above, we can see
exactly how fighting defensively can counterbalance the advantages
of having more troops. Earlier we assumed that they were facing
each other in the open and 'slugging it out', each attacking the other.
Let's now imagine that they fight again, only this time force B is
fighting defensively, from a carefully chosen and prepared position,
and A is forced to attack.

Now, instead of both sides having a strike rate of one shot in five,
A's is reduced to one in fifteen, as its forces have to concentrate on
attacking as well as firing, and B's troops are also protected behind
fortifications of some sort (trenches, palisades, sandbags, earth-
works, walls, foxholes etc.). The confidence of being protected
steadies B's men and improves their morale, and their strike rate
subsequently improves to one in three.

After round one of this engagement, A has been reduced to 1667, while B is reduced to 867. After round two, the figures are 1378 and 756.

After round three, A is down to 1126 and B to 664. After round four, the numbers are 905 and 589. Round five brings reductions to 709 and 529, and A's superiority is reduced to 1.3:1. After round six the two forces are more or less even, and after round eight the situation has reversed, with B having a superiority of almost 2:1. Such a mathematical calculation assumes that the two forces continue fighting regardless of the effect that these casualties would have on morale. As already mentioned above, however, A would probably withdraw long before this, given the huge casualties it had suffered.

THE BATTLE OF THERMOPYLAE, 481 BC

One of the best examples of the power of fighting defensively is a story known to schoolchildren throughout the western world, that of the Spartans at Thermopylae. In 481 BC, the Persian King Xerxes crossed the Hellespont into Greece with an army of about 150,000 on over 1200 ships and began a march south into central Greece.

The Greeks decided to try to hold them at Thermopylae, where access through the mountains was restricted to three narrow passes. The central one was only about 20 feet wide and the other two even narrower. They had only 7–8000 troops immediately available, commanded by the Spartan king Leonidas, and the intention was to hold the Persians until they tried to detour around them with their fleet. This would take them into a narrow strip of water called the Euboean Channel, where the huge size of the fleet would be a disadvantage and where the Greek fleet hoped to defeat them.

After waiting for five days in the hope that the Greeks would flee, the Persians attacked and ran straight into a solid wall of what were probably at the time the best fighting troops in the world. The Medes and the Cissians tried all day, but their superior numbers were of no use; only a small number could actually be brought to bear on the Spartans at any one time. In addition, the Greeks were more heavily armored and had longer spears.

In the words of Herodotus: 'They made it plain enough to any-one, that the King had in his army many men, but few soldiers.' The disgraced Medes were replaced by the King's handpicked Persian troops – the Immortals – but they were no more successful.

The fighting lasted all day and was renewed the following morn-ing in the vain hope on the part of the Persians that the Greeks would eventually have to cede when all of them had been wounded in some way. But the Greeks never wavered and were able to stand firm because man for man they could match their larger enemy. For the whole of the second day the fighting continued, and again the Persians were forced to withdraw.

Eventually, the Persians were told of a narrow track that ran from one of the narrower passes over the escarpment to their rear, and under cover of night outflanked the Greeks. When the Spartans learnt of this, Leonidas kept the Thebans and Thespians with his own men, but dismissed the rest of the allied troops and came out of the narrow pass to die.

They fought man to man until their spears were broken, and when they lost their swords they fought with their bare hands. According to Herodotus: 'No one could count the number of dead.' They were finally killed to a man by archers, the Persian infantry still unable to defeat them.

While the superior fighting skills of the Spartan hoplites were obviously a significant factor in the Greeks' ability to hold up the Persians for so long, nobody could claim that the same success would have been achieved had they been fighting on a plain. The main factor was the fact that they were defending a narrow moun-tain pass, which not only gave them the advantage of the defense but was an illustration of the benefits of the force:space ratio, largely negating the advantage that the Persians had in numbers.

THE BATTLE OF THE SOMME, 1916

The power of the defense reached its apogee during the First World War. While virtually every battle until the final stages of the war could be used to illustrate this, perhaps the best (and most infamous) example is what happened on the first day of the Battle of the Somme in July 1916. This also serves to illustrate that numerical superiority alone is no answer to the difficulties presented by a strong defense.

Two years into the war, the Western Front was deadlocked, with both sides dug in behind heavily entrenched lines that stretched unbroken from the North Sea to the Swiss border. At first the defenses were mere ditches, but as time passed they became more elaborate, with barbed wire, dugouts, firing bays and communication and support trenches.

However, masses of British volunteers were at last starting to arrive in France, and in an effort to break the deadlock, a grand assault was planned on an 18-mile front just north of the River Somme. Approximately 30,000 Germans held that section of the line, and Britain massed 150,000 troops to overwhelm them; a superiority of 5:1! However, the British high command was not leaving anything to chance. Also included in the plan was an overwhelming artillery bombardment that would literally blow the German positions to pieces, and leave no Germans alive to face the advancing infantry.

The bombardment started on 24 June and lasted a week, and on 1 July the infantry advanced, confident that no one would be left alive after such a terrifying ordeal; 66,000 men of the first wave of the attack advanced in line, with no rush, at walking pace, as British infantry had for centuries. Many regiments even took pride in 'dressing' the troops so that they advanced in a perfect line as if on the parade ground.

Unfortunately, although some parts of the German defenses had been destroyed, most had not; many Germans and their weapons had survived the bombardment. These defenders climbed out of their deep bunkers as soon as the British artillery stopped to open up a terrifying hail of machine gun fire at the same time as the German artillery began to fire. The 20–30-feet deep belts of barbed wire (which were supposed to have been blown to smithereens) proved to be uncut, and within a few hours the entire advance stalled.

As the troops advanced across 'No Man's Land', they were mown down in their thousands. The 34th Division alone suffered 6380 casualties, and many units suffered losses of up to 90 percent.

An eye-witness from the 169th German Regiment later wrote:

When the English started advancing we were very worried; they looked as though they must overrun our trenches. We were very surprised to see them walking, we had not seen that before. ... When we started firing, we just had to load and reload. They went down in their hundreds. You didn't have to aim. We just fired into them.

While the German positions were taken at the southern end of the British line, not a yard was captured at the northern end, and the ground taken was a tiny percentage of what was supposed to have been captured.

On the first day of the battle, the British suffered over 57,000 casualties, against the Germans' 8000.

THE POWER OF FIGHTING DEFENSIVELY IN BUSINESS

Over the years I have listened to dozens of brand plans from young, fresh-faced marketing managers and attended dozens of new product launches. Without exception, it was stated with confidence on each occasion that meticulous independent research had shown that consumers preferred new brand x to existing brand y, and that (say) 80 percent of them had stated they were likely to buy the new product.

The problems begin when the product finds itself on the shelf next to brand y in the real world: consumers don't do what a supposedly representative sample said they would do. Of course they might buy the product at first, out of curiosity or tempted by a special offer, but after that initial trial they normally go back to their existing brands, the ones they have used for a long time and are comfortable with.

You will recall from Chapter 1 how many of the UK's major fmcg brands have been around for decades. To look at the same subject in a different way, if we consider the first ten products to be

Table I First 10 brands to be advertised on TV in the UK

1	Gibbs SR toothpaste
2	Cadbury's drinking chocolate
3	Kraft cheese
4	Dunlop tyres
5	Woman magazine
6	Surf washing powder
7	National Benzole petrol
8	Lux soap
9	Ford cars
10	Guinness

advertised on British television (Table 1), we can see that nine of them are still household names, the sole exception being National Benzole petrol. More than 40 years later, despite dozens of brands being introduced into each of their markets and the best efforts of their competitors to destroy them, they are still around today as major brands.

In a recent book on investing called *Great Companies, Great Returns*, Jim Huguet produced a list of the 14 US companies that he would define as 'great', based on 12 different criteria (Table 2). These companies have achieved an average return 45 percent higher than the S&P 500 over the last five years, and nearly 50 percent over the last ten years. Huguet writes:

> *These companies have been in business an average of 111 years. The oldest ... was founded in 1806. The youngest ... celebrated its fiftieth birthday in ... 1999. Only three of the companies were founded in the twentieth century .... All but Medtronic have survived world wars and the worst depression this country has ever experienced. They have all flourished despite numerous recessions and market declines. They have withstood the onslaught of international competitors. Despite everything that has been thrown at them, they have survived and flourished.*

It should be emphasized that it is not sheer size that has enabled them to 'survive and flourish' (a list of the top 14 US companies by

Table 2 Great companies of America

Company	Founded
American International Group	1919
Bristol-Myers Squibb	1887
Citicorp	1812
Coca-Cola	1886
Colgate-Palmolive	1806
General Electric	1892
Gillette	1895
Johnson & Johnson	1885
Medtronic	1949
Merck	1914
Merrill Lynch	1887
Pfizer	1849
Procter & Gamble	1837
Schering-Plough	1864

size looks very different); only six of them are in the top 50 of the 1999 Fortune 500. The reason for their success is that each is so well established within its marketplace.

THE TACTICAL POWER OF THE DEFENSE: BARNES & NOBLE VS AMAZON

The Internet offers a unique way of competing with the giants of industry, in that it enables a small company to go straight to its customers without having to worry about distribution on retail shelves and expensive high-street locations.

One such company is Amazon.com, a Web-based bookshop that, unlike the vast majority of companies with Web sites, conducts 100 percent of its business via the Internet. The first Web-based company to be floated on the US market, its stock-market launch in May 1997 was a runaway success. Such was the enthusiasm for the company among investors (even though it was still loss making at the time) that the share price opened 63 percent higher than the initial offer price. The initial offer price of $18 itself gave the company a value of $421 million, significantly higher than most traditional booksellers that do make money. After only four years of operation, the company is the world's largest bookshop.

Its success has been due to the differences between the way it operates and the methods of its more traditional competition. Unlike non-Web-based booksellers, the company stocks only a limited range of bestsellers, preferring to get most books from a wholesaler once they have been ordered. Having received them, it then packs and ships them to the customer. Expensive book inventories are therefore not needed, bricks-and-mortar retail outlets are an irrelevance, and expensive high-street rents and rates are avoided. Its key assets are therefore not the books and shops, but the technology that underpins its systems.

Such has been the enthusiasm of cyberphiles that claims have been made about Amazon being a threat to booksellers not only in the US but around the world, and forecasts of closure for thousands of traditional outlets as the Internet becomes the new way to order books for the majority of the public.

As befits a newcomer to a marketplace, the company's strategy had initially been one of raiding logistics, where it concentrated on one specific sector unserved or ignored by existing bookshops, i.e. consumers who wanted (or were willing) to buy via the Internet.

However, its extraordinary growth and Wall Street success quickly attracted the attention of its large, established competitors. In June 1997, Barnes & Noble, the US's largest bookseller, opened its own online bookshop, finally realizing that online order taking and designing Web sites are actually easier than the more mundane stuff of financing, stocking and shipping the product itself. It believed that once it managed to master the new skills needed, it would automatically have an advantage over Amazon because of its expertise in the old, traditional ones. Says CEO Steven Riggio, 'There was a mystique about how difficult it was to get started on the Web, but it's quickly fading.'

With B&N adopting a blatant head-to-head combat strategy aimed at taking on Amazon at its own game, the nature of the book war changed significantly. Once the two companies were operating on a similar basis, some industry observers found it hard to see where

Amazon had an advantage. Both Web sites can get any book in print (this is nothing special; even the smallest bookseller can eventually do this) and both have deals with other sites that point browsers their way (Amazon uses Yahoo, B&N the *New York Times* Book Review).

But beyond that, B&N seemed to have a number of things going its way. In speed of delivery, the edge goes to the company that can get its hands on the books fastest and here the $3 billion per year giant should be able to win hands down. The company stocks about 400,000 frequently ordered titles in a central warehouse in New Jersey, with the result that it should be able to annihilate its competition in terms of delivery on most titles. It also deals direct with the publishers, thereby obtaining better deals and cutting out the wholesaler's margin, and this enabled it to launch its site with 30 percent discounts on all hardbacks.

Amazon fought back by matching these prices, stocking more titles and trying to improve delivery times from its wholesalers, but in doing so ran the risk of incurring some of the very costs that it had once boasted of eliminating. The launch of barnesandnoble.com seemed like another example of what happens when a larger competitor decides to take a smaller one.

However, these observers did not understand the tactical power of the defense. B&N's site had little effect, as Amazon.com is the name that people still automatically think of when they contemplate buying a book on the Internet. While B&N was successful in winning a market share in the low teens, Amazon stayed with over 50 percent, and in its first year B&N lost $30 million on the venture.

In an SEC document filed for an intended IPO, B&N stated that during the period February–August 1998 it had sales of $22 million. During the first six months of that year, Amazon's sales were $203 million!

B&N began to look for allies, and at the end of 1998 50 percent of the company was sold for $200 million (not bad for a company that was losing $30 million!) to Bertelsmann, a German media giant. This company is the world's biggest book publisher and already owns Random House, Bantam, Doubleday and Dell (the publisher, not the PC manufacturer discussed in Chapter 5). It is twice as big as its biggest competitor. In addition to having access to an Internet bookshop's 'raw materials' (i.e. the books themselves), Bertelsmann also has a huge infrastructure of warehouses, forklifts, mailing centers etc., and these resources should significantly bolster B&N's attacks.

However, students of military history know the power of fighting defensively and the fact remains that to most people who are interested in such things, Amazon is the name of which most people are aware.

B&N and Borders in the US, and Waterstones and WH Smith in the UK, will never be as committed to e-commerce as Amazon, because of their existing asset base of bricks and mortar. Because of this, most consumers will still think 'bookshops' when they hear their names, while they will think 'Internet' when they hear the name 'Amazon'. Amazon looks set to continue to defy the pundits and go from strength to strength. Although it has only around 2 percent of the US book market as a whole, it has around 75 percent of the Internet book market. Maybe one day it will even make a profit.

FOUR LEVELS OF CUSTOMER FORTIFICATIONS

An inescapable lesson from a study of great campaigns is that an army's defensive power is always increased by the use of prepared fortifications (the fact that these have often not prevented defeat does not negate this fact). The commercial equivalent is to build strong defenses around customers before the expected competitor attack occurs, turning each into a form of impregnable fortress.

There are four levels of customer fortifications:

❑ Improving service levels to give customers no excuse to be tempted to defect.
❑ Building relationships with customers so that they do not want to defect.
❑ Creating exit barriers for customers, so that defecting to a competitor incurs some kind of cost or penalty.

❑ Building entry barriers for the competition, making it difficult for it to enter the market in the first place.

IMPROVING SERVICE LEVELS: DYSON

Despite the fact that most companies appear convinced that they lose more customers because of price than anything else, research has shown time and time again that the prime reason for customers changing suppliers is poor or apathetic service. Too many studies have concluded this for it not to be taken as a fact, and one study conducted by PIMS, a Boston-based consultancy, showed that 68 percent of defecting customers were lost as a result of something that could be categorized as poor service.

It is outside the scope of this book to discuss customer service in depth, so I will restrict myself to making two points about it. The first is that in service, it is the little things that matter most. The majority of companies seem to think that if they lose a customer through poor service, it is when something major has gone wrong. Although this can obviously happen, it is not the norm. When something major does go wrong, the company will probably know about it in the first place, the customer will usually tell them about it, and if the company goes into 'recovery' mode, it can often save the situation.

The real danger is when a series of relatively unimportant, annoying little things go wrong, none of which is significant in the overall scheme of things. These errors may be so small that the customer will not say anything and the supplier will remain in ignorance about their existence. Nevertheless, they still add up and eventually the customer feels 'enough is enough' and looks around for an alternative. In looking around, he or she probably finds a better price (new customers often get great deals), and the original supplier then thinks that it lost the customer through price. However, the customer found the lower price as a result of looking around; and the reason that he or she looked around in the first place was the series of small annoying mistakes (i.e. the type of thing that is normally within employees' control).

The second point is that aiming to satisfy customers is a bad idea. Something like 90 percent of company mission statements contain some reference to 'satisfying the customer'. However, there is no identifiable link between customer loyalty and satisfaction. Consider the following:

❑ JD Power research shows that 90 percent of US drivers say that they are 'satisfied' with their current car, but no brands other than the Lexus and Saturn have a repurchase rate of higher than 50 percent.
❑ Bain & Bain research shows that between 60 and 80 percent of defecting customers described themselves as 'satisfied' with their previous supplier.

As Chris Daffy says in his book *Once a Customer, Always a Customer*: 'Satisfied customers are like lodgers; they are with you for now, until something better comes along.' According to him, customer satisfaction occurs when the service delivered is equal to what the supplier promised, or what the customer was expecting. Merely delivering what customers are expecting, however, is no big deal. After all, the customers assumed that the supplier could do this; that is why they bought from it in the first place. No company has a right to expect loyalty from a customer who is merely satisfied.

Loyalty is only generated when the service delivered exceeds what is expected, thus creating customer delight. The problem most companies encounter is that they spend much of their time, effort and resources delivering what they think their customers expect, then sit back in smug self-satisfaction once this is being achieved 99 percent of the time. Unfortunately, they then have to come to people like myself and ask why they are still losing customers by the bucketload, even though they are scoring a high percentage of ticks in the 'satisfied' column on the feedback forms they send out.

Delivering what customers expect prevents dissatisfaction and is enough to stop them from actively looking around for an alternative supplier; however, it is not enough to prevent them leaving if they are actively 'poached' by a competitor.

When looking at the results of satisfaction surveys, the only ticks that count are those in the 'more than satisfied' column (whether it is titled 'delighted' or anything else). Any other customers should be viewed as being at risk.

Service should therefore be a priority for all companies, not only those that have direct contact with the end user or that are in a recognized service industry. In addition to the tangible benefits of product quality and value for money, companies need to add value by branding the service they can provide (see the discussion on Graniterock in Chapter 6). It is interesting to note that in the US the two cars with the highest repurchase rate (Saturn and Lexus) both use company-owned retail networks rather than relying on independent or franchised dealers. This gives them complete control over the total purchasing and after-sales experience, rather than having to rely on the distribution network to deliver the type of service they themselves would want to give.

The vacuum cleaner industry in the UK was turned on its head by the introduction of a genuinely differentiated and superior product from Dyson, the cyclonic vacuum cleaner. However, a superior product is not enough to achieve sustainable market leadership. Nowadays product innovations are very short-lived, and competitors can copy new features in months where an innovative company would once have had a breathing space of years. No matter how superior a company's best product is, somewhere a competitor has something on the drawing board that will match (if not surpass) it. Competitive SWATs built around product performance alone are therefore very vulnerable, for when that competitive product is introduced, the company's point of differentiation disappears overnight.

Dyson was always aware that its competition would one day bring out their own cleaners using cyclone technology, and to prepare for that day the company set out from the start to deliver outstanding customer service. Most service in the industry was poor or average, with customers having to carry their (sometimes heavy) appliances back to the retail outlet where they were bought or to an independent repairer once the warranty had expired. The service the customer received was then 100 percent in the hands of the retailer or repairer rather than the manufacturer.

In his autobiography *Against the Odds*, James Dyson writes:

> *I was adamant from the outset that the retailers who sell our machines would not be involved in the customer service loop. ... I felt that the customer service relating to our machines was our own responsibility and also that giving a customer the highest level of service is ... part of the Dyson proposition.*

The company has its own helpline, the number for which is prominently displayed on every cleaner, to save the customer the inconvenience of searching for a long-lost instruction manual. This is open seven days a week, from eight until eight, and is staffed by employees whose number one aim is to help the customer rather than defend the company against criticism. Customers with a broken or damaged machine are told that it will be collected the following day, and it comes back fully repaired two days later, having had a free service thrown in. If required, a replacement cleaner will also be provided for the duration of the repair.

The result is delighted customers, who will not only repurchase from Dyson rather than a competitor when the time arrives, but who also act as advocates for the company and recommend it to their friends and relatives. Dyson claims that 64 percent of its sales come via recommendations of this sort.

Now that Electrolux has introduced its own bagless cleaner, it will be interesting to see if the Dyson defense is successful.

BUILDING CUSTOMER RELATIONSHIPS: NESTLÉ BUITONI

Improving service levels ensures that customers are not actively given a negative reason to defect. The second level of customer fortification gives them a positive reason to stay. It should be noted that this is not the same as a loyalty scheme; with these the customer's loyalty is often to the scheme itself rather than to the company running it. When consumers can collect Air Miles from a wide variety of suppliers such as Sainsbury, Shell and NatWest Visa, they may choose to spend their money with them not because they feel that they are the best suppliers in their particular industries, but because there is a short-term reward for doing so.

Any loyalty is better than no loyalty, but companies should be looking to build loyalty to themselves. One way of doing this is by price, but as we have seen, if a company targets price-conscious customers it should not be surprised when they drop it like a hot potato when an even cheaper alternative becomes available.

If it does not have a competitive SWAT, the best way for a company to build long-lasting loyalty is via relationships, so that customers feel that the company is 'their' supplier.

An outstanding example of this is Nestlé and its pasta brand Buitoni, purchased by the company in 1988. Nestlé quickly gave Buitoni the strategic aim of becoming the world's leading brand of Italian food. In the UK, while the brand had almost twice the market share of the second leading brand, it faced the problem of a rapidly growing own-label market, which has over 60 percent of the market. The main problem was lack of brand loyalty, as most 'new entrants' to the dry pasta market would buy a brand initially because of the reassurance that this gave them, but switch to own-label once they became comfortable with cooking it. To many people, a pasta is a pasta is a pasta.

Lacking a competitive SWAT to justify the price differential other than that used by most brands when competing with own label, i.e. 'quality' – something that shoppers increasingly do not believe; personal experience shows them that most own-label grocery products are of a very high quality, and many suspect that they are produced by the branded manufacturers anyway – Buitoni felt that the normal 'mass-marketing' techniques were no longer cost effective or appropriate, and became one of the first fast-moving consumer goods (fmcg) companies to try a 'one-to-one' approach.

Its aim was to build a relationship with lovers of Italian food based on common interests, to establish a genuine dialogue with them rather than relying on the traditional one-way approach of advertising, and to establish itself as the authority in Italian cuisine, thereby creating a bond between the company and its customers that hopefully would be strong enough to prevent their defection to own label.

The 80/20 rule applies to all industries, in that a small percentage of heavy users account for the majority of sales and profit, and Buitoni's first task was to identify just who the consumers of its pasta were. Over an 18-month period all advertising, be it TV, press or radio, featured a telephone number asking pasta lovers to identify themselves; in return, respondents received a free 20-page recipe booklet and a loyalty promotion.

After the 18 months, a total of 200,000 names had been collected and the 'Casa Buitoni' Club was launched. Every respondent was sent a personalized invitation to join with a free-reply postcard, simply asking for a Buitoni barcode to be attached. Over 20 percent joined, giving an initial membership of over 40,000, and over 9000 of these filled in a detailed questionnaire in the first issue of the Club's quarterly newsletter. Over 5000 responded when volunteers were sought for a special consumer panel for use in product testing.

Although the theme for the Club is 'Share the love of Italian food', the common interest on which the relationship was to be based was not just a love of Italian food, but of all things Italian. The full-color quarterly newsletter is full of pasta recipes, exclusive offers, competitions, money-off coupons and features on Italian life, wine and culture in general. It adds genuine value for customers while at the same time subtly reinforcing their shared interests.

A free careline (heavily featured on every pack) is provided for members to enable them to communicate with Buitoni on anything at all to do with its products, recipes or even Italy overall. Consumers have telephoned to ask for advice on where to holiday in Italy, or even for suggestions of Italian names for their children! In 1998 a Web site was introduced to provide an on-line version of the magazine.

There is no guarantee that any of these members buys Buitoni pasta (in theory, they could belong to the club and buy own label). Nestlé accepts that some of its spend will therefore be wasted, but it points out that a large percentage of traditional, mass-marketing spend is also wasted (remember Lord Leverhulme's dictum that 'Half of my advertising is wasted; I just don't know which half'?). While the Club is therefore run as an 'act of faith' to a certain extent, the company is convinced that it is both successful and cost effective. Although Nestlé will not produce market share figures, it is adamant that the relationship built with its key pasta users is a key deterrent to customer defection.

CREATING EXIT BARRIERS FOR CUSTOMERS: FREQUENT FLYER SCHEMES

The creation of relationships aims at making customers want to stay with the supplier in question because of an emotional bond. An added fortification is the creation of exit barriers for customers, i.e. something that meant that they would suffer materially if they did defect. Perhaps the best-known of these are the frequent flyer schemes run by many major airlines.

Following the deregulation of the US airline industry in 1981, and facing attack by new, low-cost companies such as People Express, the established airlines faced a serious problem in preventing customers 'defecting' to competitors. They finally came up with frequent flyer miles.

The first company to introduce these was American Airlines, which announced its AAdvantage program in May 1981. This encouraged passengers to build up 'credits' each time they flew with AA and then to redeem them against other flights. Each flight with the company therefore acted as an incentive to remain with it for the next one.

The cost to AA was minimal as long as it had empty seats, but the perceived value of the flights to the customer was very high. The good news was that the people most likely to become loyal were also its most profitable customers, the frequent business passengers.

In order to ensure that non-paying passengers did not displace paying ones, AA restricted the number of seats on any one flight and the flights on which they could be taken. It acted to prevent the sale of credits.

While the program was a truly innovative idea, the problem was that it was not sustainable as a competitive SWAT. Any airline could do it and, within weeks of AAdvantage's launch, United Airlines announced its own program called Mileage Plus. Within three months, every major American airline had a similar scheme. However, nearly 20 years later AA's program is still the world's largest with 30 million members (United, the number two, has 23 million, and BA's Executive Club a mere 2.5 million).

The introduction of other programs did not mean that AAdvantage ceased to have value. Even when a raft of such schemes exist, there is still a strong incentive for passenger loyalty after they have clocked up a few thousand miles. Of course, passengers could belong to several different programs (much as many people in the UK have both Tesco Loyalty and Sainsbury's Reward cards), but this would only be worthwhile for a small minority of very frequent flyers, and for these each program had added incentives.

Passengers flying with AA can achieve Gold status if they fly 25,000 miles per annum and Platinum if they fly 50,000; once they reach these levels they receive unlimited first-class upgrades, a special reservation service and companion upgrades. Thus even once the credits have been cashed, the incentive is still there to fly with AA to maintain the privileges to which they have become accustomed.

An added, and probably unforeseen, benefit of such programs is that they reduce price competition among the major carriers. As each major airline develops its own base of loyal passengers, the temptation to go after market share via price cuts becomes less attractive. Similarly, raising prices within reason is less likely to drive customers into the arms of the competition, especially if the flyers' companies are paying rather than themselves.

Smaller competitors without such schemes, such as the no-frills airlines discussed in Chapter 5, complain that the programs are anti-competitive. They assert that the schemes subvert corporate travel policies, because despite whatever the finance director attempts to dictate about travel expenses, senior managers are going to book with their 'favorite' airline when they can to clock up more miles.

The programs work to such an extent that some have raised serious concerns about their effect on limiting competition. Attempts have even been made to 'level the playing field', such as the German competition regulators' ruling that Lufthansa's program be widened to include a small competitor called Eurowings.

BUILDING BARRIERS FOR THE COMPETITION: WALL'S ICE CREAM

The fourth level of customer fortification is the creation of barriers that make it difficult for competitors to get a toehold in the market in the first place. An example is Bird's Eye Walls (owned by Unilever), the clear market leader in the UK ice-cream market, with a share of approximately 70 percent of the £300 million wrapped impulse market. The numbers two and three in the market are Mars and Nestlé (which purchased Lyons Maid in 1993).

Walls has achieved this position of dominance by building almost insurmountable barriers to entry to ensure that its competition is permanently doomed to minor-league status. It has freezer cabinets in the vast majority of outlets selling wrapped impulse ice cream, which are installed with a contractual agreement that only Walls products can be displayed in them.

Until 1979, the agreement also stated that no other freezer unit could be displayed in the outlet, but an investigation by the Monopolies & Mergers Commission (now known as the Competition Commission) deemed this illegal. Since then outlets have been allowed to keep more than one freezer, but in practice few do; they simply don't have the space.

At the time, Lyons Maid was an almost dormant competitor, but the market was shaken up by the entry of Mars into the marketplace in 1989 with an ice-cream version of the Mars bar and the Dove bar. Walls responded by bringing out an alternative to Dove called Magnum. The latter soared in sales and is now the number one brand; Dove was withdrawn from the marketplace because of a lack of distribution – Mars simply could not get it into enough outlets due to the ubiquitous Walls cabinets. Although Mars brought out its own freezers and had these installed alongside those of Walls in the likes of motorway services shops, the vast majority of corner shops did not have the space for a second cabinet.

The situation was compounded by the fact that Walls has a network of regional distributors who 'police' the cabinets and supply its products exclusively. Possession of a cabinet binds the retailer to purchasing from the distributor; if it wants to buy elsewhere, it loses the cabinet.

Mars had the whole issue reopened by the MMC in 1993 (to no avail), again in 1995 and yet again in 1998. The Commission said that Walls had to offer all wholesalers the same terms as it offered its distributors in order to encourage competition. However, Walls responded by launching its own in-house distributor network, run for it by subcontractors. Yet again it had escaped.

The company's clever use of exclusivity (which would be illegal in some other countries) and a tied distributor network have meant that for decades its market position has been impregnable. Any impulse brand lives or dies on its distribution, and competitors' brands have just not been able to achieve sufficient levels to threaten Walls.

THE IMPORTANCE OF SECURING THE FLANKS

One of the most important principles of defensive warfare is to guard the flanks, traditionally seen as the weakest point of any defensive position.

THE GULF WAR: OPERATION DESERT STORM, 1990

In August 1990, 100,000 Iraqi troops crossed their southern border into Kuwait, ostensibly to prevent that country from producing more oil than it had been allocated under OPEC agreements thereby causing oil prices to plummet. Kuwait's entire population was smaller than Iraq's armed forces, and its army had not even been mobilized, the government confident that a diplomatic solution would be found to the problems it had with its much larger neighbor. However, although this made Iraq's task easier, Kuwait never stood a chance against such overwhelming numerical superiority and it would have been occupied almost as quickly even if the forces had been ready.

Outraged by such a naked display of force against a small state but also concerned about the security of oil supplies (and about what Saddam Hussein would do next if his military adventure went unpunished), the international community formed a coalition of forces from a wide variety of countries. Eventually nearly 700,000 troops massed in Saudi Arabia with the aim of liberating Kuwait, and although the US provided 60 percent of them (and 70 percent of the combat aircraft), contingents existed from countries as diverse as Niger, Bangladesh, Argentina and Pakistan.

Saddam Hussein missed a golden opportunity to improve his position before the coalition was able to move its 'heavy' forces into position. Had he invaded Saudi Arabia immediately after Kuwait, his troops would have been faced with only a token, lightly armed US force backed by the Saudi airforce. Such a stroke would have removed the coalition's invasion 'launchpad' and made Kuwait's liberation impossible without either an amphibious assault or an invasion of Iraq itself. However, Saddam allowed this window of opportunity to slip by, manly due to the fact that he felt he could legitimize Kuwait's invasion but would not be able to do the same over its larger southern neighbor. He also seems to have thought that the US was weak and would not fight for Kuwait, but might do for Saudi Arabia.

Saddam's only conventional military experience had been the eight-year war against Iran, which he had eventually won by having his troops retreat and draw the Iranians into 'killing zones'. Stopped by massive obstacles and flanked by pre-positioned tanks and artillery, the young, inexperienced Iranians had been massacred.

Saddam envisaged a similar battle being waged in Kuwait, and as talks and various diplomatic initiatives stalled, the Iraqis dug in behind seemingly formidable defenses, preparing for what he famously referred to as 'the mother of all battles'. Over 200,000 troops, including the elite Republican Guard, erected huge defensive

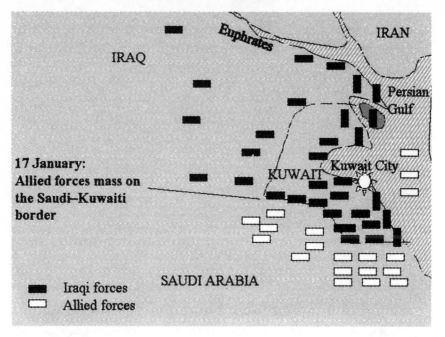

17 January:
Allied forces mass on
the Saudi–Kuwaiti
border

IRAQ

IRAN

Euphrates

Persian
Gulf

KUWAIT

Kuwait City

SAUDI ARABIA

■■ Iraqi forces
☐ Allied forces

walls of sand dozens of feet thick, topped with barbed wire and
fronted by minefields and trenches filled with oil that would be
ignited once an attack materialized. There was also the ever-present
fear of Iraq using chemical weapons (something it had done in the
Iraq–Iran war during the 1980s) and Saddam boasted that the
enemy would 'drown in their own blood'. The western media
(fueled by the opinions of armchair strategists and retired senior
military officers) speculated that coalition casualties would be huge,
often quoting figures of 20–30,000 in the first two weeks after an
invasion.

Faced with such seemingly impregnable defenses, the coalition
commander, US general 'Stormin' Norman' Schwartzkopf, was
undaunted. He had no intention of attacking the Iraqis frontally, as
Saddam seemed to think. He said later:

> *I was worried about the barrier they were building and the troops
> they were digging in behind them. The worst case would be for our
> troops to go in there and get hung up on the wire and having chem-
> ical weapons dumped on them.*

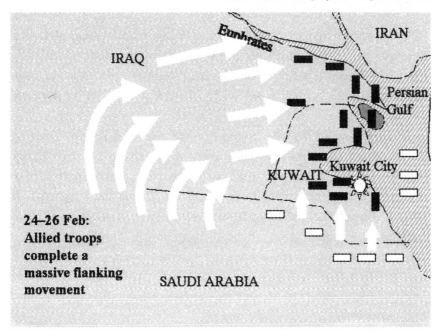

IRAQ

Euphrates

IRAN

Persian Gulf

KUWAIT Kuwait City

24–26 Feb: Allied troops complete a massive flanking movement

SAUDI ARABIA

His plan was to move 200,000 US, British and French troops as much as 300 miles to the west in secret, to deliver what he called a 'left hook', driving deep into Iraq behind Kuwait to prevent Iraqi reinforcement or retreat, and also attacking the Republican Guard by surprise, hitting it in its right flank. At one briefing he said:

> *A war in the desert is a war of mobility ... It's not a war of straight lines drawn in the sand where you dig in and say, 'I will defend here or die.'*

This plan also called for the implementation of a doctrine called 'AirLand Battle', which called for air attacks on the enemy's rear areas to cut off supply lines and destroy command-and-control centers in order to isolate the battlefield and the enemy frontline troops.

Thus on 16 January Operation Desert Storm began as the most powerful demonstration of air power since the dropping of two atomic bombs in 1945. Over the next five weeks a relentless aerial bombardment battered both Iraq and its forces inside Kuwait, with almost 90,000 tonnes of bombs being dropped and up to

3000 missions being flown per day. Radar installations, airfields, headquarters and frontline units were bombarded relentlessly until approximately 35 percent of Iraq's combat aircraft had been destroyed and between 40 and 50 percent of its tanks and artillery.

Inspired by the way Montgomery had deceived Rommel during the battle of El Alamein in 1942 as to his intended point of attack (see Chapter 2), Schwartzkopf kept up an elaborate deception plan of his own designed to make Saddam think that the main assault would come from the front and from the sea. A force of 17,000 Marines conspicuously practiced amphibious landings and an armada of 31 ships patrolled the coast, while 460 troops had the job of patrolling the Kuwaiti border 'acting' like a full division of 16,000 men, with loudspeakers broadcasting tank noises and dummy vehicles and artillery pieces.

On 23 February, with Saddam blind to what was happening on the allied side of the border, the US, British and French troops earmarked for the task began a massive flanking movement westward. The following day, as US and Arab troops attacked the Iraqi defences frontally at selected spots, these flanking troops raced deep into Iraqi territory and wheeled around the Iraqi flank along the Euphrates river.

The supposedly impregnable defenses proved anything but. As allied aircraft burned the oil from the Iraqi trenches using napalm and others were simply filled in by tanks shoveling dirt with bulldozer blades, allied troops cut passages at carefully selected weak points and motored through, often without meeting opposition.

Completely taken by surprise, the Iraqi defense virtually collapsed. By 27 February, Kuwait City had been liberated and a solid wall of allied troops cut off the remaining Iraqi troops from escape. To have continued would have been like shooting fish in a barrel, and President Bush called off his troops. Within three and a half days more than 29 Iraqi divisions had been destroyed, in addition to 3000 tanks. The 'mother of all battles' had lasted only 100 hours. Schwartzkopf later said:

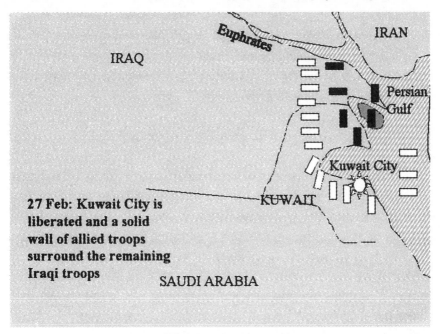

IRAQ

IRAN

Euphrates

Persian Gulf

Kuwait City

KUWAIT

27 Feb: Kuwait City is liberated and a solid wall of allied troops surround the remaining Iraqi troops

SAUDI ARABIA

After the third day ... we knew we had them ... it was literally about to become the battle of Cannae, a battle of annihilation.

(See Chapter 9 for how Hannibal completely destroyed a Roman army with a double envelopment.)

The battle was won primarily because Saddam had become fixated with the idea that the main attack was going to come from the front and the sea, and had put his troops in fixed positions facing these fronts. He thought that an attack from the west was impossible, and that the number of men required for such an attack could not have been moved quickly enough for him not to have had advance warning. He had ignored one of the most basic rules of defensive warfare, which is to secure the flanks. To give the final words to General Schwartzkopf:

When we knew he couldn't see us any more, we did a massive movement of troops all the way out to the west ... because at that time we knew he was still fixed in this area with the vast majority of his forces, and once the air campaign started, he would be incapable of moving out to counter this move, even if he knew we made it. There

were some additional Iraqi troops in this [western] area, but they
did not have the capability nor the time to put in the barrier that had
been described by [him] as an absolutely impenetrable tank barrier
that no one would ever get through.

SECURING THE FLANKS COMMERCIALLY

The commercial equivalent of securing an army's flanks is recognizing a company's weak points as the most likely route of a competitive attack, and either shoring up the defenses in advance at those points, or responding aggressively when such an attack materializes. The continued success of established companies depends on their recognizing and reacting to competitive threats as and when they occur. Examples abound of companies (and whole industries) that have been destroyed because they failed to react to attacks from existing competitors, new entrants or even substitutes.

Not only should companies never be complacent about competitive attacks, they should actually attack themselves before the assault comes from outside. A company should know the strengths and weaknesses of its products and services better than the competition (sometimes it fails to do so as a result of complacency or arrogance), and a continual, honest appraisal of these will reveal the best points for the competition to attack. Is it price? Quality? Ease of use? Service? Reliability? Delivery? Choice? Range? Speed?

Whatever it is, you can be certain that if you are able to identify it today, the competition will inevitably do so at some time in the future. It may not be tomorrow, next week or next month, but it will happen. In fact, it is probable that right now someone, somewhere is planning something that will severely weaken your competitive position. When it happens, what will you do about it?

If you cannot identify the most likely directions of competitive attacks and do not know what you will do if or when they take place, you are not doing your job properly. A general would not wait until the enemy attack took place and then allocate his defensive forces accordingly. He looks at the terrain, identifies the most likely route of attack and then allocates his forces to cover those areas.

In fact, rather than wait for the attack to take place, it is a far better strategy to introduce the product or service yourself before the competition has a chance to do so, and in doing so attack yourself. Most companies resist doing this because it inevitably leads to cannibalization of existing sales, but at least that cannibalization goes to you and not someone else. If you were placed in a position (perhaps an arcane court sentence imposed in a foreign land) where you could not avoid being shot in the foot, but were given the choice of either doing it yourself or having the official executioner do it, which would you choose? Personally, I would do it myself, taking a small-caliber pistol and shooting off only my little toe. If I left it to the executioner, he might take the foot off at the ankle using a sawn-off shotgun!

Nintendo's refusal to introduce a 16-bit machine to compete with Sega's (see Chapter 9), for fear of cannibalization of its 8-bit machine, gave Sega a three-year monopoly of that part of the market. The whole of the British motorcycle industry perished because it ignored the Japanese threat; Harley-Davidson nearly suffered the same fate (see below). Detroit's 'Big Three' auto manufacturers ignored a similar threat, thinking that 'small cars will never catch on; people want cars that only do five miles to the gallon', even when the price of petrol was skyrocketing after the fuel crises of the mid-1970s.

SECURING THE FLANKS: KINGFISHER VS WAL-MART

Although Kingfisher (the UK retail group that owns Woolworth, Comet, Superdrug, MVC and B&Q) denies it, the driving force behind its failed 'merger' (read takeover) with Asda, the country's fourth-largest food retailer, was a fear of Wal-Mart, the world's largest retailer, 'invading' the UK.

Retailing has become global over the past decade as the most successful companies expand their winning formats overseas. The most successful retailer in the world is America's Wal-Mart, which has recently moved into Germany and is reported to have its eyes on the UK. Wal-Mart (see Chapter 9) is a general merchandiser with

huge discount warehouses where shoppers can buy virtually anything they want at rock-bottom prices. Its combination of range,
value and excellent service has made it a favorite with US consumers, and with an April 1999 market value of £131 billion, it
dominates the world retail league, being more than twice the size of
the number two company, Home Depot (also American, with a
value of £58 billion).

Woolworth itself is a general merchandiser, but it has a limited
range and its mostly high-street stores are tiny compared with the
US company's out-of-town behemoths and even though B&Q,
Comet, MVC and Superdrug might be able to match Wal-Mart's
range in their chosen areas of expertise, they sell their products
under different roofs while it provides a 'one-stop shop'.

Kingfisher has recently opened its first out-of-town superstore in
Edinburgh called Big W, which combines the group's retail chains in
one outlet, but what this format lacks when compared with Wal-
Mart is food.

Food retailing has been central to Wal-Mart's growth for the simple reason that it brings customer traffic. Shoppers visit DIY stores
and electrical retailers several times per year; most visit food stores
weekly and it is this frequency of visit that makes food retailing so
important. While shoppers are buying their weekly groceries, it is
convenient for them to buy the various other non-food items they
need during the same visit.

Some have criticized Kingfisher's choice of Asda because it is only
the fourth-biggest food retailer, but these critics are missing the
point. Asda's average store size is 42,000 sq ft, twice the average size
of market leader Tesco (20,000 sq ft). In addition, Asda also has the
highest proportion of non-food sales, with half of its 9 million sq ft
of floor space devoted to general merchandise, especially its hugely
successful clothing range developed by George Davis, the founder of
Next.

The merger with Asda would have made Kingfisher the eighth
biggest retail group in the world with a value of £17.3 billion. While
it would still have been dwarfed by Wal-Mart, it would have had the
benefit of fighting defensively and the purchase of Asda would have

secured its flanks and shored up its defenses in its most vulnerable area.

Unfortunately for Kingfisher, the announcement of the merger caused Wal-Mart to have a closer look at Asda itself and it liked what it saw. Moving quicker than the slow-footed Kingfisher probably thought possible (a deal between Asda and Kingfisher had been mooted for years), it put in a cash bid worth £6.7 billion, far more attractive to Asda shareholders than the doomed merger deal, and snatched the company from under the competition's nose.

HONDA VS HARLEY-DAVIDSON

In the late 1950s, Harley-Davidson was in the supreme position in the US motorcycle market. Over a period of 60 years it had destroyed its US competition (the last competing firm closed in 1953) and held 70 percent of the US market. To most bikers, Harley was virtually a US institution.

In 1959 Honda decided to enter the US market and to observers, taking on Harley appeared to be a *kamikaze* attack, or commercial suicide. To have attacked Harley head on would have been just that, as there is no way that their much smaller bikes could have made major inroads with that company's traditional customers, even though they were actually of better quality.

Honda therefore chose to fight Harley with a **head-to-head logistics** strategy. It also decided to attack it on terrain where its traditional strength, its loyal customer base among existing US bikers, was irrelevant. Honda identified an inherent weakness in this; the US motorcycle market had not shown much growth over the years, partly because the price of a high-powered Harley could be higher than that of a car, but partly because the public image of motorcyclists was so poor.

The majority of the US public had never been on a motorcycle and thought of bikers as leather-clad degenerates straight out of Marlon Brando's film *The Wild One*. Adding to this image was the fact that most Harley dealerships were located in rundown parts of town and their appearance lived 'down' to their image. While this image was an essential factor in Harley's dominance of the existing market, with customers who reveled in their 'bad boy' image, it was also acting as a brake on any growth in the market.

There was no way that an attack by Honda on Harley's traditional market using a head-to-head combat strategy could be successful. Instead, it first secured a beachhead by concentrating on a sector of the market that had been ignored by Harley, respectable college kids who were desperate for a form of transport other than their parents' car, but who could not afford a car of their own.

In Japan, a small, overcrowded country with busy roads, motorcycles were used by millions of 'normal' people everyday as a convenient, cost-effective method of commuting to work or college, and Honda thought the US market was also suitable for that kind of usage. In the first year, however, it sold only 167 vehicles, and Harley-Davidson ridiculed both its products and its approach as unsuitable for the US public. Harley had tried to launch low-cc bikes twice itself (in 1925 and 1949) and had failed on both occasions, and this experience led it to believe that it couldn't be done and that Honda was doomed to failure. However, its previous attempts had failed partly because it had priced the bikes not much lower than its traditional ones, and the public had rejected them as poor value for money.

Honda, on the other hand, positioned the bikes as an inexpensive, fuel-efficient, cost-effective method of transport, ideal as the answer to campus parking problems. This was as far as possible from the negative image previously associated with motorcycles, and the company used advertising featuring nice, acceptable, clean-cut young people with bylines such as 'Go happy, go Honda', 'You meet the nicest people on a Honda' and 'Honda days, not holidays'.

It was aiming at non-traditional bike owners, young people aged 16–26, who would probably not have even thought of purchasing a motorcycle or who would have discounted such an idea due to the high cost. And it was incredibly successful in this, with almost one-third of its first-time buyers aged under 20. It also offered a wider range of colors and models than Harley (14 by 1965).

Honda calculated that Harley would be unable to compete successfully against its own products and approach, because the very thing that gave it strength in the existing market – i.e. the greasy, 'tough-guy' image – was a weakness when it came to the new market. Harley found itself unable to react, but was also complacent because an upturn in the motorcycle market in general meant that its own sales didn't suffer too badly.

However, once Honda had established a reputation for quality that far surpassed that of Harley, it moved on to the next market sector in line with a raiding logistics strategy. It introduced larger machines to compete directly and enable new users who wanted to trade up in terms of horsepower to stay with Honda if they wanted to.

The results of this strategy were spectacular. In 1964 Honda sold 270,000 bikes and by 1965 it had 80 percent of the market. The whole market expanded in size. Whereas in 1960 there had been 400,000 registered motorcycles in the whole US, by 1964 there were 960,000. This figure increased to 1.4 million by 1966, and 4 million by 1971. Although some of this growth went to Harley-Davidson, that company's rapid expansion of production caused its already mediocre quality to worsen and its share of the overall market plummeted.

Harley's traditional strengths were simply of no use in this new, expanded market, and when Honda's market share eventually fell, it was not to Harley but to other Japanese manufacturers. By 1977, Harley's share had fallen from 70 to 6 percent, largely because of Honda's strategy of deliberately choosing an area of the market where the US company's traditional strengths were of little use. Instead of fighting back and defending its 'home turf' with vigour, Harley fell victim to the 'Three Cs' of complacency, confidence and conceit, and refused to treat the activities of the Japanese company seriously. The results were disastrous, almost leading to bankruptcy.

NEW COKE

Responses to competitive attack need to be appropriate, however. In attacking their existing products and services, companies need to be careful not to throw the baby out with the bathwater. Probably the best example of a company doing this is Coca-Cola's launch of 'New Coke'.

During the 1970s, after years of remarkable growth, Pepsi was slowly narrowing the gap between itself and Coke. Its innovative marketing campaigns called on the 'Pepsi Generation' to accept the 'Pepsi Challenge', and its TV ads trumpeted the assertion that people preferred Pepsi over Coke by a factor of 3 to 2 in blind tests. By the end of the decade, Coke still had 24 percent of the total soft drinks market to Pepsi's 18 percent, but by 1984 this lead had halved to only 3 percentage points (Coke was actually 2 percent behind Pepsi in grocery stores). What was worse, this had happened while Coke was spending $100 million per year more than Pepsi on advertising!

The problem was more than just slick Pepsi marketing. To Coke's horror, it appeared to be the taste of the product itself. Research was showing time and time again that Pepsi's advertising claims were true: young people actually seemed to prefer the slightly sweeter taste of Pepsi in blind tests. Terrified that its original recipe was no longer the 'secret weapon' it had always been and that Pepsi would eventually push it into the number 2 slot, Coke reacted by developing a new product tasting more like Pepsi, and by 1984 it was beating the latter in blind tests. Just to make sure, Coke then ran the biggest taste test ever conducted. It spent $4 million testing the new product with 191,000 people in 13 cities, and the result was that 55 percent of people preferred the new taste to the old.

'New Coke' was launched in April 1985 with a great fanfare, and within 24 hours 81 percent of the US public had heard about the launch (a greater percentage than had heard of Neil Armstrong's landing on the moon, 24 hours after that had happened!).

Then everything started to go wrong. Within four hours of the product's hitting the shelves Coke had received 650 calls of complaint, and by mid-May the figure had grown to 5000 a day. Some 40,000 critical letters and calls were received, the majority objecting to what they saw as an American symbol being changed. One such letter, typical in its tone, said:

It was nice knowing you. You were a friend for most of my 35 years.
Yesterday I had my first taste of new Coke, and to tell you the truth,
if I had wanted Pepsi, I would have ordered Pepsi, not Coke.

Loyal consumers stockpiled the old product, its price skyrocketed, and some even announced plans to sue the company! By July, the percentage of people who preferred New Coke to 'the real thing' was down to 30 percent, and on 11 July Coke relaunched the original product as 'Coke Classic'. It was an about-turn of such importance that ABC actually interrupted its television programming to announce the news.

The whole event was viewed by many as a public relations success, due to the massive media coverage that the company had achieved, worth hundreds of millions of dollars, and the wave of public support for the original product that had been unleashed. On the back of it, in 1985 the company achieved a sales growth of 10 percent and a profit growth of 9 percent.

Coke should be congratulated for having the courage even to contemplate changing its biggest 'sacred cow', the product recipe itself, but amazingly it failed to recognize that a 55/45 split in favor of change was not a high enough figure. By aiming at the 55 percent (many of whom may not have been won over anyway; they may have continued buying Pepsi), it risked alienating the diehard 45 percent who actually did not like the new, sweeter taste.

A much more successful approach would have been to launch a new, sweeter variant of Coke (it already had the variants Diet Coke and Cherry Coke), giving consumers a choice between the two tastes. Those who preferred the 'real thing' could still have had it, while those who preferred the Pepsi taste but still liked the brand values associated with Coke could have opted for the alternative. The approach the company did take was virtually guaranteed to fail.

Self-diagnostic questionnaire

1 What are the strengths or weaknesses of your company that a competitor could take advantage of?

2 If you were in that competitor's shoes, how would you conduct the attack? Establish a small group of people to brainstorm how this attack would take place. From which existing competitor (or substitute) is it most likely that a serious attack on your company will come?

3 How likely is it that such an attack will happen?

4 How can you pre-empt such an attack by introducing the necessary product/service/approach yourself?

5 What would be the cost of cannibalization if you did so?

6 What would be the cost if a competitor did it instead?

7 Is service an integral part of your company's proposition? Would your staff agree with your assessment if you asked them?

8 What are the top six reasons for customers switching suppliers in your marketplace?

9 Ask your customers to compare your service levels with those of your competition. How do you stack up? Are you merely matching your customers' expectations, or do you regularly exceed them?

10 Can you genuinely say that your staff are customer oriented? What training programs do you have in place to ensure that they are?

11 What could you do to build a genuine relationship based on adding value and a mutual interest with (at a minimum) your biggest customers? What common interest/bond do you have with your customers?

12 Is there any kind of loyalty/frequent-use reward scheme that you could use to build exit barriers for your existing customers?

13 Are there any barriers to entry that you could build to deter new entrants from coming into the market?

4

THE IMPORTANCE OF
POSSESSING A SWAT

THE MOST IMPORTANT LESSON OF WARFARE IS THAT POSSESSION OF a superior weapons and tactics system (SWAT) will render any strategy (even the wrong one) more likely to be successful.

The search for a SWAT has led to combat tactics undergoing numerous transformations over the past 2500 years, although many of these have been cyclical in nature. Prior to the development of artillery, there were four basic weapons systems: heavy cavalry, light cavalry, heavy infantry and light infantry ('heavy' troops have usually been armored and relied on shock action, closing with the enemy to fight hand to hand with spear, sword or axe; 'light' troops have usually been more lightly equipped, possessed greater mobility and relied on missile power such as arrows, slings or javelins).

While it has not been a prerequisite for success that an army contained all four weapons systems (the Roman system, which can hardly be termed unsuccessful, had only two in any significant numbers, for example), those that managed to accomplish this invariably were successful.

Those that achieved success without all four were usually able to do so due to the absence of an enemy armed or organized to exploit that lack (when Rome finally met such a enemy, it suffered one of the worst military defeats in its history; see Chapter 6), or because geographic terrain dictated against the practical development of all four (e.g. cavalry has never played a major role in very mountainous countries).

Each of the four systems has achieved pre-eminence in different periods, in different armies or on different terrains, and history has shown that each is both superior and inferior to one or more of the others when used in isolation. The wise general has always known that his task was to decide on the optimum combination to use depending on the forces he was facing and the tactics they would use.

For example, it has repeatedly been demonstrated that heavy cavalry has been unable to defeat properly trained, led and motivated heavy infantry. The Greek phalanx, the Roman legion, the Scottish *schiltron*, the Spanish *tercio* and the Napoleonic infantry square all repulsed heavy cavalry charges on numerous occasions. However, heavy infantry on its own could do little to defeat heavy cavalry; it has nearly always needed the support of light infantry or light cavalry to do so (see the discussion of the battle of Crecy in Chapter 7).

On the other hand, when heavy infantry formed into one of the above formations in order to repulse a heavy cavalry charge, its massed ranks became extremely vulnerable to the firepower of light infantry or cavalry and, in later years, of artillery. Therefore heavy cavalry backed by any of these systems could be successful in defeating heavy infantry.

Thus well-trained and disciplined heavy infantry could defend itself against attack by heavy cavalry, but was vulnerable to missile fire from light cavalry or infantry. Light cavalry, also vulnerable to light infantry, needed the support of its heavy counterparts, and the light infantry needed protection from heavy infantry to withstand these attacks.

Like the children's game of 'paper, scissors and stone', each could be victorious depending on the enemy that it was up against.

During periods of history where no particular army possessed an advantage, or in specific wars where all participating armies were homogeneous, victory normally went to that side with a significant numerical superiority, or to that fighting defensively, with both sides 'slogging it out' like two equally powerful stags locking antlers.

A good example of this is the American Civil War, a conflict lacking in the brilliant use of tactics, where forces were more often than not thrown at each other in frontal attacks regardless of the ensuing carnage. There was a striking preponderance of indecisive victories, where one army or the other was defeated but not destroyed, and

Table 3 Major battles of the American Civil War

Battle	Defending forces	Attacking forces	Result
First Bull Run,1861	Confed: 32,500	Union: 35,000	Indecisive Confed victory
Shiloh,1862	Union: 51,000	Confed: 40,000	Union victory
Seven Pines,1862	Union: 26,000	Confed: 26,000	Indecisive
2nd Bull Run,1862	Confed: 54,000	Union: 63,000	Decisive Confed victory
Antietam,1862	Confed: 45,000	Union: 87,000	Indecisive Union victory
Fredericksburg,1862	Confed: 78,000	Union: 116,700	Decisive Confed victory
Stones River, 1863	Union: 43,400	Confed: 37,700	Indecisive
Chancellorsville,1863	Union: 130,000	Confed: 60,000	Decisive Confed victory
Gettysburg,1863	Union, 93,500	Confed: 77,500	Decisive Union victory
Chickamauga,1863	Union: 57,000	Confed: 66,000	Indecisive Confed victory
Chattanooga, 1863	Confed: 30,000	Union: 56,000	Decisive Union victory
The Wilderness,1864	Confed: 61,000	Union: 118,000	Indecisive
Spotsylvania,1864	Confed: 50,000	Union: 100,000	Indecisive
Atlanta,1864	Confed: 53,000	Union: 100,000	Decisive Union victory
Nashville,1864	Confed: 30,000	Union: 55,000	Decisive Union victory
Five Forks,1865	Confed: 10,000	Union: 25,000	Confederate surrender

left to regroup and fight another day; the victorious army was simply too exhausted to follow up its success.

At Antietam, for example, 'the bloodiest single day in American history', almost 25 percent of Lee's Confederate troops were casualties, but he was allowed to get clean away to reinforce for another day. Likewise at Gettysburg, the bloodiest battle in American history and this time a decisive victory for the Union, Lee suffered losses of 36 percent but again was allowed to retreat and escape.

The real problem facing both sides was that they were too alike! Armed with almost identical weapons and similarly composed, neither had any real advantage over the other, unless it was in numbers or the fact that it had managed to adopt a strong defensive position. What was needed was a breakthrough in tactics or weaponry to give one side a superiority of some kind, but this did not happen and the result was a series of bloody battles that cost the lives of hundreds of thousands of Americans, in a war of attrition that only ended when the South was literally too exhausted to fight any more.

DEVELOPING A COMPETITIVE SWAT

The real advantage in battle therefore lies with the side that has a superior tactical or weapons system of some sort. The same is true in competitive strategy.

All too often, companies launch 'attacks' on their competitors when they have no advantages whatsoever. They have products with the same (or similar) features and benefits, the same (or even higher) prices and the same (or even less) marketing support. And yet they expect customers and consumers in their thousands to leave the products they have been using or consuming and switch to theirs, for no better reason than that they wish it to be so.

This could be called the 'Tinkerbell' approach to competitive strategy, where there is a belief that if everybody really, really wishes hard enough, something will happen (i.e. the company will beat its competition). All the evidence suggests that in the real world this simply doesn't occur. As we have already seen, almost nine out of ten new product launches fail and not always because there was anything wrong with the product; many failed products are just as good as others that are successful.

Long-established companies or brands automatically possess all the advantages in their established markets, as was explained in Chapter 2. Being 'just as good' isn't good enough! To succeed, a product or company has to be *better* than its competition. It has to be of better quality, more reliable, look better, cost less, have additional features, perform better, have better advertising etc., etc. It doesn't have to have all these advantages, of course, but it does need at least one of them.

All companies therefore need to be continually engaged in searching for that 'something' that makes them different from the competition, for that competitive SWAT system that enables them to stand head and shoulders above the rest.

Most organizations recognize the impact that this can have on the customer and act swiftly to prevent their competition from achieving an advantage whenever something different is introduced to the marketplace. If the competition introduces a model with new features, they do too. If it offers extended credit, they do too. If it reduces prices, they do too, and so on.

There is nothing wrong with aping the competition as long as this is compatible with your organization's overall marketing strategy and positioning, but such activity must be recognized as being defensive in nature. Far fewer organizations seem concerned with using a competitive SWAT offensively, to make themselves different. Most will talk about it, but few achieve it. The proof is in the plethora of 'me too' products and companies that are almost identical to those of the competition. There are usually minor differences, but these may be noticeable only to the companies themselves and can be invisible to the customer.

WHY IT IS A COMPANY'S OWN FAULT IF ITS CUSTOMERS ARE OBSESSED WITH PRICE

The result, of course, is that customers, unable to identify any significant and worthwhile differences for which they are willing to pay a premium, make their purchasing decisions based on price. After all, they have to make a decision based on something and if the only visible difference is price, then it will be on that. This leads people in many organizations with which I work (especially salespeople) to make comments like: 'all our customers seem to be interested in is price'.

To such people I make the point that while individual customers might be price oriented for a number of valid reasons (usually economic in nature), if customers in general exhibit the same tendencies then it is usually the organization's own fault!

This is the case for two reasons. First, there is no differentiating factor that has sufficient value to customers to make them willing to pay a premium over the price of the product or service offered by the competition, and it is the responsibility of the organization to create one. Successful companies do not bemoan the fact that customers see no difference between them and the competition; they go out and make a difference.

Second, most companies who think like this tend to behave in a way that creates a self-fulfilling prophecy. Thinking that customers are interested only in price, they use price as their main (and sometimes only) marketing tool, offering discounts, promotions or permanent low prices in an attempt to win business. This rewards customers for basing their purchasing decision on price and therefore reinforces such behavior in the future.

THE COMPETITIVE SWAT MATRIX

What I term competitive SWATs are often referred to by others as sources of competitive advantage, and there are three generally accepted generic routes to achieving that: low-cost leadership, differentiation and focus, each of which is dealt with in some detail in Part II.

When Michael Porter first introduced the concept of competitive advantage in his book *Competitive Strategy*, he wrote:

> *...achieving competitive advantage requires a firm to make a choice. ... Being 'all things to all people' is a recipe for strategic mediocrity and below-average performance, because it often means that a firm has no competitive advantage at all. ... A firm that is 'stuck in the middle' will compete at a disadvantage because the cost leader, differentiators, or focusers will be better positioned to compete in any segment.*

Events have since overtaken this rather simplistic view, as examples now abound of companies that have managed to combine the best of both low-cost leadership and differentiation strategies. The point of differentiation itself may have been a major source of cost reduction, or cost reengineering has led to the company being differentiated in a way that is valued by the customer.

While some companies following low-cost leadership establish a low cost base and produce a no-frills product, such as the airlines described in Chapter 5, many such as Dell Computer, Direct Line insurance (Chapter 5) and Amazon (Chapter 3) have reengineered themselves in a way that has differentiated them from the competition and established a significant cost advantage.

What Porter calls 'strategic mediocrity' occurs when companies pursue neither low-cost leadership nor differentiation, or both half-

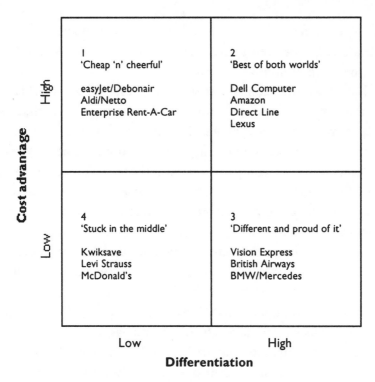

Figure 2 The competitive SWAT matrix

heartedly. It is by doing this that they find themselves 'stuck in the middle', unable to decide what they stand for in the marketplace, and find that their customers are in a similar quandary.

If we take Porter's approach and update it, Figure 2 shows the initial choices open to a company before the choice between a focus or mass approach is considered. The words 'high' and 'low' on each axis refer not to a company's absolute position, but its position relative to the competition. Therefore a company with a low cost base but which operated in a market where such a position was commonplace would have no advantage over its competition, and would therefore find itself in the bottom half of the matrix, regardless of its focus on costs.

In box 1, we find companies that have structured themselves so that they have done without a lot of the costs that their more traditional competition has always taken for granted. Their products or services will tend to be basic and without 'frills', but they will have one redeeming feature, low cost. Their approach to achieving low-cost leadership has been to remove costs rather than to reengineer the company in an innovative manner.

In box 2 we find companies with the best of both worlds, i.e. those that are differentiated from their competition but that also have a distinct cost advantage. This position may be arrived at from either angle. Sometimes an approach to removing costs ends up differentiating the company, for example with Direct Line insurance or First Direct bank. Sometimes an attempt at differentiation ends up cutting costs as well, for example with Amazon or Dell Computer.

Most companies in this box will be ones that have adopted this strategy from the outset. Established companies normally find it difficult to move into this box without setting up a completely new subsidiary (for example, British Airways has created Go to compete with its no-frills competitors, Debonair and easyJet).

Box 3 is for companies that are highly differentiated but in a way that may even add costs to their operations. Compared to the competition, their costs, and therefore also their prices, will be high. However, their point of differentiation adds value for their customers in such a way that they are willing to pay the added premium. The best examples here would be heavily branded companies such as British Airways, luxury goods suppliers such as Mercedes-Benz or 'designer' goods such as Armani or Versace.

Box 4 is unfortunately where most companies in most markets find themselves, i.e. without any real cost advantage relative to the competition and also undifferentiated in the eyes of the customer.

To take one sector, consider high-street banking. Can you think of a significant difference between any of the high-street banks that adds value for the consumer? The reason that most of us stay with the same bank all their life is not because we think they are fantastic, but because we can't see any difference between them and therefore no reason to change!

No company plans to be in box 4. They are pushed there by the activities of their competitors. Three examples are outlined below where this has happened: Kwiksave, Levi Strauss and McDonald's.

KWIKSAVE

Supermarket chain Kwiksave is a company that for many years possessed a competitive SWAT based on low-cost leadership in box 1 but has recently been forced downwards into box 4, due to the arrival of new entrants to the market that were able to undercut it on price.

Throughout the 1980s, Kwiksave concentrated purely on selling major brands, unlike its competitors that were increasingly introducing more and more own-label products. However, the differences between them were more deeply rooted.

Selling mainly dry grocery products, Kwiksave employed a 'pile it high, sell it cheap' strategy while the others deliberately tried to move upmarket, and prided itself on its 'cheap 'n' cheerful' approach. The average Kwiksave store was smaller than a normal Tesco, Sainsbury, Asda or Safeway, because Kwiksave had no superstores (with its limited range, there would not have been much point).

Its stores were basic, with products displayed on simple racking in cardboard cases cut open with a knife. Costs were kept to a minimum as an obsession, with the resultant savings being passed on to the public via low prices. If Kwiksave could not be guaranteed to be the cheapest in the high street on a given product, that was often removed from the range. This resulted in strong terms from suppliers, as the limited range offered meant that the company could often offer chosen suppliers volumes out of all proportion to its position in the overall marketplace.

The company pursued a raiding logistics strategy aimed at price-sensitive consumers who did not have a high level of disposable income, a market sector that appeared unattractive to its more 'upmarket' rivals. While the major players fought each other for the top end of the market, Kwiksave had the bottom end almost to itself. With the major players unwilling to reduce their margins below 8 percent and Kwiksave willing to accept 5 percent, the company was able to carve a name for itself based on value for money.

Then the UK market was 'invaded' by European companies like Aldi, Lidl and Netto, used to continental margins of about 2 percent. These companies were attracted by what they saw as rich pickings, and they undercut the whole market on price. While their strategy *vis-à-vis* the market as a whole was one of **raiding logistics**, with regard to Kwiksave it was one of **head-to-head combat**, in that they were going head to head for exactly the same customers.

Their stores were even more basic than Kwiksave's, their service almost non-existent and their staff few in number. Shoppers had to queue for long periods in cramped aisles, and their choice was often limited to brands that no one had heard of (many of these were proprietary brands, in that they were manufactured specifically for the stores but did not carry their names). But they were cheap, considerably cheaper than the rest of the market, and to many shoppers on limited incomes that was what counted above all else.

A frisson of fear ran through the industry as a whole. Fearing the loss of thousands of customers, even the two giants Sainsbury and Tesco responded by introducing lines of tertiary brands that were even cheaper than own label. As it turned out, their fears were groundless, since shoppers used to superstores, range and service could not be wooed to the new arrivals with their queues and small, crowded stores with skeleton staff.

The company that was affected, however, was Kwiksave. As the majors became more competitive on price some of its customers 'traded up', and tens of thousands defected to Aldi and Netto. When a company sets out to attract price-conscious shoppers, it should not be surprised if it loses them when a cheaper competitor arrives on the scene.

Suddenly, for many of Kwiksave's shoppers, there was no longer any compelling reason to shop there. If they were motivated by low prices, either because of low income or because they just didn't like spending their income on groceries, there were cheaper alternatives. If they were motivated by superstores, wide range, own label and service, they probably never went to Kwiksave anyway. Unless Kwiksave happened to be their nearest supermarket and therefore offered convenience, why go there?

After struggling for several years, Kwiksave finally posted two years of poor financial results, its profit dropping from £125 million in 1996 to £2.8 million the following year. The chain immediately announced a cost-cutting program, including the closure of 400 stores and the shedding of thousands of staff.

Finally, in February 1998, a 'merger' was announced between Kwiksave and another middle-ranked chain, Somerfield. The reality was more like a takeover of the former by the latter. The combined chain announced that some Kwiksave stores would be switching fascias and others would be closed down, and it must be asked for how much longer the red and white of the Kwiksave logo will adorn UK high streets.

LEVI STRAUSS

This privately held, 150-year-old company is the original maker of denim jeans, its '501s' first being produced in the 1840s. Having run into difficulties in the early 1980s, the company managed to turn itself around by closing plants, expanding overseas and focusing on its core products. At first things went well and award-winning advertising, the launch of the 'Dockers' casual trouser range and a concentration on foreign sales all boosted business, sales and profits, which rose by $7 billion and $700 million respectively over the following decade.

However, the company's share of its core US market (males aged 16+) virtually halved between 1990 and 1998, falling from 48.2 percent to only 25 percent. Its insular approach meant that it had missed out on a number of trends that all had negative effects.

The market share of own-brand jeans such as those owned by the big department stores rocketed from 3.2 to 20.4 percent. JC Penney's Arizona Jeans Co. range is now worth over $1 billion, only a decade after its launch. Sears Roebuck's Canyon River Blues range is worth over $250 million after only four years, and Federated Department Stores' Alfani range hit sales of $100 million in its first season. All of these ranges offer high-quality jeans at a significant price discount to Levi's.

Levi's philanthropic approach to its staff in an industry better known for sweatshops and indentured immigrant labor is well known, but its downside is a cost structure that saddles the company with a big cost disadvantage and makes its product expensive even by national brand standards. For example, Levi's sell in the US for around $30, compared with Wrangler's $20. Partly as a result, Lee and Wrangler's share of the core market increased from 22.1 percent in 1990 to 31.9 percent in 1996.

Customers not attracted by lower prices have been enticed away by the designer labels that have entered the market. US designers such as Tommy Hilfiger, Ralph Lauren, Calvin Klein and Donna Karan have been joined by Italian designers such as Armani, Versace, Dolce & Gabana and Moschino, who have all turned to casual clothing. In US department stores in 1997, overall sales of jeans declined by 3 percent in volume terms; those of 'designer' jeans grew by 28 percent!

In addition, Levi's have been around so long that they are viewed by many teenagers as something their parents wear. They have been turning to brands like Diesel and JNCOs (huge baggy jeans with 40-inch bottoms and 17-inch pockets) and products such as bell bottoms and shiny nylon jeans in fluorescent orange. Research from Teenage Research Unlimited shows that the percentage of US teenage boys who consider Levi's a 'cool' brand has fallen from 21 percent in 1994 to only 7 percent in 1998.

The results have been devastating and in November 1997 the company announced the closure of one in three of its US factories (reducing the total from 33 to 22) and the firing of 7000 employees. As you might expect, this was accompanied by brave words from company spokespeople about being on top of the problem and having plans to turn the company around. The closures were seen as an unfortunate 'one-off' that had happened as a result of Levi's having taken its 'eye off the ball'.

However, that has proven not to be the case. Sales in 1998 fell by 13 percent and less than 18 months later, in February 1999, another announcement said that half of the remaining factories would be closed and a further 6000 jobs lost.

Despite the fact that it is still very profitable and has a very positive cash flow, Levi's has suddenly found itself in box 4, as for many people there is no real reason to buy its product any more. The brand has become neither one thing nor the other.

McDONALD'S

Named as the world's biggest brand in one recent book, it is diffi-cult to think of McDonald's as being in box 4, but that is exactly where the company finds itself in its home market in the US. With over 21,000 outlets in over 101 countries (a new branch opening somewhere in the world every three hours) and $32 billion in sales, there is no doubt that McDonald's will remain the world's biggest fast-food hamburger chain for the foreseeable future, but in the US there are signs that it is steadily losing ground to rivals.

For over 40 years the world's appetite for Big Macs has seemed insatiable and the company's Golden Arches fascia is a familiar sight across the globe. Abroad, the brand is everything that the US stands for, a symbol of democracy and choice. When the first Moscow branch was opened, Russian customers queued around the block for hours to buy a burger and fries. But in the US, such symbolism is meaningless and the reality is that at home the company is only managing to grow via an aggressive, on-going campaign of new store openings that frequently cannibalize existing sales (often to the fury of franchisees). Year-on-year growth in existing stores, the true measure of success, was down about 5 percent in 1997.

Ironically, the opening of new stores is itself one of the things that is hurting like-for-like sales. In 1996 the number of McDonald's out-lets grew by 6.4 percent, but sales by only 2.9 percent. Burger King's units, on the other hand, grew by 6.9 percent, but its sales increased by 9.2 percent. In 1997 over 2500 new branches were opened by McDonald's, two-thirds of them outside the US, and virtually all of the company's growth is coming from these foreign markets, where its outlets outnumber those of competitors like Burger King by a ratio of five to one.

The fact that McDonald's still dwarfs its competitors is down to the unarguable fact that it has more outlets than anyone else, rather than that its offering is more appealing to customers or adds more value. The sheer ubiquity of the Golden Arches is what gives the company its competitive advantage. Yet some observers feel that this is the only thing that McDonald's has got going for it.

Recent research revealed that nearly 30 percent of customers who chose the chain as their favorite cited convenience as the most important factor, with only 45 percent citing the products' taste as the deciding factor. In contrast, 82 percent of Wendy's fans and 76 percent of Burger King's customers did cite taste as the most important factor. The inescapable conclusion is that taste is not as important as convenience (read 'location') for McDonald's customers. So what happens when a Burger King or Wendy's outlet opens nearby, and convenience is no longer a differentiator?

McDonald's competitors have long focused on product as their competitive SWAT, correctly identifying that the weakness in McDonald's strength is its famous conveyor-belt, batch-manufacturing system, where product is made in quantity and then kept under the hot lamp until someone asks for it. This is fine at busy periods when it will only stay there for less than a minute, but what about slower times when it may be there for quite a while?

Adopting a **head-to-head combat** strategy (as befits a strong number two), Burger King has tried to turn McDonald's uniformity into a weakness. It has advertised for some time along the theme of 'It's your burger', stressing that it make your food as it is ordered, to your requirements, with its ads showing simple, mouth-watering close-ups of the product.

Unwilling (or unable) to accept that consumers might actually be seeing something wrong with its basic offerings, McDonald's first tried to differentiate by broadening its range with products aimed at adults. In 1997 it launched the Arch Deluxe, a 'sophisticated' burger with a secret sauce of mayonnaise and two mustards (and an optional slice of bacon), designed to appeal to adults supposedly more concerned with taste. However, this was high in fat, high in calories and expensive, and consumers decided that if they were going to eat unhealthily and have a burger, it might as well be a basic one for 99 cents as opposed to a 'sophisticated' one for $1.79. Chastened, the company then resorted to what is often the last stand of those who have ran out of anything better to do – discounting.

Its 'Campaign 55' (named after 1955, when the company was founded) offered a burger for 55 cents if the customer also bought hash browns and a drink (hamburger chains have longed worked on the principle of giving the burger away, selling the fries and making a profit on the drink). However, the communication of the offer was ambiguous if not misleading, and consumers did not realize that there were any restrictions on the 'burger for 55 cents' aspect; they were confused and annoyed in their thousands when they learnt that they also had to buy other products to benefit from the offer. The resulting bad publicity forced McDonald's to pull the promotion after only six weeks, in an embarrassing climbdown.

The company now seems reluctantly to have accepted that the competition appears to have a better product, and it is now planning to abandon the batch-cooking system for a 'just-in-time' system that focuses on one order at a time, just like the competition. However, it is planning to go further. Research shows that McDonald's has the best record in terms of speed of delivery, and the company is determined that this should not be lost by the change of system.

Vice-President Jack Greenberg says: 'You can get made-for-me in a lot of places, but if you can get it at the speed of McDonald's I think it will revolutionize this business.' Using specially designed software to communicate the order instantly to the kitchen, the plan is that a burger will be produced with hot, fresh and moist ingredients within 90 seconds, faster than it takes for the customer to add fries and a drink to the meal and then pay for it.

If McDonald's can add speed to hot 'n' fresh, it may have achieved the holy grail of the burger industry and moved itself out of box four into box three, differentiating itself from its rivals on both product and speed. But Burger King is already working on improvements to its own system, and the question has to be asked whether such a move would be at best a short-term one. Only the next few years will provide the answer.

The Three Routes to Possessing a Competitive SWAT

In deciding which of the routes to a competitive SWAT to follow – low cost, differentiation or focus – a company needs to take into account three main factors. The first is an analysis of the *competitive forces* at work in its market(s). This will help clarify the routes to competitive advantage already chosen by various competitors, enabling it to identify the areas of opportunity available to it. This is discussed in more detail in Chapter 5.

The second factor is *customer value*, the company needing to ask itself which of the possible options will create the most. It is at this stage that the likely costs of the strategy should be taken into account, together with the potential premium that could be passed on to the customer. A strategy that could not be made profitable without passing on the entire premium should be examined critically, as it will by no means be certain that this will be possible once competitors respond.

Whether this is possible at all is a question of the third factor, *sustainability*. A strategy which, when identified by competitors, could be not only imitated but also improved will obviously never be sustainable. Therefore in considering whether the strategy is open to imitation, the company must ask itself whether it would be able to pursue it in a way that customers would perceive to be better than the competition.

Core Competencies

Ultimately, whether a company will be able to be better than the competition will depend on whether one or more of the skills necessary for the implementation of the strategy is a core competence of the company involved.

Hamel and Prahalad, in their seminal book *Competing for the Future*, define a competence as 'a bundle of constituent skills and technologies, rather than a single, discreet [one]', but add several qualifiers to this before it can earn the adjective 'core'. First, they say that it must make a disproportionate contribution to customer value, and the distinction between core and non-core competencies depends in part on the distinction between core and non-core customer benefits.

Second, it must also be competitively unique, or nearly so. The company does not have to be the only one in its market to possess the competence for it to be core, but it cannot be so if every competitor possesses it. In every market there will be skills the possession of which is a basic requirement for participation. These merely allow a company to take part in the race: they do not guarantee it a place on the winners' rostrum.

Third, the competence must be extendable. While a competence might be deemed core within a single business, in that it provides customer value and is competitively unique, from the point of view of a corporation it will not be so unless it is extendable across various business units, and can be used to provide a range of different products or services.

Honda's core competence in engines, originally developed in the motorcycle market, has enabled it to expand into the car, outboard motor, lawnmower and snowmobile markets. Likewise, Sony's core competence of miniaturization, developed from the production of miniature radio transistors for Bell Labs, has enabled it to introduce the Walkman, pocket TVs and pocket CD players.

This approach complements traditional competitive theory in that a core competence can be a source of competitive advantage, but it approaches competition from a slightly different perspective. Most traditional competitive strategy analysis has focused on particular products and services, and the issues of pricing, positioning, signaling, differentiation and cost reduction are considered in this context.

However, competition between specific products or services is merely a temporary and superficial expression of a much deeper competition between companies over competencies. Brands, products and services don't compete; companies do! Competencies span both products and (within a corporation) individual business units, and losing (or winning) the battle for competence leadership can have profound implications for a whole range of products.

The development of core competencies might take years, or even decades in some instances; it took JVC 20 years to perfect those that contributed to its success with VHS. It is not something a company can suddenly do overnight, having decided that an analysis of the marketplace dictates that possession of a specific competence is a prerequisite for the most attractive of the strategy options available. To an extent, therefore, a company's choice of options is significantly restricted by the issue of what core competencies it has and, as importantly, does not have.

However, just as a company's choices today will be limited by decisions it made several years previously, so its choices (and fortunes) in the future will be affected by those made today. While most executives would agree that their marketplace today is very, very different from the one in which they competed in a decade ago, few appear to realize that it will probably be even more different again a decade hence. Even of those who have acknowledged this, only a minority spend more than a superficial amount of time trying to understand how it will be different. Hamel and Prahalad call this industry foresight, and see this as giving a company:

> the potential to get to the future first and stake out a leadership position. ... Industry foresight allows a company to control the evolution of its industry and, thereby, its own destiny. The trick is to see the future before it arrives.

Many British and American companies appear to be like stereotypical incompetent generals, preparing to fight the next war with the tactics of the last. Praise for the car industry in the West's belated attempts to turn to 'lean manufacturing' ignores the fact that Toyota, Honda, Nissan *et al.* had already been doing this for up to 40 years! Fighting the competitive wars of the first decade of the twenty-first century with the tactics of the 1980s is hardly the epitome of foresight.

Looking to the future and realizing that what has made you profitable in the past will not necessarily do so in the future was behind GEC's decision to sell its Marconi electronic systems business to

British Aerospace in 1998. Although critics said at the time that this was akin to selling the company's 'jewel in the crown', it was all part of a long-term plan to expand in high-growth sectors of telecommunications equipment.

Lord Simpson (GEC's managing director) stated immediately afterwards that he intended to restore the company's market value to the level enjoyed before the sale. He has since been on a spending spree across Europe and especially in the US, with the money received from BAe, to boost its currently small presence in the fast-growing data networking and Internet-related equipment business. He says:

> *We still have plenty of firepower left. At the moment, we are still an ugly duckling in the telecoms market ... but I believe in five years' time we will emerge as a beautiful swan.*

While the cues and trends are there in any market for companies to observe, Hamel thinks:

> *to create the future a company must first be capable of imagining it ... [and] to develop a powerful visual and verbal representation of what the future could be.*

IDENTIFYING THE FUTURE BEFORE IT ARRIVES

To be able to do this, companies must ask themselves the following questions.

What are the demographics of my specific market(s)? Is the market(s) currently, or will it/they become, dominated by any specific age group? Are there any identifiable behavioral trends in that age group?

Faith Popcorn identified 10 key trends affecting consumer behavior across the developed world, one of which she terms 'down-ageing'. She defines this as a refusal to accept the traditional limitations forced on people by growing old. In an era where the female readers of one US magazine voted the 70-year-old Sean Connery 'the sexiest man alive', people are refusing to accept that even septuagenarians are 'past it'. The last thing many senior citizens want is to be marketed to as OAPs. They may be 65+ chronologically, but they think of themselves as 45+.

What trends in behavior can be observed across all age groups? Popcorn identifies a number of these, from 'cocooning' (where people retreat from the big, bad world outside into their own private cocoon – great for anything to do with security, home entertainment, take-out food, home shopping etc.) to 'small indulgences' (where people treat themselves to a slice of the high life when they can't afford the whole thing – luxury chocolates, Mont Blanc pens, Gucci bags etc.).

Are there trends in other marketplaces that will raise customers' expectations in general and therefore affect your own? Many companies make the mistake of benchmarking their service levels, for example, against competitors in the same industry. Customers, on the other hand, increasingly benchmark a company's service against the best service they have received from anywhere. Thus a newspaper could find itself being compared to British Airways, First Direct, Tesco or Marks & Spencer, Wal-Mart, Nordstrom or Disney.

What is happening technologically in both your own industry and others? For many companies today, the writing is already on the wall for their existing products and services. Somewhere, someone is developing (or has already developed) a technology that will make theirs redundant. To take a few examples: CDs have largely replaced cassettes, which earlier replaced vinyl records. Radial tires replaced cross-ply. The typewriter was replaced by the wordprocessor. Composite car bumpers have replaced metal ones. Endo-surgery has replaced open surgery. The PC has ousted the mainframe. The fax replaced the telex, and is in its turn being replaced by e-mail.

Do you know what developments are taking place in your industry (and complementary ones) that could replace or make redundant the technology you are using? Identifying the core competencies that are necessary for success in today's marketplace is not enough. The successful organizations of the future will be those that are able to identify the competencies required 10 years' hence, and to work towards their development.

HEWLETT-PACKARD PRINTERS

It is especially difficult to identify the core competencies that may be required tomorrow if the company in question is not in trouble. In the early 1990s, the inkjet printer division of Hewlett-Packard (HP) was amazingly successful by any measurement. Its market share (more than twice the size of the number two's) was over 50 percent and its factories worked at full capacity, selling every printer and ink cartridge they could make. Its products were in so much demand that they were virtually all on allocation, as there were never enough to meet requirements.

Most companies at this stage would suffer from complacency, but HP decided to reengineer itself completely and turn most of its systems and processes on their heads.

The reason was that it identified that future growth in the market would come not from the business market, on which it had traditionally concentrated, but from the fast-growing home PC market. Inkjet printers were a less expensive alternative to lasers – although the latter were coming down in price, threatening their profitability – and at the same time they were perfect for home use.

The problem was that the systems, processes and attitude that had been fine for the business market were totally inappropriate for the consumer market, and HP had to learn a whole new range of competencies to enable it to take advantage of the opportunity.

For example, in the business market HP manufactured the best possible product, charged what it wanted and delivered when it could. Business customers were willing both to pay for the extra features and also to wait until the product became available, due to HP's high reputation in the market.

Many consumers, on the other hand, had never even heard of HP; the rest thought the brand name stood for high prices and certainly would not put off a purchase if the company's product was unavailable. If the HP printer wasn't on the shelf, they would simply buy one from a competitor. To most, the purchase was a quick 'add-on' after the PC had been bought and neither a great deal of time nor thought went into it. Few would pay a premium price just because the printer carried the name 'Hewlett-Packard'.

Being able to deliver product when the market wanted it at a competitive price was a completely new competence that had to be learnt from scratch. HP's salespeople now had to be able to go to the likes of Wal-Mart and commit to a promotion at a certain month of the year and guarantee the delivery of x thousand units. The company increased the amount of regional manufacturing that it did to take account of seasonal and regional differences, built new factories overseas and employed contract manufacturers to help meet demand at peak times.

Another new competence required was flexibility. HP used to have five basic models for the business market, but it quickly learnt that it needed a much bigger range. It now has 75, each aimed squarely at a certain segment of the market. This was achieved by having a small number of common platforms that were then customized by adding different features when required. The generic platforms are delivered to distribution centers, where the extra features are added before distributing the printers onwards to retailers. This means that a platform intended to be product x can be changed to product y as late as possible if demand changes for some reason. It also allows platforms to be shipped between distribution centers if demand increases suddenly in one part of the world.

Because consumers' decision about what to buy is so quick (research showed HP it was 3–5 minutes), store salespeople had little time to 'educate' them and HP also had to learn new skills of merchandising and communicating information quickly and efficiently via point-of-sale material.

HP is a perfect example of how the competencies that worked well for a company in the past are not necessarily those that will work well in the future.

THE FUTURE OF RETAILING

Electronic commerce is currently growing at such a rate that Michael de Kare-Silver forecasts in his book *e-shock: the Electronic*

Shopping Revolution that by 2005 it will account for about 20 percent of shopping. He also points out that with low margins and high fixed costs, a drop in sales of only 10–15 percent could force many retailers into bankruptcy. Yet how many retailers are aware of the Internet tidal wave that is about to engulf them? How many have an e-commerce strategy? How many are actively developing a competitive SWAT to defend themselves against what will be a wave of virtual retailers entering the marketplace?

Another of Faith Popcorn's key trends is called '99 lives', as we all increasingly feel as if we have too much to do and too little time to do it in. This is an age when virtually all menial tasks can be outsourced to others, from walking the dog to returning videos, and people are increasingly loath to spend their valuable time on chores.

Shopping can be divided into two types. One these is chore shopping, by which I mean two things. The first is the purchase of items such as groceries. For the vast majority of people, doing a weekly shop for groceries is a mundane task that they would happily delegate to somebody else; they get no pleasure out of doing it – pleasure perhaps from eating the food, but not from the process of buying it.

All of the major UK grocery multiples are now experimenting with home shopping (with orders placed via the telephone or Internet) and Iceland has a fleet of 700 vans covering the country. The company is outperforming the rest of the industry sector financially, and identifies home shopping as a significant contributor to that success.

The second type of chore shopping is when consumers have to go out of their way to a shop merely to pick something up. No browsing is involved; the consumer knows what he or she wants and simply enters the shop, picks it up and pays for it. This does not necessarily relate only to low-price items or routine purchases; it can even apply to luxury items. If consumers know what they want and do not need specialist advice or help with finance, the sheer process of getting in the car (or on the bus/subway/train), traveling to the shop, paying at the car park, struggling through crowds, waiting to be served, finding staff, queuing at the checkout etc., etc. is an inconvenience.

The process whereby consumers visit a retailer, choose goods from a selection on display, pay for them and transport them home has basically remained unchanged for thousands of years; people buying from market stalls in Assyria or ancient Egypt went through the same basic process that we do today. But now there is no need for that to be the case, and electronic shopping and home delivery will revolutionize chore shopping. In the future we will shop when we want to.

The second type of shopping is leisure shopping, where pleasure is obtained and visiting the shop is almost a leisure activity. Huge US-style malls such as the Bluewater complex in Kent or the Trafford Centre in Manchester site cinemas, restaurants, bars and other leisure activities (tenpin bowling, fairground attractions etc.) along-side retailers and provide a temperature-controlled environment to enable visitors to enjoy their time shopping. Book superstores in the US provide armchairs and settees for browsing and coffee bars where customers can get refreshments as they read, turning book buying into a leisure activity and the stores into meeting places.

Increasingly, shopping will polarize between these two extremes. Consumers will purchase routine or mundane items electronically and have them delivered to their homes, and only bother to visit bricks-and-mortar premises if the retailer can give them something back in return in terms of entertainment or enjoyment. Even cars can be bought via the Internet nowadays, and if you think that people will always need to visit shops to try on clothes, stop for a moment to think about mail-order companies that have operated successfully for years!

While the likes of Tesco and Sainsbury are toying with the Internet, they still have a huge vested interest in bricks-and-mortar shopping and, although they have the resources to do so, they will be unable (or unwilling) to pursue e-commerce with the energy and vigor it requires. In most industries revolutions and the development of new core competencies come from new entrants rather than existing players, and it was Amazon, not Borders or Barnes & Noble, that launched Internet shopping in the book trade. While many booksellers are venturing on to the Internet (see Chapter 3), one cannot help but feel that they would prefer it if Internet selling failed.

In the future, successful retailers will therefore fall into two camps. They will provide a hassle-free, convenient service to save us the 'bother' of chore shopping, or they will find new ways to entertain us and make our shopping experience with them enjoyable. Unfortunately, most retailers currently fall somewhere between the two, in that they still require customers to visit them to pick up goods, and yet manage to make it an unenjoyable (occasionally even mind-numbingly boring) experience in the process.

Self-diagnostic questionnaire

1 Do you feel as if the majority of your customers are only interested in price? If so, does your organization act in a way that reinforces this behavior and therefore creates a self-fulfilling prophecy?

2 Why should your customers buy from your organization on any grounds other than price?

3 Is your range/service/quality/expertise etc. really better, or are you just believing your own corporate hype?

4 When was the last time you thoroughly examined your competition's range/service/quality/expertise etc. to see if your long-held preconceptions and prejudices still hold water?

5 Where would you place your company on the competitive SWAT matrix? Ask some of your customers if they agree.

6 What is the source of competitive advantage for each of the competitors in your marketplace? Be honest with yourself and admit if they are better than you in any area. Your view will probably be subjective; ask your customers (and your competitors' customers) what they think. Locate your competitors on the matrix.

7 What core competencies does your organization possess that enable you to be better than the competition?

8 What opportunities would exist if you were able to extend those competencies into another marketplace?

9 What changes are happening in your marketplace, and what core competencies will you require in 2/5/10 years' time to enable you to remain successful?

PART II

HOW TO DEVELOP A SWAT

P ART II LOOKS AT THE MOST IMPORTANT OF THE THREE LESSONS of warfare in more detail – how to develop a SWAT. Each of the following three chapters looks at a highly successful military SWAT, and how it was specifically developed to take advantage of, and therefore be superior to, the other 'competing' systems of its time. Each also looks at one of the three ways to achieve a competitive SWAT on the business battlefield, using examples of companies that have been successful in doing so.

Chapter 5 considers how Alexander the Great built the world's first combined-arms army to overcome the 'competing' military systems of Greece and Persia; and how to achieve a competitive SWAT in business via the route of low-cost leadership.

Chapter 6 examines how the Roman legion enabled Rome to build one of the greatest empires the world has ever known; and the commercial route of differentiation.

Chapter 7 discusses how the use of the longbow enabled England to defeat a much larger, richer and stronger opponent in successive battles during the Hundred Years' War; and achieving a competitive SWAT via focus.

5

ALEXANDER THE GREAT – LOW-COST SWATS

O NE OF THE MOST OUTSTANDING EXAMPLES OF A SWAT CAN BE found in the army of Alexander the Great, which was the first to use all four of the weapons systems outlined in Chapter 4 in a systematic, combined manner. Prior to its development, there had been two dominant systems in the ancient world. The Persians (used to the wide open spaces of central Asia) had one based mostly on light, missile-firing cavalry and infantry that fought its foes from a distance; the Greek system was based almost exclusively on heavily armored infantry (fighting shoulder to shoulder in a tightly packed formation called a phalanx), which relied on shock action.

The Greek system had proved itself superior in a number of battles, although each system had its advantages. Alexander (building on work done by his father) combined the best elements of the two into the world's first combined-arms army that would demonstrate its superiority over the competitive system time and again.

Despire its superiority over the Persian system, the Greek phalanx nevertheless had two main weaknesses, namely its lack of flexibility and its inability to defend itself from attacks on its flank. Its strength and power derived from the momentum achieved by all of its members pushing forward; if attacked from the front and flank simultaneously, this momentum disappeared and much of its effectiveness evaporated. The Persians had been unable to capitalize on this because their cavalry was mostly of the light variety. An army with heavy cavalry using shock tactics would be able to take advantage of these weaknesses, especially as the Greeks had almost nothing in the way of cavalry themselves.

While heavy infantry could withstand an attack from heavy cavalry, the secret to success would be the use of a combination of both heavy infantry and cavalry, the former to 'pin them down' from the front, the latter to attack them in the flank or rear.

Unlike southern Greece, Macedonia's climate of glen and plain had provided lush pasturage on which its feudal nobility could rear horses by the thousand, enabling them to develop significant numbers of cavalry. Learning from his experiences fighting the barbarian tribes to the north, Philip developed a force that relied on shock action rather than missile power for effect. Over light cavalry, the Macedonian heavy cavalry enjoyed the same advantages that heavy infantry had over light in shock combat. They therefore acted more like heavy infantry on horseback, charging straight for their opponents with an iron-tipped lance made of tough cornel wood, and cutting a swathe through them like a knife through butter. These were called the companion cavalry as they were led personally by the king in battle, and were therefore his companions in combat.

These men were superbly trained and drilled to act as a unit. They were subdivided into squadrons, each with its own professional officers and NCOs, something unheard of in an age when cavalry was normally just a horde of similarly armed individuals charging in an undisciplined mass. Its basic unit was not a block but a triangular wedge, apex first. As each rider could see the squadron commander at its point, the unit was able to change direction mid-gallop by taking their cue from him.

In order for heavy cavalry to be used effectively against enemy heavy infantry, however, it was essential for the enemy phalanx to be immobilized first. This could have been achieved simply by attacking it with a similarly armed phalanx, but Philip was too much of a military innovator to be satisfied with that. Instead, he improved on the basic phalanx by establishing a body of heavy infantry called the 'foot companions'. These were organized into six brigades each approximately 1500 strong, and were composed of professional soldiers, unlike the part-timers of the Greek city-states. Incessant training meant that they could march in columns, rectangles or wedges, broadening or thinning their ranks as required, and by marking time, they could wheel and advance at an angle and face about.

The ancient world had never seen anything like it. In order to enable the Macedonians to outfight the Greeks, they were armed with the *sarissa*, an extraordinary pike up to 18 feet long that had to be held with both hands. This in turn necessitated a smaller shield than that used by hoplites, but this did not matter much as the whole idea of the *sarissa* was that the enemy never got to close range anyway. Because of its length the points of the first five ranks projected beyond the front line. Each short hoplite spear facing them, therefore, would be met by five Macedonian ones, their phalanx resembling a metal porcupine bristling with quills.

Because all Greek infantry tended to drift to the right, or shielded side, commanders usually placed their best troops on the left, with the result that they never met in the battle. In order to keep infantry at their allotted place in the line so that the Greeks could be held in place, the Macedonian right was strengthened by placing there the 'shield bearers', the army's best troops.

In isolation, both the infantry and the cavalry were probably the finest the Ancient World had ever seen, but what made them formidable was Philip's (and then Alexander's) ability to use them in conjunction with each other. Cavalry had never been able to charge down a solid line of steadfast heavy infantry, so the foot companions and shield bearers were used to pin down the enemy infantry, while the cavalry drove off the enemy horsemen and then (instead of pursuing them from the field, as was normal) had the discipline to regroup, change direction and cut diagonally into them using their wedge formation. The cavalry acted as a hammer striking the enemy on the anvil of the foot companions.

Alexander fulfilled his father's ambition by defeating the Persians and establishing an empire the like of which the world had never seen, all before an untimely death from natural causes at the early age of 32. The battle of Issus shows vividly how this superb war machine was used to inflict a crippling defeat on an enemy not only vastly superior in numbers, but also fighting defensively.

THE BATTLE OF ISSUS, 333 BC

In 333 BC, Alexander the Great left Asia Minor (modern-day Turkey) and headed southwards down the eastern coast of the Mediterranean to enable him eventually to head east and confront the Persian King Darius, who had allowed him to roam relatively unchecked through his empire for two years after beating a Persian army on invasion. However, unbeknownst to Alexander, Darius had outflanked him (it is not known whether this was deliberate or accidental) and ended up in his rear, cutting him off from his bases in Asia Minor.

Darius had intended to shadow Alexander southwards down the narrow coastal plain and then attack him from the rear once he had headed east on to the more open ground on the other side of the coastal mountains. Although he had not had time to summon his whole army, he had collected the entire Persian and Medean feudal levy. Contemporary historians' claims of an army of 400,000 men can be discounted as exaggeration in order to magnify Alexander's subsequent success, but there is no doubt that Darius significantly outnumbered the Macedonian army. He would certainly have had between 150,000 and 200,000 men.

Attacking Alexander on the other side of the mountains would enable him to use his superiority in cavalry to good effect, but this plan depended, of course, on Alexander continuing south. Although he would not have known the exact size of the Persian army, Alexander would have been well aware of his numerical inferiority and the threat that it posed. However, for a short time he had the opportunity to negate the advantage that Darius's numbers gave him, by fighting where he was. The plain was only about one and a half miles wide, and if he could engage the Persians there, he would be able to secure his flanks on the mountains and the sea and thus prevent them from being attacked. He would force battle on Darius in a location where his numerical superiority would have no advantage.

At dawn Alexander turned northwards and retraced his steps until he met the enemy, who (despite their numerical superiority) decided to fight defensively, and assumed a position along a narrow stream called the Pinarus. Darius placed his 30,000 Greek mercenary infantry in the center to face the Macedonian phalanx with his 60,000 *kardakoi* (Persian heavy infantry) to their left and right, and massed 30,000 of his cavalry on the right wing, where the opportunity existed to charge along the beach and turn Alexander's left flank. About 3000 cavalry and some light infantry were placed on the left wing and the rest of his untrained infantry levy was stationed to the rear.

Darius's plan was obviously to hold the center and left wing while his cavalry swept along the beach and took the Macedonian phalanx in the rear. Alexander's plan was almost a carbon copy. Despite the Persians' strength there, he placed only a few thousand Thessalian and other allied cavalry on the left under his second-in-command Parmenion, his 9000 foot companions and 3000 shield bearers in the centre and his 1800 companion cavalry on the right commanded by himself. His various contingents of allied light infantry were dispersed along the line, his total force numbering about 40,000.

Although on the left wing Parmenion would be heavily outnumbered, his success in holding off what were bound to be heavy attacks from the Persian cavalry was crucial to Alexander's plan. Like all good plans, this was simple. While Parmenion held the Persians on the left and the foot companions and shield bearers the center, Alexander himself would lead the companion cavalry in an attack on the right. After he had routed the lighter-armed cavalry there, he would wheel to his left and take the Greek mercenary infantry in the flank and rear.

Speed was of the essence, as the Macedonian phalanx would encounter some difficulty in crossing the river to their front without opening holes in their ranks that could be taken advantage of by the Greek hoplites facing them. If this happened there was a serious chance that the plan would fail. By mid-afternoon everybody was in place and, with the Macedonian war cry of *alalalalalai* echoing across the plain, the companion cavalry kicked their horses into action.

The Persian cavalry on both flanks also charged, as did the foot companions, and battle was joined. On the left, Parmenion was successful in holding off repeated attacks from his much greater enemy, as lack of space meant that a large proportion of the Persians could not actually engage his Thracians and Thessalians, and had to mill around rather aimlessly at the rear. Extra numbers are of little importance if it is impossible to bring them into action.

In the center, the phalanx was having difficulty crossing the river and gaps began to open into which the Greek mercenaries poured, challenging the phalanx's widespread reputation for invincibility. However, Alexander and the companion cavalry made short work of the cavalry and archers to their front, who gave way at the first charge. Leaving his light cavalry to pursue them, he wheeled left as planned and cut a swathe through the *kardakoi* at an angle, effectively cutting their rectangular formation into two triangles. Those to the rear immediately fled, leaving those to the front to the mercy of the shield bearers, and the companions, who were disciplined enough to resist slaughtering them as they fled, continued onwards until they could attack the Greek mercenaries who were hard pressing the Macedonian infantry in the center.

The Greeks were forced to look to their rear and, once the Thessalians managed to get around the Persian cavalry facing them on the left and join in the attack, Darius fled the field. Abandoning his shield and chariot, he escaped to fight again another day and Alexander had complete control of the battlefield. The massive untrained infantry levy to the rear fled without even having had to lift a weapon.

Alexander had won one of the greatest victories of the ancient world, against a numerically superior foe fighting largely on the defensive. To have attacked such an enemy would have been madness to many people, the only option being to withdraw and fight again on another day. However, such were the skill and discipline of the Macedonian army, and the tactical brilliance and personal courage of its commander, that he was able to ignore two of the most basic lessons of war, the superiority of numbers and the tactical power of the defense.

LOW-COST LEADERSHIP AS A SWAT

The pursuit of cost leadership within a market is perhaps the most clear-cut of the three generic strategies identified in Chapter 4. However, this is not the same as mere cost reduction. All organizations should be involved in the reduction or elimination of unnecessary costs; those wishing to pursue a strategy of low-cost leadership must be prepared to go much further. To be the low-cost leader in a market requires an obsession with cost, so that your organization develops similar skill and discipline to that making the Macedonian army so successful.

There are three main approaches to low-cost leadership:

❑ reducing costs without affecting the fundamental structure of the company
❑ reducing costs per unit manufactured
❑ changing the structure to eliminate certain costs altogether.

COST REDUCTION

Many companies attempt to reduce their costs by increasing productivity, factory shutdowns, staff redundancies and a general 'squeezing' of budgets across the board, without altering the fundamental structure of the company itself.

An increasingly popular area of traditional cost reduction is in purchasing. Approximately 55 percent of an average company's revenue is spent externally on purchased goods and services, and yet most concentrate their cost-cutting activities almost exclusively internally. One of the most commonly quoted reasons behind mergers and acquisitions is increased purchasing power, which will generate theoretical savings of x million per annum.

In recent years, companies have also been using location more and more as a source for reducing costs by moving production to countries with lower labor costs, something that is benefiting the UK, as German and French companies move there to avoid crippling costs.

However, annual rounds of budget cutting and supplier squeezing can only produce so much in the way of cost savings before they begin to affect quality and service. An example of what can happen comes from General Mills and its handling of the brand Lacoste in the US. When diversification was in vogue the company bought the US rights to the brand in 1969 for $30 million, and over the next decade built a full range of clothing with the famous crocodile logo with annual sales of $400 million.

General Mills then made the mistake of thinking that marketing fashion items was the same as breakfast cereal and, in an attempt to improve profitability by reducing costs, stopped importing shirts from France, manufacturing them instead in low-cost Hong Kong. The drop in quality was immediately apparent and sales began to slow. In response, the company relaxed its distribution policy and dumped massive amounts of stock on retail discounters, thus destroying the brand's cachet. Over the three-year period 1982–5, sales fell from $400 million to $50 million. The brand limped along for another decade with sales steadily falling, until the French company Devanlay (10 percent owned by the Lacoste family) bought back the US rights to the brand name and crocodile logo.

REDUCTION OF COSTS PER UNIT

The traditional way of reducing costs per unit has been via economies of scale, described by Porter as:

> *...arising from the ability to perform activities differently and more efficiently at larger volumes, or from the ability to amortize the cost of intangibles such as advertising and R&D over a greater sales volume.*

The reverse side of the same coin is the benefit derived from progression along the learning curve, as costs of an activity decline over time due to the learning that improves efficiency.

Where significant economies of scale and learning benefits can be obtained from higher volumes, many organizations (especially

Asian ones) are willing to supply other companies – even competitors – with product on an original equipment manufacturer (OEM) basis. Canon, for example, sells laser printer engines to Apple and Hewlett-Packard, among others, which has helped it become the world's leading producer of such engines.

Most Japanese and Korean companies are only too willing to follow such a strategy, producing microwaves for General Electric, videos for RCA, computers for ICL, engines for Ford or flat screens for Apple. Bear in mind that these are not companies whose strategy is to do this exclusively; they will all have their own brands that use the same components.

Hamel calls these intermediate products 'core products', and points out that Asian companies often have a greater core product share than brand share. Thus Canon's share of the world laser printer engine market is greater than its brand share of the laser printer market. Industries are often much more concentrated at core product level than at brand level.

For example, while many, many companies produce laptop computers, only two (Sharp and Toshiba) produce the flat screen displays used in them in any significant volume. The aim of many such companies is to create a virtual monopoly in the area of the core product, where it becomes more worthwhile for competitors to purchase from them rather than manufacture themselves. Apart from generating profits, the higher volumes achieved help to reduce those companies' costs, enabling their own branded models to earn higher margins or to be sold at a lower price than those of their competitors.

However, low-cost leaders don't merely have tight controls on budgeted expenditure. They examine every aspect of their business to identify not only ways of cutting costs, but of eliminating them altogether by developing new ways to run their organization, which Porter calls 'reconfiguring the value chain'. This involves structuring the company in a way that is fundamentally different to competitors, and that generates a significant cost advantage.

ELIMINATION OF COSTS VIA RESTRUCTURING

The third and most radical way of reducing costs is to restructure the company so that it quite simply does not have a lot of the costs that its more traditional competitors take for granted. In most industries there are a set of implicit assumptions about 'the way things are done'.

For example, in bookselling the assumption was that (as in other retail markets) bricks-and-mortar outlets stocked a limited range and consumers had no option but to travel to those outlets to study the range on offer and make a purchase. Anything not in stock would be ordered as a special item, sometimes taking a number of days or even weeks to arrive.

In PCs, the assumption was that all manufacturers made product according to their own forecasts and sold it via value-added resellers (VARs), who sometimes stocked the product for months before unpacking and personalizing it according to the needs of the business customer.

Normally such assumptions are only challenged by new entrants to the market, who do not have the blinkered mentality common among long-standing competitors. The bookselling model was ripped to pieces not by an established bookseller but by Amazon, which introduced selling via the Internet.

Likewise, the PC market assumptions were questioned not by Compaq, IBM or Hewlett-Packard, but by Dell Computer, with its direct-selling model.

DELL COMPUTER

Dell Computer has gone from being number eight in the global PC market in 1994, to number seven in 1995, number five in 1996 and number three in 1997 (behind only Compaq and IBM), a position it retained in 1998. Over the same period, sales have climbed from $3.4 billion to $18.2 billion and profits from $140 million to £1.5 billion. At its peak, the stock price had increased an incredible 29,600 percent since 1990 (from 23 cents to $68).

This meteoric rise has come not from creating fantastic new technology, but from the rather mundane business of assembling and selling personal computers. This is an industry where price competition is cut-throat and products are technologically obsolete only months (if not weeks) after being delivered, and where the competition contains such giants as IBM, Compaq, Digital and Hewlett-Packard.

Dell's success is due to the fact that it simply does things differently from the rest of the industry. The conventional use of value-added resellers hits the manufacturer two ways. First, their margin adds to the final cost of the PC, and second, the manufacturer has to offer them price protection. If the value of a PC drops while in their inventory, then the manufacturer makes up the difference, and this can add up to between 10 and 15 percent of the cost.

Now look at Dell's *modus operandi*. The company does not use resellers but sells direct to its customers, 90 percent of whom are businesses, schools or government agencies. It also only builds machines after the order for them has been received, enabling them to be personalized exactly to the customer's requirements.

Until 1997 these orders were taken by telephone, but Dell has now added the Internet to its armory, and is one of the most successful companies selling in this way. According to Dell, 80 percent of the people who have bought over the Internet have been new customers.

The benefits of operating like this are enormous. Dell has no finished goods inventory, and in an industry where inventory depreciates by 1 percent a week, that alone gives it a big cost advantage. The cost of PC components drops by about 32 percent a year. As Dell carries about 70 days' less inventory than its more traditional competition, this translates into a 6 percent cost advantage.

The company is obsessive about this issue, and is continually looking for ways to reduce it still further. In 1993, Dell had $2.6 billion in sales and $34 million in inventory; in 1997, while sales had increased to $12.3 billion, inventory had actually fallen by a third, to $23 million. The company is now looking to measure inventory in hours rather than days.

This enables it to keep pace with technological developments, shipping every machine with the latest high-tech components.

Dell can take the reseller's margin out of the finished price, this factor alone giving it an advantage of about 7 percent. Its direct marketing and sales expenses add about 1 percent, which gives it a net saving of 6 percent.

Also because Dell does not work through resellers, it has direct contact with 100 percent of its customers. If they suddenly start asking for something, Dell knows about it immediately. Being this close to the customer prevents it from making expensive mistakes by developing products that are not really required.

Finally, Dell gets paid not by the reseller, but by the end users, many of whom are the likes of Shell, Ford or Boeing, companies with a higher credit rating than Dell itself. Its small business and individual consumers pay by credit card, which means that Dell has their money before production has even commenced.

These advantages mean that Dell can undercut the competition significantly on price (without hurting profits), but its other weapon consists of its service and speed of delivery. In 1998 it was able to deliver eight customized, fully loaded Power Edge servers to the New York stock exchange in 36 hours to enable it to handle higher trading volume as a result of the Asian crises, and 2000 PCs and 400 servers loaded with the customer's own software to 2000 Wal-Mart stores in six weeks.

In 1997, the Woolwich Building Society in the UK put to tender an order for 2700 PCs and 800 servers, the choice initially being between IBM, Dell and HP. Once IBM dropped out on price, the other two were nearly identical, but while HP wanted to deliver everything to the company's headquarters, Dell was willing to deliver them, ready to boot, to each of the 450 branches, at no extra cost. It won the order. The Woolwich estimates that it saved about £0.5 million by choosing Dell.

Price differences mattered less when customers were inexperienced and needed hand holding, but nowadays experienced corporate buyers (who account for most of Dell's sales) are willing to bypass the resellers. Compaq, IBM and HP (whom Dell recently usurped as number three in the market) cannot copy the company's model without alienating the resellers on whom they depend. That doesn't mean that they are not trying, nevertheless.

IBM has already tried (and abandoned) a plan to sell direct, and instead now ships many of its machines to resellers in a semi-finished state, allowing them to complete the manufacture. However, this ties it into its resellers even more tightly and removes much of the value that it has hitherto added.

Compaq has announced that on any new models, machines will not be built without firm orders, and is also planning to deliver more of them direct. But while it is struggling to assimilate DEC's 50,000 employees into its own company (it bought the company for $9.6 billion), it cannot afford to alienate the resellers completely, something that a move into direct selling would surely do.

To Michael Dell, selling direct is something you either do or you don't; there is no half-way house:

> *Balancing is very, very tough. The notion that you can sell these products direct and these other products elsewhere does not work.*

If he is correct, then his direct sales model is relatively free from competition, as it is unlikely that Compaq, IBM or HP would ever have the courage to alienate their resellers completely. His choice of a terrain on which his competition cannot fight has given his company a virtually impregnable position in the market.

Direct Provision of Financial Services

Until the mid-1980s, the insurance market in the UK was dominated by big groups and staid brokers, but the market was turned on its head by the creation of Direct Line in 1985. This was the first insurance operation to sell its services over the telephone, and although other companies have since copied its *modus operandi*, it remains today the largest and best known of the direct providers.

It revolutionized the way financial services are sold, eliminating the need for high-street branches, commission-paid financial advisers and glossy literature, by replacing all of this with a friendly voice. Although the initial investment for a direct provider is expensive, requiring as it does computer systems, call centers and highly skilled staff, the overall costs are lower because the need for high-street shopfronts is eliminated. This lower cost base enabled Direct Line to beat its rivals significantly on price.

Shortly after Direct Line's foundation, Midland Bank opened First Direct, the UK's first telephone bank. One of the executives who set up the new operation said:

> *We had discovered it was expensive to get new customers by discounting. What we needed was a lower-cost way of making the product. At the same time, we were appealing to the baby-boom generation, who were comfortable dealing on the 'phone.*

A willingness to accept lower margins than traditional financial service providers is an additional reason that the direct providers can at times offer mortgages and personal loans at a full 1 and 4 percent lower respectively, and interest on instant-access accounts up to 2.5 percent higher. Traditional providers are very vulnerable to attack, as all the customer has at home is a few pieces of paper and little direct contact with them that can be used to generate loyalty.

The most recent major entrant into the direct provision of financial services is Virgin Direct, owned by Richard Branson. Founded in 1995, its growth has been amazing, due to its tactic of providing very simple products and undercutting the competition on virtually every front. Branson says:

> *The big insurers are dinosaurs. All they want to do is cry that it's unfair. They've been unfair to consumers for hundreds of years. They're all struggling with the job of introducing the telephone into their cumbersome, conventional sales approach. Enlightened customers should not have to pay for the privilege of being sold to. ... Gradually there will be a complete shift to direct sales of financial services.*

While the traditional financial service providers have long viewed their ubiquitous high-street presence as a source of strength, the associated high costs have now been revealed to be a major weakness. However, they are saddled with them, and there is not a great deal they can do. Nearly all of them have cautiously entered the direct market, but they have tended merely to dip a hesitant toe in the water, their 'branch comes first' culture preventing them from diving in headlong.

THE SKY'S THE LIMIT: THE RISE OF THE NO-FRILLS AIRLINE

In the US, low-cost airlines account for about 30 percent of all flights. Companies such as Southwest Airlines, Tower Air and ValueJet (renamed Trojan Air following the Florida DC-9 crash) steadily made inroads on the share held by their higher-cost rivals. Southwest alone has 250 Boeing 737s in its fleet.

Over the past four years in Europe, over 88 airlines have been founded. More than 30 of these have subsequently gone into receivership, but the remainder are virtually all low-cost, no-frills airlines such as Debonair, easyJet, Ryanair and Virgin Express.

All of these companies share a number of important characteristics. They tend to use lower-cost airports and avoid the expensive fees of Gatwick and Heathrow. EasyJet flies from Luton and Liverpool, Debonair from Luton and Ryanair from Stansted. Virgin Express does use Gatwick and Heathrow, but is planning to launch services from Birmingham, Manchester, Glasgow and Edinburgh.

In some ways this use of regional airports benefits customers, as check-in times can be shorter, parking is cheaper and baggage recovery generally quicker, and both Luton and Stansted are almost as easy to reach from central London as the two 'giants'. The airlines themselves enjoy shorter turnaround times, easyJet claiming that its aircraft spend a third more of their lives in the air than those of BA.

They sell most of their tickets direct to the public, avoiding the commissions paid to travel agents (easyJet and Virgin sell 100 percent direct, the former actually boasting that it has never paid a penny to anyone in commission). Passengers are not allocated seats, but pick up their (reusable) tickets at the gate and sit anywhere, on a first-come, first-served basis.

There is no entertainment and little or no refreshments in-flight. Debonair is more low-frills than no-frills, offering coffee and a muffin, and Virgin provides soft drinks.

In addition, they use the lowest number of cabin staff allowable by air transport regulations, without impinging on safety. The average age of easyJet's fleet is seven years, and by the end of 1999 it will have the youngest fleet in the air. The average age of Virgin's planes is under five years. All planes have to meet the standards set by the Civil Aviation Authority, regardless of the fares they charge.

They also pay their staff less than established airlines, and in only flying short routes avoid the need for expensive overnight stays. They also do without expensive uniforms, easyJet for example dressing its staff in orange jeans and sweatshirts.

At first, traditional airlines such as British Airways ridiculed these companies as operating for 'peanuts', stating that there was no money to be made in that part of the market, but their success has forced it to think again. EasyJet currently carries about two million passengers per year, and when Ryanair was floated on the US and Irish stock exchanges the listing was 18 times oversubscribed.

Franco Mancassola, founder of Debonair, says that budget carriers such as his own are an 'unstoppable force', adding:

> *It's like the seeds of democracy in a totalitarian state. You can ignore it but it won't go away. The landscape of aviation will never be the same again.*

Having identified one particular part of the airline market as their target, i.e. short-flight, price-sensitive passengers (usually flyers not putting the cost of the flight on an expense account of a company they don't own), the no-frills carriers are all pursuing a **head-to-head logistics** strategy whereby they are concentrating on one part of it at a time, with new routes being added gradually and cautiously.

BA already operated in the low-cost sector in France and Germany, where its subsidiaries Air Liberté and Deutsche BA are the biggest competitors for Air France and Lufthansa. Its reluctance to introduce such an operation in the UK seems to have been due to a fear of cannibalization of its main business rather than a reluctance to enter the low-cost sector *per se.*

BA's strategy then changed as it launched its own low-cost operation, Go. Just as traditional armies faced with guerrilla adversaries have often concluded that the only way to fight them was with similarly armed and equipped troops (such as the American LURPs in Vietnam, or the UK's Special Air Service), BA has concluded that the only way to fight the no-frills operators is to fight 'fire with fire'.

Given the huge resources at BA's disposal, one could be forgiven for assuming that it will be able to concentrate these and generate a force:space ratio high enough to crush the other low-cost operators (the airline has a history of attempting to put competitors such as Laker Airways and Virgin Atlantic out of business). However, many observers are sceptical of BA's ability to abandon its traditional high-cost approach, and think that the airline will merely subsidise Go via BA's main operation rather than operate on a true low-cost basis. Mancassola says: 'A dinosaur can only create another little dinosaur.'

Mancassola *et al.* will be keeping a close eye on BA to make sure that such cross-subsidization does not take place, and will take the matter to court at the first signs that this is happening. Already Stelios Haji-Ionnaou, the owner of easyJet, has challenged the company to make public its losses.

The skies facing the no-frills operators are not completely blue, however. In the US after the deregulation of the industry in 1978, between 80 and 85 percent of the new businesses launched went out of business. While Go's initial routes are not in direct competition with the other carriers there is little danger of this, but the real threat will come when two or more carriers begin to compete head to head on the same route.

At that point, the 'enemy' will cease to be BA and the other 'traditional' airlines and become another no-frills carrier. Then the strategy will become **head-to-head combat,** and that is when the casualties will occur. Until that date, however, it looks likely that the low-cost airlines will continue to steal business from their higher-cost, higher-priced rivals.

LEXUS VS BMW AND MERCEDES

Pursuing a low-cost leadership strategy does not automatically mean selling a standard, no-frills product. A good example of this would be the strategy pursued by Toyota in its launch of the Lexus car into the luxury car market, competing against BMW and Mercedes. In the US, these German imports had had considerable success in taking market share in this segment from Cadillac, the traditional US prestige car. The average age of Cadillac owners was increasing, the brand being seen as stuffy and conservative, and younger, affluent buyers were moving to the two German brands in their thousands.

Toyota has long been recognized as the most efficient car manufacturing company in the world, but its concentration on mass-produced, low-cost models meant that as its customers grew more affluent as they got older, they had nothing to trade up to. In 1983, therefore, Chairman Eiji Toyoda challenged its engineers to develop the 'best car in the world', using Mercedes and BMW as the benchmark. This has been described by some as trying to get 'Beef Wellington at McDonald's', but Toyota was prepared to invest six years and $500 million to make it possible.

The German approach from BMW and Mercedes was very much one of differentiation. Both invested heavily in their brand names and both had carved out very profitable niches that to a point did not even compete directly with each other, BMW drivers tending to be younger.

The manufacturing approach of both was the opposite of the Japanese low-cost one, as typified by this comment from Edzard Reuter, the former Chairman of Daimler-Benz (owner of Mercedes):

> *We continually study our position and we always come to the con-*
> *clusion that we should stay away from mass production. The*
> *economies of scale wouldn't help us ... [and] we have a culture of*
> *engineering and product differentiation that would make it difficult.*

Both companies at the time were incredibly engineer led, and their products engineered to high specifications almost regardless of cost; increased costs would just have to be borne by the customer! For example, the BMW engineers decided that the complex rear axle on the 1989 850i needed a bigger part to improve road holding. The Japanese approach would have been to reengineer the entire axle so that the improved road holding was achieved, but the cost remained the same. BMW's approach used the larger part and doubled the cost of the axle to about $3000.

The Mercedes S-class has 88 electric motors that adjust virtually everything, including a rear-view mirror that is only 12 inches from the driver's nose. These 'improvements' led to the cost of the Mercedes top model increasing from $44,200 in 1980 to $125,000 12 years later. The engineers decided what the customer actually wanted. It was only recently that Mercedes' motto 'the best or noth-ing' was changed to 'the best for our customers'. This concentration on building cars almost by hand in a country that has some of the highest labor costs and benefits and the longest holidays in the world has an enormous impact on the cost of the vehicles.

Toyota's approach was to be totally different. Using its core com-petencies in low-cost, highly automated production, it planned to build a car that would match (or even surpass) that of its rivals but at a fraction of its cost. Toyota had virtually invented the just-in-time production system. With traditional mass production, parts and finished cars were turned out in large batches and pushed 'downstream' into inventory levels on dealers' showrooms. With JIT, cars are not built until there is an order for them. Dealers use computers to order cars directly from the factory, the customer get-ting his or her built-to-order car within 7 to 10 days.

The company also had a number of other advantages over its competitors, including a network of committed, competent and high-quality suppliers. Its product-development efforts were also organized differently, with a senior engineer in charge of the complete development of a new car, instead of the industry norm of only being responsible for a clearly defined part of it. This organizational benefit meant Toyota could develop a new model in less than four years, compared to General Motors' five and Mercedes' seven. This allowed it to correct mistakes more quickly, cut costs and keep it better abreast of market trends. At a time when Mercedes was experimenting with robots for the first time, as much of Toyota's process as possible was already automated.

All of this meant that Toyota had a huge cost advantage over BMW and Mercedes. In an ideal world, this would mean that the company could earn profits that were significantly above average, by charging the same prices as they did. But the Lexus did not have the brand name of either of the other two companies.

People who spend more than $20,000 on a car are not buying transportation alone. They are making a statement about their income and taste. Extensive research showed Toyota that it had little chance of attracting the sixty-something owners of Cadillacs and Lincolns. In addition, before the brand had had a chance to establish its own reputation and image, it had as little opportunity with people who had previously invested a small fortune in high-priced Mercedes and BMWs, to whom anything else would be a letdown. Toyota decided to aim for the affluent younger buyer who aspired to one of the German cars but could not yet afford one. This was later refined to a target audience of 43-year-old males with a household income of $100,000.

Wanting a more sophisticated approach than it had used in the past, Toyota invested in a completely new dealer network with new showrooms (something Honda was pioneering with the Acura). The Lexus LS 400 was launched in late 1989 at a price of $44,000: expensive, but a bargain compared to the Mercedes S-class at almost $30,000 more. Nor did the cheaper price tag denote lower quality.

The JD Power report of 1991 ranked the Lexus (together with Nissan's Infiniti) as best brand against two measurements: the least number of problems reported in the first 90 days of ownership, and customer satisfaction after one year. Mercedes ranked fourth and third, and BMW fourteenth and tenth. The Power report concluded: 'Luxury owners appreciate status and prestige but buy reliability.' This reputation for quality and low-cost maintenance, and the launch of other Japanese luxury cars such as Honda's Acura and Nissan's Infiniti, hit BMW and Mercedes hard.

RISKS OF A LOW-COST STRATEGY

In theory, a low-cost strategy does not necessarily mean translating these cost advantages into low prices. Where such reductions can be achieved through such factors as economies of scale, preferential access to raw materials or the possession of proprietary technology, the low-cost producer may be able to offer the customer a product or service that is comparable to that of its higher-cost competitors, and charge similar prices. Where this happens, the low cost base will translate directly into significantly higher profitability than that enjoyed by the competition. Even where this is not achievable, proximity in what is offered will still lead to above-average returns.

In practice this tends not to happen. Where products or services are comparable, the result is that customers buy on price. As low-cost producers have more scope to cut prices, they invariably do. Also, many organizations achieve their low-cost leadership through the elimination of 'unnecessary' differentiating features rather than the factors mentioned above, and the result of this is that they tend to provide a standard, no-frills product. This then needs to be sold at a significantly discounted price to the differentiated products or services offered by the competition, and a common pitfall is that the discounts offered offset the cost advantage, thus resulting in average or below-average profitability.

Sometimes changes in technology can eliminate an organization's leadership almost overnight. It is therefore essential that the low-cost leader is fully aware of any technological developments that could result in this, and is far-sighted enough to be aware of how the market's requirements might change in the future.

A third risk comes from a reduction in sales. Often low product margins are tolerable or acceptable provided that high volume is leading to high plant utilization and generating high profits overall. When sales volumes fall for any reason, it is very easy for black ink to change quickly to red on the P&L account.

The fourth is that customers' requirements can change over time. The standard, no-frills product of today can easily become a by-word for low quality tomorrow as differentiating factors that once were viewed as optional become expected as the norm. In the car industry, for example, it was not long ago that electric windows were found only as standard features on expensive executive cars. Today most middle-range cars have them and it will not be long before they will be expected as the norm on even low-priced, budget cars. A similar trend, although not yet so advanced, is happening with air conditioning.

The most common threat, however, occurs when more than one organization in the market chooses to pursue the low-cost strategy. Success really requires an organization to be *the* cost leader rather than *a* cost leader. When a market has several competitors trying to share this position, the usual result is a price war, with prices being cut closer and closer to the bone as each tries to achieve dominance and force the other to abandon its strategy.

In extreme cases this can destroy the profitability of the whole market, as even differentiators are forced to reduce prices as the gap between them and the low-cost producers widens to the point where customers start to question the size of the premium they are paying.

HARRIS QUEENSWAY

The tale of Harris Queensway is a cautionary one of how a low-cost strategy can fall apart when the risk factors outlined above come into play. Philip Harris grew a family-owned chain of three carpet shops in London into an empire of 440 stores with a total sales area of 4.6 million square feet, sales of £109.2 million and operating profits of £12.36 million. This was achieved through the implementation of a deliberate 'pile it high, sell it cheap' strategy that targeted budget-conscious consumers.

Operating costs were kept to a minimum, with most stores being huge low-cost, edge-of-town, retail 'sheds' with low rates and overheads. Low priority was given to the merchandising and display of product, with the marketing proposition unashamedly based on low, low prices. The acquisition of Queensway Discount Warehouses in the mid-1980s diversified the company into furniture, something that was reinforced by the later acquisitions of Times Furnishings and the Ultimate electrical chain (running the electrical departments as concessions within Debenhams department stores and a handful of Queensway branches). The group's pretax profit peaked in 1987 at £42.1 million.

However, Ultimate was never profitable and in 1988 the bubble burst for the rest of the group. For three successive years profits fell and the now Sir Phil Harris was forced to leave the company. Ultimate and Times Furnishings were disposed of and the company was renamed Lowndes Queensway. Despite attempts at rescue it ceased trading in 1990.

Several things had gone wrong. A recession, high interest rates and a downturn in the housing market all meant that consumers were spending less on carpets and furniture. Most consumers replace household items either when they are worn out or when they are moving home, and in times of recession even these tend to be postponed. The size of the market decreased considerably.

In addition, competitors with healthier balance sheets and more cash, such as MFI, Allied Carpets, Cantors and department stores, all responded by becoming more price driven, offering lower prices, extended credit and interest-free deals. Lowndes Queensway was already operating on paper-thin margins and rock-bottom prices and could not respond by lowering prices further.

Finally, consumer expectations had changed. The 1980s were a decade of retail innovation, when such companies as Body Shop, Next and Habitat changed customers' expectations about what a retail chain should offer. The merchandising and display of product were improved, as were the design of stores and the service and advice on offer from salespeople.

Lowndes Queensway, however, did not even pay lip service to these developments until it was too late. Rather than identifying what the real needs of customers were, the company's strategy was totally sales led, with all marketing executives being sacked once the group hit financial difficulties. People still wanted low prices, but they wanted them in attractive stores on well-merchandised product, with professional salespeople at hand if required.

Self-diagnostic questionnaire

1 Which of your company's competitors offer the lowest prices in your markets?
2 How do they achieve this? Have they reconfigured their organization, thereby giving themselves a substantially lower cost base? Or are they simply willing to accept lower margins?
3 If it is the former, what areas have they changed/eliminated? Exactly where do they have a cost advantage over your own company?
4 Is there any way in which you could restructure your company to eliminate many of the costs that you now take for granted?
5 If you were starting up a brand new company selling the same products/services as you do now, how would you structure it?

6

THE ROMAN LEGION –
DIFFERENTIATED SWATS

A FTER ALEXANDER'S DEATH HIS EMPIRE SPLIT INTO SEVERAL smaller ones, each commanded by one of his generals. It would be interesting to know what might have happened had Alexander lived longer, as such an ambitious and adventurous man would undoubtedly have turned his attention westwards (before his death he had made known his intention to return to North Africa and conquer Carthage), and would inevitably have come into conflict with the newly emerging power of Rome.

In its early days, Rome's enemies were the other city-states of Italy, often the descendants of Greek settlers who therefore fought in the Greek fashion. Later on Rome would also clash directly with the Macedonian descendants of Alexander during their conquest of Greece and in the Carthaginian Wars, as Carthage fought very much in the Macedonian manner. All of this meant that a system of warfare needed to be developed that would enable it to combat the Macedonian system effectively.

WEAKNESSES OF THE MACEDONIAN SYSTEM

For all its effectiveness under Alexander the Great, the Macedonian phalangial system did have its weaknesses.

First, its success relied on its ability to hold its formation without creating gaps. Thus if the right wing started to drift to the right (as it invariably did), either the whole phalanx had to follow suit or a gap would be created. In addition, it was almost impossible to control an advance over rough ground without creating gaps. For the foot companions, with both hands busy holding the *sarissa*, such gaps could be deadly, as an opponent armed with a sword would have free rein to create havoc once inside the Macedonian line.

Second, the phalanx had no reserve. All of its members engaged in the attack and once contact was made they were effectively contained *in situ*, unable to do anything else or react to unforeseen events.

This was compounded by the fact that Alexander's (and his successors') style of leadership was very personal. He led the companion cavalry himself, which meant that he was unable to direct control of events once battle was joined. The initial disposition of troops therefore governed the events of the subsequent battle to some extent. Contemporary historians would have us believe that the course of Alexander's battles always unfolded exactly as he had planned; if this was so, then it was a tribute either to his genius or his fortune (or both). Had events unfolded differently, his ability to redirect his forces and change the original plan would have been severely hampered because of his leadership style.

Finally, not all members of the phalanx were effective, with most of them too far from the enemy line to be able to use their weapons without endangering their own men in front of them. There was therefore a considerable waste of manpower.

THE PERFECT FIGHTING MACHINE

The reaction of Rome to these weaknesses was to develop a system that was more economical in the use of troops and that provided far more flexibility, articulation and the ability to react to unforeseen events. Like the city-states of Greece, Rome depended on a city militia for its armies. This levy (or *legio*, which gave the legion its name) was called on in times of emergency and disbanded afterwards; the armies therefore tended (again like the Greeks) to be comprised mainly of infantry, with a small force of cavalry provided by the aristocracy. However, it was there that the similarity with the Greek phalanx ended.

By the end of the fourth century BC Rome was deploying its infantry in three separate lines, each divided into a number of maniples (or 'handfuls') three ranks deep containing two centuries, although these were comprised of 70–80 men rather than the 100 that their name implies.

Eschewing the use of the spear or pike as a shock weapon, legionaries were armed with two javelins called *pila* (singular *pilum*) and a short stabbing sword called a *gladium*. *Pila* were designed to bend behind the head once they had struck a hard object, thus dragging an enemy infantryman's shield to the ground and rendering him defenseless, as well as preventing him from reusing it. Offensive tactics consisted of throwing the *pilum* and closing quickly to fight hand to hand with the sword. Legionaries were armed with a helmet, breastplate, leg greaves and a large oval shield two and a half feet wide and four feet high. Reinforced in the center and around the rims with iron, this provided an effective defense whether in sieges, fighting Greek phalanxes or Celts wielding huge two-handed swords.

These maniples were then organized into cohorts, and ten of these together (some 4500 to 5000 men) would form a legion, the equivalent of a modern-day division.

The subdivision of the legion into maniples enabled a degree of articulation and maneuverability never before seen in the ancient world. For the first time the individual was freed from the restrictions of fighting in mass formations while still having the benefits and reassurance of support for his flanks and rear. To wield the *gladium* effectively, each legionary needed about six feet of cleared space to his right, so each line of men was staggered to cover the gaps made. In turn, gaps were left between maniples in line that were covered by other maniples 100 meters to the rear.

ADVANTAGES OVER THE PHALANX

The effect was a chessboard formation that had a number of advantages over the phalanx. First, it anticipated the creation of the gaps so feared by the phalanx by allowing for them systematically in advance. In the manipular legion, before the Romans closed with their opponents in combat, parts of the second line would move forwards to fill the gaps left in front.

Second, when the third line moved forwards in turn to fill the second line's gaps, the rest constituted a reserve, something almost unheard of before then, when every fighting man was usually committed to battle.

Third, Roman generals would distance themselves from the actual fighting, viewing their role as one of strategic direction of the battle, and were therefore able to direct the reserve as and when they deemed appropriate.

THE LEGION PERFECTED

In their development of the manipular formation, the Romans had improved on the phalanx but had not yet developed a total combined-arms system to match that of the Macedonians. In the first and second Punic Wars Rome suffered a number of humiliating defeats, largely due to the Carthaginians' use of cavalry that was able to drive the Roman horsemen from the field with ease and attack the infantry from the rear.

This deficiency in cavalry was beginning to cost Rome dearly, but it knew that its 'core competence' lay in its ability to train and organize infantry. One of the first-known examples of 'outsourcing' then occurred, as Rome left its cavalry requirements largely to its allies and, with the help of Numidian cavalry, eventually achieved a decisive victory over Carthage.

Having 'cut their teeth' on the Carthaginians, the Romans went on to achieve several distinctive victories over the Macedonian system in Greece and Asia, again using cavalry supplied by allies.

This was despite improvements to the phalanx. The Macedonians had extended the *sarissas* of their fifth rank to a length of over 20 feet and shortened those of the first four by varying degrees so that all five spear points projected at the same distance. As two phalangists could occupy the same linear space as one legionary, this meant that 10 spears would confront each individual Roman soldier, making victory theoretically inevitable, for as the Roman Polybius wrote, 'it is impossible for a single man to cut through them all in time once they are at close quarters'.

This 'inevitable' victory assumed, however, that the phalanx could maintain its formation. If it could not, and the Romans could exploit the gaps created, the lightly armored phalangists (most having to use both hands to wield their enormous spears) would be massacred. The Roman infantryman was trained to fight as an individual and, with the space his formation gave him, he was able to turn, twist and duck in a way that no member of a phalanx ever could. Exploiting the inevitable gaps that opened up in the phalanx, this flexibility enabled him to come to close quarters with his enemies and, once there, they had no defense against his razor-sharp sword.

At the beginning of the first century BC, the consul Marius made further changes to refine the legion. The most important was making the cohort rather than the maniple the basic tactical unit. The usual formation of the legion was three lines, with four cohorts in the first and three in the second and third, staggered in the usual chessboard pattern.

If the first line faltered or was in need of assistance, the next line would advance through the six-foot intervals between each legionary to relieve them, and the third line was kept back as a

Structure of a Roman legion

Century (eight contubernia of ten men)   Maniple (two centuries)

Cohort (three maniples)

Legion (ten cohorts)

reserve. The picture was therefore one of constant movement by ranks within lines and also between the lines themselves. Every infantry army the Romans encountered, be they African, Greek, Syrian, Jewish, Gauls, Spanish, German or British, all succumbed to the might of the Roman legion backed by a relatively small force of cavalry.

No opponent trying to defeat the Romans by taking them on in an infantry battle ever came close to success. To most of the known world at that time (and to the Romans themselves) they seemed invincible. The weapons system that could defeat a legion backed with allied cavalry did not seem to have been invented.

THE BATTLE OF CARRHAE, 53 BC

Despite this, there were obviously occasions on which Rome was defeated; the point is that nobody was able to defeat them using a similar, infantry-based model. It is worth looking at one of the rare occasions on which Rome was defeated, when it made the error in the first century BC of invading Parthia and met a weapons system unlike anything it had ever encountered. The Parthians had been forced by the vast open plains of their country to develop a military system that was exclusively mounted, and for the first time the Roman military machine faced an opponent that had no intention of playing it 'at its own game'.

The Roman general Crassus was dismissive of his enemy, regarding his only problem as being 'the tedium of the march and the trouble of chasing men who dare not come to blows'. This was foolhardy in the extreme; the one area in which the Romans had encountered difficulties was in fighting cavalry, and the Parthians possessed both heavy and light cavalry, the former heavily armored (both man and horse) and armed with a lance so long and heavy that the Romans nicknamed it the 'bargepole'. These forces were provided by the Parthian aristocracy, whose retainers provided the mass of light cavalry armed with bows.

Although Caesar once said that he preferred to use hunger rather than steel, Roman generals inevitably pursued a **head-to-head** combat strategy when they went to war, confident that their SWAT could defeat whatever was thrown at it. Given the 'superiority' of the legion, the logical strategy for the Parthians to follow would have been a raiding one of either type, harassing it as it advanced without giving battle as the Persians did several centuries later (see Chapter 10).

However, perhaps because they wanted the propaganda value of having defeated the Romans in head-to-head combat rather than by what the Romans themselves would have regarded as subterfuge, they also chose to adopt a head-to-head combat strategy.

The Parthians allowed Crassus to march far into Mesopotamia before revealing themselves. On seeing them the Romans confidently formed a defensive square, and the Parthians wisely chose not to charge with their heavy cavalry. Instead, they simply showered the Romans with arrows from all sides, not even having to aim carefully, since 36,000 men made a huge, densely packed target they could not miss.

Crassus had included 4000 cavalry (mostly Gauls) in his army and on learning that his enemy had an almost inexhaustible supply of arrows, he sent 1300 of these with 5000 infantry and 500 archers to attack the Parthians. This cavalry faced the same fate as the lightly armored Persian cavalry facing Alexander's companions 200 years previously. Hopelessly outweighed by the heavy cavalry, the Gauls were routed and forced to take shelter with the infantry, which then was subjected to the same terrifying shower of missiles that the main body of Crassus's army had endured. Virtually all of them were killed or wounded and when they finally lost all effectiveness as a fighting force, the Parthian heavy cavalry charged and finished them off, except for 500 who were taken prisoner.

Then the same fate was meted out to Crassus and the rest of his army. When the Romans crowded together tightly enough for their shields to overlap and provide an effective defense, they made an ideal target for the charges of the heavy cavalry, and when they stayed apart in order to avoid this, they were picked off by the archers. The massacre lasted until the following day, but eventually the entire army was destroyed or taken prisoner.

What the Parthians had that many other Roman opponents did not was a weapons system (and a terrain) ideally suited for fighting heavy infantry. History had shown that heavy infantry was able to defend itself against heavy cavalry. By forming in a group, protected by armor and shields, the heavy infantryman had a number of advantages: a firm foundation from which to fight, the ability to concentrate on fighting over anything else (like having to control a horse without the benefit of stirrups), depth and a square formation that left no side unprotected. But the formation of such a group made them 'sitting ducks' for either light infantry or cavalry armed with missiles.

While the heavy Greek infantry at Marathon had been able to charge the Persian foot archers and put them to flight, no such option existed for Crassus, as the Parthians had the vastness of the Mesopotamian plains behind them and could simply retire until the charge had spent itself. But mounted archers are at a distinct disadvantage to foot archers, who have a steadier base from which to operate and, like heavy infantry, the luxury of being able to concentrate on one thing at a time. Had the Romans had a larger force of archers, these would have been able to keep the Parthian horse archers at bay while relying on the protection of the heavy infantry from the heavy cavalry. Once again, the Romans had been defeated due to an over-reliance on heavy infantry alone.

The Parthians were unable to capitalize on their success and replace Rome as the dominant power of the time because their weapons system was only of use on territory that allowed the free-ranging movement of cavalry. An attempted invasion of Syria failed when it became apparent that they had no means of besieging cities, and could not even operate effectively in forested terrain, leaving the area soon after losing a considerable number of men in an ambush.

COMMERCIAL DIFFERENTIATION

Commercial organizations looking to create a SWAT by differentiation seek to be unique in some way that has value to their customers (if this is not the case, then the company is *different* rather than being *differentiated*) and for which those customers will be willing to pay a price premium. If this premium exceeds the costs incurred in being unique, the strategy will lead to above-average profitability. Even if the customer will not pay a premium, the other benefits of the strategy are increased sales at the same price and more loyalty from customers in slack times.

The point of differentiation can be virtually anything, provided that it creates value for the customer. In the case of a retail outlet or bank, it could be location, for example. It could be scale, with customers seeing value in dealing with the 'biggest in the market'. IBM built its empire partly on this factor, with the slogan 'Nobody ever got fired for buying IBM', the implication being that the company's size meant security.

It could be nationality. Part of Harley-Davidson's appeal to its customers is that it is seen as an American institution, for example. It could be additional product features, quality, speed, customer service, range, convenience, ease of doing business; in fact anything at all that adds value or that the customer perceives to add value.

VISION EXPRESS

Many companies have differentiated themselves by providing their customers with additional products or services that they did not even realize they wanted until they saw them on offer.

An excellent example of this that added perceived value for the customer is Vision Express's guaranteed provision of spectacles within one hour. After all, how many customers really need new spectacles within an hour? Only a very few, such as those who have lost or broken their originals and do not have a spare set; nobody else actually needs them that quickly. However, Vision Express has experienced extraordinary success by providing this service because the customer perceives it to be a great idea, and that is what counts.

Although many other opticians' chains now offer the facility, the one-hour spectacle superstore was pioneered by Vision Express and its founder, Dean Butler. Not an optician by trade (he was a marketing executive working for Procter & Gamble), Butler became interested in the industry when helping design an advertising campaign for a friend who owned a small optician's chain and was having difficulty competing with a rival. He saw that the production of the spectacles itself only took about 30 minutes, but people were having to wait about two weeks for them as they had to be sent off to a laboratory and then returned.

The obvious solution was to make the spectacles on the premises, but this entailed investing in expensive manufacturing equipment, and having larger premises to accommodate it. The traditional view was that this just couldn't be done.

Convinced that it could, Butler left Procter & Gamble in 1984 and opened the first branch of Lenscrafters, offering a one-hour service. The idea was successful and within three years he had four stores, eventually selling them to the US Shoe Corporation for £4.7 million. As part of the deal, he negotiated a 2 percent cut of the profits for five years, and stayed to help the chain grow to 231 stores.

Unable to compete in the US as part of the sale agreement, Butler then took the concept to Europe and set up Vision Express in Nottingham in 1988, launching his business with distinctive advertising. Customers were soon won over by the idea of spectacles within one hour, regardless of whether they needed them that quickly or not.

At the time, the optical industry was very old fashioned and conservative, and had only been deregulated three years earlier. Prior to that, advertising had not even been allowed, which prevented companies from reducing prices because even if they did so, they couldn't tell anyone about it!

Vision Express's innovative approach took the industry by storm, and the idea was so popular with the public that the chain quickly grew to over 200 stores in the UK and also Italy, Poland, Belgium, Luxembourg, Argentina and the Philippines, with profits of over £20 million. In 1997 it was purchased by Grand Optical Photoservice (GPS), the fastest-growing opticians' chain in France, which also offers a similar service. Together the two chains have 347 stores, and they plan to quadruple in size over the next 10 years.

SNAP-ON TOOLS

The Snap-On Tools Corporation (based in Kenosha, Wisconsin) sells high-quality tools to mechanics and auto dealers, achieving almost legendary status among its customers and a cachet for its products rivaling that achieved in their own markets by Rolex and Rolls-Royce. The company has earnings of over $1.5 billion and profits of over $130 million, and has reached this through a focused strategy that clearly differentiates it from its competition in three areas.

First is the quality of the tools themselves. To its customers, Snap-On tools are the standard by which other tools are measured. Made by hand from only the highest-grade steel, most of the tools are backed by a lifetime warranty; but more important than the warranty itself is the customer's knowledge that the tool quite simply is not going to break. It is common for mechanics still to have tool sets 25 years after their purchase. Ownership of Snap-On tools sends a strong signal that the owner is a professional, and the tools are often proudly displayed in workshops.

Second is the relationship between the company and its customer base. Snap-On has avoided diversification into the DIY or construction sectors and is totally focused on auto-repair shops. The company has nearly 6000 franchise dealers who visit a customer base of 325,000 weekly in vans. Each van is essentially a mobile retail unit, carrying around $100,000 worth of inventory, and the weekly visit enables the franchise dealer to sell additional tools on a regular basis.

Third, and to many customers the most important, are generous credit terms. Snap-On charges about double the prices that a retail DIY store would charge, and a chest full of its tools could cost up to $10,000. The company therefore makes it easy for its customers to afford the tools by offering interest-free credit on most sales. Customers simply pay a fixed amount, in cash, each week when the dealer calls.

However, nearly 90 percent of vehicles today are computerized, and even the small independent needs more and more sophisticated equipment to meet their growing complexity. This puts additional strains on the finances of most independent customers (a computerized diagnostic system costs $40,000), so these more expensive items are sold via formal loans from the company's financial services arm. While interest is charged on these, credit is extended to customers who might not qualify for it elsewhere, literally enabling many customers to stay in business.

The bond developed over a long period of regular calling and the trust demonstrated by Snap-On ensures that the company achieves a much higher percentage of the average customer's business than do any of the competition.

DIFFERENTIATING A COMMODITY: GRANITEROCK

Companies that sell what in their view are commodities often claim that their product cannot be differentiated, and that there is no difference between their product and the competition's. The product or service that cannot be differentiated does not exist!

If the product itself is a commodity, then the services surrounding it can be differentiated – after-sales support/advice, delivery, ordering systems, reliability, lifetime warranties etc.

One example is Graniterock, a company based in California that produces rock, sand, gravel aggregates, asphalt and ready-mix concrete, and sells other building materials such as bricks, concrete blocks and wallboards. Its industry has traditionally been regarded as a commodity business, with the key determinant for customers being price.

Graniterock, however, has managed to differentiate itself clearly in terms of quality and service. As on-time delivery of ready-mixed concrete is important to its customers the company has benchmarked itself against Domino's Pizza, on the grounds that both companies deliver perishable product, and has an on-time delivery performance of 95 percent, something unheard of in the industry.

It has also taken the unprecedented step of trusting its customers. If a customer is dissatisfied with any product or service, they are simply asked to reduce the sum they pay by an amount that compensates for the dissatisfaction. The amount deducted is left up to the customer. The annual cost of this is only about 0.2 percent of sales, about one-tenth of the industry average; and in case you might be cynical enough to think that the number of complaints received would increase considerably, they actually reduced by 31 percent following the introduction of the system. This approach also communicates to the customer the fact that Graniterock is confident about its product (after all, you couldn't offer that if you didn't have a good product).

WEAKNESSES OF A DIFFERENTIATION STRATEGY

The key risks in a differentiation strategy are fourfold. First, the extent of differentiation can be narrowed or even eliminated through imitation. Amazon's differentiation has been weakened by Barnes & Noble's introduction of an Internet service (see Chapter 3) and Vision Express is no longer the only company to offer to manufacture spectacles in one hour (although it is still the only major chain that offers the service in every store, enabling it to advertise its core proposition heavily in a way other chains cannot).

Second, the point of differentiation may cease to be valued by customers, or they may be swayed by other differentiating features offered by competitors. The financial difficulties experienced by Nike in 1998 are a good example (see below).

Third, cost proximity to the competition may be lost, with the result that a large pricing differential opens that is sufficient to cancel out the value offered by the differentiation in the customer's mind. A company that is starting to find itself in this position is Intel. For years the company has been able to charge up to five times more than its competitors because of its virtual monopoly of the microprocessor market (see Chapter 2), and the fact that its products have always been technologically superior to theirs. Now for the first time, competitors such as AMD have begun to introduce products that are as good (or nearly as good) as Intel's at a fraction of the cost, and the question has to be asked whether, if they can overcome the delivery problems that have plagued them, Intel can continue to achieve its traditional price premium.

Fourth, competitors following a focus strategy may achieve even greater differentiation by specializing in one segment of the market, something which is looked at in depth in Chapter 7.

Finally, the point of differentiation may not add value from the customer's point of view. Here the company is different, but not differentiated.

The ease with which competitors are able to do any of these things is contingent on how well the strategy has been thought through, and this depends on three things.

First, just because a company is different does not mean that it has achieved a competitive advantage. To do this, the point of differentiation must reduce the customers' costs, improve their performance or reduce their risk of failure. The most valued points of differentiation will be those that can be seen and measured easily by customers while also being heavily signaled. Signals such as brand name, market share/position and heavyweight effective advertising act as barriers to entry and are difficult for competitors to break down.

The important role that value signals can play is often overlooked by companies that prefer to rely on the 'facts', i.e. the performance of the product itself. This is the 'better product will win' fallacy, and ignores the fact that many purchases, even theoretically hard-nosed business ones, are made at least in part on subjective criteria. Companies who ignore value signaling are open to attack by competitors who use this route to play on this aspect of customer behavior.

Second, sometimes a company differentiates a product or service too much, and tries to charge a premium that is higher than customers are willing to pay. If quality is higher than is actually needed, competitors with the correct level but a lower price will be better positioned to satisfy the customer's needs. A higher than acceptable price premium may also need to be charged when a company's costs are not at least in proximity to those of its competitors.

Third, the difficulty of imitating a differentiation strategy is partly a function of how many points of differentiation exist. Obviously, a company with one point of differentiation is more susceptible to attack than one with many, as imitation in the latter case will necessitate widespread changes in competitors' behavior.

NIKE

It might seem strange to use Nike as an example of what can go wrong with a differentiation strategy, since it is one of the world's most successful companies, but in 1998 it announced its first quarterly loss in 13 years, as a result of what appears to be a decline in the popularity of its products. It seems that the Nike logo no longer adds the value that it once did for consumers.

Before the company's establishment in 1971, training shoes had been footwear for athletes only, but the jogging boom of the 1970s created a whole new market, encouraged by the establishment of speciality retailers like Athlete's Foot and Kinney's Foot Lockers and the launch of specialist magazines.

Nike's invention of a new 'waffle' sole and the subsequent development of 140 models by the end of the decade (allowing for difference in sex, age, weight, running speed and skill level) catapulted it to success over the heads of established competitors like Adidas. By 1981 it had over 50 percent of the market.

Then in the 1980s the shoes became a fashion item, and Nike responded with a marketing strategy aimed at persuading kids to wear the same shoes as their sporting idols. By getting professional sportsmen and women to wear the product, the company also managed to get otherwise unachievable exposure and advertising. An advertisement in *Sports Illustrated* could be purchased for $50,000, but the only way to get on the cover was on the feet of the sportsman in the photograph. Phil Knight, Nike's founder, said:

> *The secret of the business is to build the kind of shoes professional athletes will wear, then put them on the pros. The rest of the market will follow.*

This strategy is an extremely expensive one. In 1997 Nike spent $5.6 billion on marketing, including $4 billion on sponsorship of stars such as Michael Jordan ($70 million), Ronaldo ($10 million) and even whole teams (Nike clothed 10 of the national teams playing in the 1998 soccer World Cup), the 10-year sponsorship deal with the Brazilian national football team costing $400 million. This is affordable, as the shoes can cost as little as 46p to make in China, yet sell for over £50 per pair in the UK.

Recognizing that about 80 percent of all sales of sports shoes or clothing are bought as fashion items, some competitors, such as LA Gear, tried to diversify into fashion clothing, but Nike stuck to its sporting roots, establishing itself as a sports brand. This did not seem to matter, as the line between sportswear and fashionwear virtually disappeared, following a generational shift towards casual and functional clothing.

In 1988 Nike overtook Reebok to become brand leader, and by 1991 it had become the first sportswear manufacturer to gross more than $3 billion in annual sales; by 1997 that figure had trebled to $9 billion. In 1998 the company boasted a 33 percent global share of the training-shoe market (40 percent in the US).

However, Nike's very success brought two major problems. First, the more a company becomes identified with fashion, the more at risk it is from trends. Fashion goes out of fashion, and there are always competitors waiting with a more up-to-date image.

Second, when you are as successful as Nike, and parents and even grandparents wear your products as well as teenagers, how fashionable can you really be? The company's famous advertising line 'Just Do It' was an anti-establishment, eighties way of saying 'to hell with everyone else', but the company had actually *become* the establishment.

A clear opportunity existed for a competitor to capture the youthful, anti-establishment market, but LA Gear (which had attempted to move into fashion clothing) filed for bankruptcy and Reebok and Adidas had both copied Nike's strategy of focusing on sport.

The challenge, when it came, was not from another sportswear manufacturer, but from fashion clothing. Teenagers turned not to a different brand of trainer with a more youthful image, but away from them altogether. In the US (and to a lesser degree the UK also), the wearing of trainers suddenly became less fashionable and teenagers turned to leather boots and shoes by companies such as Caterpillar and Timberland and Reebok-owned Rockport (in 1997, Rockport's turnover was $500 million).

The effect was dramatic as sales fell and Nike was left with an inventory mountain the size of a medium-sized Himalayan foothill in sports shops around the US, with top-of-the-range shoes normally selling for $160 being reduced by 50 percent to clear. Fourth-quarter earnings in 1997/98 fell by 69 percent from $237 million to $73.1 million, and it was announced that the company would shed 1600 jobs and embark on a cost-cutting program to slash $1 million in annual costs.

The company has announced plans that will enable it to bounce back, including new products, new advertising and a new, softer advertising line ('You Can' instead of 'Just Do It'). The probability is that a company as professional and successful as Nike will succeed in this. The surprise is that it did not appear to see the problem coming, despite several signs. Over two years previously the company's Hollywood division, whose job is to place products with celebrities, announced that it was having difficulties and that it could not even give its trainers away.

Internal discussions were held about the company's waning popularity, but the decision appears to have been taken to stick collective heads in the sand and ignore the warnings. Nike claims that discounting is a temporary phenomenon and will disappear once the inventory glut has been removed. At the time of writing Wall Street is less sure and is worried that the company's insistence on maintaining its sponsorship spend can only exacerbate the situation, given that sales forecasts are flat for the next 12 months.

It is too early to tell whether the company's short-term woes are temporary or an indication of worse to come. It is just possible that Nike's 'recovery' plans could resemble the shuffling of deckchairs on the *Titanic*.

THE GREYHOUND BUS COMPANY

An example of a company paying the consequences for trying to differentiate itself in a way that did not add value for its customers is the US bus company Greyhound. A few years ago, it decided to bring itself into the twentieth century and introduce a computerized operating system called Trips. Customer service had been adversely affected by cutbacks and downsizing, and the company was also suffering from competition from low-cost airlines in many areas.

Trips would allow a sophisticated reservation system and efficient fleet scheduling that in theory would enable Greyhound to compete effectively, and on the announcement that this was going to happen the company's stock soared on Wall Street, nearly doubling in the next six months.

Unfortunately, operating computerized systems was not only not a core competence of the company, it was not even a competence. Standards of service actually dropped, with the result that customer traffic fell by 12 percent in one month. Tickets took several minutes to print, keystrokes could take nearly a minute to register on the screen, and the staff were poorly trained. Computer-generated errors often lost luggage and left customers stranded at terminals, and competitors took advantage of the situation by putting on additional buses.

The worst mistake, however, was that even an efficient and fully working system would not really have added much value for Greyhound's customers. Its average customer earned only $12,000 per year and many didn't have credit cards to make a reservation even if the system had worked. The existing value chain was quite simple: people turned up for a bus, and on the rare occasion that one was full, they waited at the terminal for the next one. Very low-tech, agreed, but simple and something they were happy with. Trips was an expensive disaster because nobody had stopped to think whether it would actually add value or not.

Self-diagnostic questionnaire

1 Identify each of your main competitors (and also those companies that offer substitute products) and identify which of them (if any) has a significant point of differentiation. Ask your customers to do the same; sometimes they will see differentiation where you cannot through corporate myopia or a refusal to accept that a competitor night do something better than yourselves.

2 Identify ways in which you can narrow the gap between yourselves and the competition.

3 Are there any customer needs in your market (either explicit or implicit) that are currently unserved? Could you differentiate yourself in a way that would meet or exceed these needs?

4 List as many points of potential differentiation as you can, and rank yourselves and the competition against them.

5 Identify what you consider to be your company's core competencies. Ask your customers if they agree.

6 Link these with the potential points of differentiation to identify any natural links.

7 Check any chosen route of differentiation against the two prerequisites of customer value and sustainability. Ask your customers if they would value the differentiation. Would you be able to sustain it, or could the competition easily catch up?

7

THE ENGLISH LONGBOW –
FOCUSED SWATS

IN THE CENTURIES FOLLOWING THE FALL OF ROME, INFANTRY
eventually became totally subservient to cavalry. The empire dis-
solved into a number of separate, fragmented kingdoms, which
meant that there was no longer any formal administrative military
machine, armed forces being organized purely on a local basis.
More and more fortifications were built to protect rural populations
and commercial centers, and each local landowner maintained a
standing army of knights and men-at-arms.

Each landowner's loyalty, however, was to himself and his immediate lord rather than to the king. When the great barons obeyed
their feudal summons to serve in the king's army for a given number
of days per year, the resulting royal armies were a hotchpotch of
forces with no common bond, organization or training.

The whole period was one of complete stagnation in military
thought, strategy and tactics. Feudal armies were characterized by
indiscipline and insubordination, with a hierarchy of command
based on social status rather than ability, and with tactics replaced
by blind frontal attacks whenever and wherever the enemy was
sighted, with no reconnaissance and without any effort to attempt
flanking attacks. Warfare was regarded as a noble pursuit, for
noblemen, in which a man of honor might display his courage and
fighting prowess to the world.

Friendly infantry were discounted as being there to 'make up the
numbers', the equivalent of cannon fodder and very definitely tenth-
class citizens rather than comrades-in-arms. Enemy infantry were
regarded as a disorganized rabble to be ridden over in order to

attack the enemy cavalry. They were untrained, poorly armed and only collected together for the duration of the campaign; unsurprisingly they had poor morale and little motivation to fight other than saving their lives.

DAVID VS GOLIATH

The predominant power in western Europe at this time was France, which never made any attempt to develop effective light or heavy infantry, relying completely on frontal attack by heavy cavalry. But the effectiveness of cavalry was also paradoxically being undermined by the gradual replacement of chainmail by fuller plate armor. While this did improve effectiveness by making the rider more immune to injury, the full weight of the armor on both man and horse (140–150 lb) reduced the cavalry to a lumbering mass capable only of 'charging' frontally at a fast trot and unable to make sudden stops or starts. When thrown into confusion or faced by more agile opponents, these knights were to prove helpless.

France's nobility were considered to be the cream of western chivalry. However, during the fourteenth and early fifteenth centuries they suffered a series of resounding defeats at the hands of a much smaller and less powerful neighbor.

That neighbor was England. Early in the thirteenth century the English throne had been forced to give up much of the territory it held in northern France, and disputes over other English-ruled territory in France and the right of succession to the French throne itself were to bring the two countries into conflict for the next 200 years. At first it seemed to outsiders like a David and Goliath contest in which England had no chance of success. France was larger, more powerful, better armed, more populated, richer and possessed the finest body of cavalry in Christendom.

Knowing that England and her allies could never match France and her allies in the numbers of horsemen necessary to stand a chance in a cavalry battle, the English needed an alternative method of dealing with what had proven so far to be the almost irresistible charge of the French nobility. They were therefore forced by necessity to develop a SWAT that would capitalize on the inherent weaknesses of the French.

THE 'DISCOVERY' OF THE LONGBOW

Edward I discovered this 'secret weapon' while campaigning to conquer the Welsh during the 1270s. It was the longbow, a weapon decidedly superior to either the old, composite bow or even the crossbow. As long as a man's height, when fired by an expert the longbow had the same destructive power as a crossbow – at one point the English came across an arrow that had been fired into a four-inch-thick wooden door and that had succeeded in penetrating it and protruding through the other side – but it had the advantages of a much higher rate of fire and a longer range. A skilled bowman could fire three or four times faster than a cross-bowman, and at long range could have two arrows in the air simultaneously.

The disadvantage of the longbow was that it needed an incredible amount of skill to fire accurately and that it took a long time to obtain that skill. This long training meant that it was never popularized in France, even when its destructive power had been demonstrated. Thus for two centuries the English and Welsh held a monopoly and ultimately developed the best light infantry in the world.

Prior to the extension of the longbow's use outside Wales, however, there had already been one demonstration of how determined infantry could defeat a larger, mounted opponent. In 1297 the Scots, in rebellion under Sir William Wallace, had soundly defeated the mounted English at the Battle of Stirling Bridge by using predominantly heavy infantry armed with long pikes. While much of the Scots' success was due to the blinding incompetence of the English commander in allowing himself to be duped into battle on unsuitable ground, this was the first indication that motivated infantry-men could actually stop cavalry.

The following year, however, Edward I himself commanded an army that invaded Scotland, and completely routed the Scots even though they had chosen a well-defended position at Falkirk. The Scottish heavy infantry was formed in round *schiltrons*, with stakes linked by rope placed in the ground to help keep them in position. Armed with long pikes, they proved impervious to attack from the English cavalry, thus demonstrating once again forgotten lessons from antiquity.

Unfortunately for the Scots, Edward was keen to try out his new longbows and unleashed his archers with devastating effect. In scenes that must have been similar to the Parthian massacre of the Romans at Carrhae, the Scots were used as target practice by the bowmen until sufficient gaps occurred in their *schiltrons* to effect a successful charge from the cavalry, which broke the Scottish formation and routed them.

THE BATTLE OF CRECY, 1346

The system was further refined by Edward's grandson, Edward III, who invaded France in 1346 with approximately 20,000 men during the Hundred Years' War to assist his hard-pressed allies in Flanders. Following a raiding logistics strategy with no specific political objective, he ravaged northwestern France to the outskirts of Paris in an orgy of looting and pillage for a month until, warned of the approach of a large army under the French king Philip VI, he turned northeast towards the Low Countries.

Philip had approximately 60,000 men under his command, consisting of 12,000 heavy cavalry, 6000 Genoese crossbowmen, 17,000 light cavalry and a 25,000-strong rabble of undisciplined infantry. With such an enormous host under his command, he had a clear head-to-head combat strategy and intended to bring Edward to battle and inflict a crushing defeat on his small army.

Faced with odds of 3:1, Edward tried to avoid battle and head for Flanders, but Philip dogged his every move. Finally realizing that battle could not be avoided, Edward waited until he had crossed the Seine so that there was no major obstacle to his rear if he was defeated, and then chose as a battleground the sloping countryside near the village of Crecy-en-Ponthieu. Lacking good heavy infantry of his own, Edward improvised by dismounting his knights and men-at-arms and using them as infantry, something that would have been unthinkable to the honor-obsessed French.

It was important for success that there should be no possibility of a flanking attack from the French (however unlikely that might be), so Edward anchored his flanks: the right against a river and the left on trees in front of a village, further strengthened by hastily dug ditches. His army was formed in three roughly equal 'battles' or divisions, two to the front and one in reserve to the rear, and a large number of holes a foot wide and a foot deep were dug in the ground in front of each division to break the momentum of the French charge.

The French army was strung out in one long, disorganized column (when it left Abbeville the van was eight miles out of town before the rearguard had left!). The French nobility were so confident of victory that they had already shared out the potential English prisoners of rank between themselves and calculated the ransoms that they would demand for their release. No light cavalry screen was in place for reconnaissance purposes, and at about 6 pm the French host literally 'bumped into' the English position.

Since it was late in the day and much of his cavalry had yet to arrive, Philip wisely chose to postpone battle until the next morning, but the blood of the French cavalry was up and they insisted on attacking immediately, each wanting to be first in the charge. Unable to control them, Philip reluctantly agreed, but insisted on a 'softening up' of the English line from the Genoese crossbowmen. Tired after having marched all day, they had the late afternoon sun in their eyes. Firing once at extreme range, their bolts fell short of the English line. Then the English archers returned fire with such devastating effect that the Genoese, who had never experienced such firepower before, broke and ran.

Incensed by what they saw as cowardice, the French cavalry launched themselves forward, cutting and hacking a path through the retreating men. Instead of attacking the bowmen themselves, they aimed at the dismounted men-at-arms. Whether this was because they regarded them as a more 'noble' target or because the archers were positioned on terraces that made such an attack impossible is not known, but the charges lost all impetus under the shower of thousands of arrows, the horses stumbling among the freshly dug pits in advance of the English line. There were as many as 15 French attacks, each stumbling hard on the heels of the one before, with the result that the ground in front of the line must have been one of appalling confusion, each fresh attack being swamped by the retreating knights already repulsed. Some cavalry made it through to the English men-at-arms where a short, sharp fight ensued, but there was never any doubt as to the outcome.

The slaughter continued well into the night, until eventually the French accepted defeat and retired from the battlefield. The English line obeyed Edward's orders throughout the night and stayed in line, and when morning came they counted the dead. In the valley in front of them lay over 1500 dead lords and knights, and about 15,000 men-at-arms, crossbowmen and infantry. The English losses were about 200 dead and wounded.

The English mixture of light and heavy infantry could resist attack from any combination of weapons systems and was the perfect defensive system, one which could have beaten even the Parthians who had destroyed Crassus's legions at Carrhae.

Unfortunately for the French, the lessons to be drawn from this battle were completely lost on them. They refused to accept that England had won because of the longbow, and instead put it down to the fact that the English men-at-arms had fought dismounted.

At Poitiers 10 years later they therefore dismounted their cavalry to fight the Black Prince on foot. However, all this did was remove the one advantage that they possessed when attacking (shock) and they were again slaughtered. This time the French king Jean 'le Bon' was actually captured and taken back to England.

Then at Agincourt in 1415, in a virtual rerun of Crecy, an English army of 6000 completely routed 25,000 Frenchmen. They had failed to realise that the victory at Crecy was due to a combination of dismounted knights and archers rather than the use of the former alone.

FOCUSING ON ONE SECTOR OF THE MARKET

Choosing focus as a route to developing a competitive SWAT on the business battlefield entails choosing one particular segment of a marketplace and focusing on that, sometimes to the exclusion of all others. This is the equivalent of achieving local numerical superiority on a battlefield even though you may not have numerical superiority overall. By doing this, a company can achieve a competitive advantage in its chosen market segment even though it does not possess one overall.

A market segment is formed out of a combination of a product variety (or varieties) and groups of customers. Thus a segment could be created by selling a wide range of products or services to one particular type of customer, or one product to the whole marketplace. The first would be customer oriented, the second product oriented. A third could be created by selling one product to one type of customer, and would therefore be a combination of the two.

In most markets there will be a variety of ways in which customers can be segmented. Saga holidays, Club 18–30 and the *Oldie* magazine have segmented their markets by age and targeted a very specific age group. Nissan has done it by sex, strongly targeting young women with its advertising on the Micra, while Volvo targets the safety conscious. Both American Express and Aldi segment their markets by income level, the former concentrating on high earners and the latter focusing on the budget conscious.

Other methods of segmenting consumer goods markets might be by household size, religion, nationality, language, class, lifestyle and psychographics, education level, frequency of use and purpose of purchase (e.g. own use or gift). Industrial or commercial markets could be segmented by size, technological sophistication, use of product, strategy, price sensitivity, method of ownership, financial strength, rate of growth or order pattern. Different methods will be appropriate for different markets, or for different suppliers.

One small retail outlet (the first in an intended chain of 50) called Girl Heaven opened in the UK in 1999 dedicated to selling thousands of items ranging from 25p to £70, all aimed squarely at little girls. The shop also offers a 'Princess makeover' (where parents can bring in their daughter and have her dressed and photographed as a princess) and has staff demonstrating the latest dance steps and make-up tips.

Yet another way of segmenting a market is via channels of distribution, which requires the identification of all existing and potential methods of supplying a product to the ultimate user. Channels can have a significant impact on costs. For example, the decision to 'go direct' rather than through distributors will usually necessitate a large direct salesforce. A concentration on direct mail as the main selling channel will have severe implications for a company's whole logistics system.

Market segments should be identified irrespective of current competitive activity. It is important that the would-be focuser does not concentrate purely on the traditionally accepted view of a market's structure. The tendency is to concentrate on previously recognized segments, while in most markets there will be opportunities both for new products and services and for new potential customers.

It is these unrecognized segments that often provide the most potential because they give the company the opportunity to be the first to tailor its services to its customers' specific needs. Occasionally completely new channels of distribution can be identified and developed, as Dell was able to do with personal computers (see Chapter 5).

It should be noted that just as being differentiated *per se* does not differentiate a company or product, neither does focusing on a segment as such provide you with one. To say to customers 'buy from me because I only sell product *x*' or 'buy from me because I only sell to people like you' without telling them why your specialization benefits them will not be very successful.

For a focus strategy to be successful there are therefore two prerequisites. The first is that the customers in the segment must have specific needs that are different in some way from those of the rest of the market. For a petfood manufacturer to decide, for example, that it was going to concentrate on producing food for animals owned by women would not give it a competitive advantage unless female petowners had recognizably different needs from their male counterparts (and realized that they had them).

The second is the ability of the focuser to serve those needs better than broader-based competition. This is done by following either a low-cost or differentiation route, giving two variants of a focus strategy: cost focus and differentiation focus. The customers in the segment still have the option of buying from those competitors that are broad based, and it is therefore essential still to have either cost leadership or a point of differentiation if customers are to recognize a benefit in dealing with a specialist.

The first variant focuses on the differences in costs in some segments, and the second on the special needs of that segment. The need for some point of differentiation other than the specialization itself is exacerbated when one or more imitators enters the segment. Obviously, when more than one company is focusing on a market segment, then a company needs some way of differentiating itself against the new entrant.

The success of this strategy depends on the special needs of the segment being poorly served by broad-based competitors. If this is not the case, and those needs are being adequately served, then focusing itself will not create any extra value for the customer.

L'EGGS

Sarah Lee is a broad-based conglomerate that owns companies selling everything from cheesecake to vacuum cleaners, shoe polish to meat products. One of its most successful possessions is Hanes, the number one department-store pantyhose brand in the US. Hanes was looking for alternative distribution channels, as US women were shopping less frequently at department stores, and decided on supermarkets as a potential alternative. After all, most women would go to a supermarket at least once a week and the exposure this would give its products would be immense.

The only problem was that supermarkets didn't sell pantyhose.

Rather than attempt to sell its existing range of tights and stockings, Hanes created a new brand that would only be sold via supermarkets. The product was called L'eggs, and to reinforce the brand name it was packaged in four-inch white plastic eggs and displayed in eye-catching merchandising equipment. It was an immediate success, and the access gained to a primarily female customer traffic made the brand the number one in the country, with sales of approximately $650 million, about 25 percent of the total pantyhose market.

SCANDINAVIAN AIR SERVICES

An example of a differentiation focus is the airline SAS. When Jan Carlzon took over as President in 1980, the company was in its second year of losing money. After 17 profitable years, it was heading for a $20 million loss. At the time the entire airline industry was in trouble and the markets for both passengers and freight had stagnated. SAS identified that it needed to be able to be profitable even in bad times. Unnecessary costs had already been cut to the bone, and if the airline was to survive, its only option was to increase revenue.

Recognizing that the most stable sector of the market was business travel, SAS established a new aim of being 'the best airline in the world for the frequent business traveler'. Instead of regarding expenses as something to be minimized, however, Carlzon looked at them as resources for improving competitiveness. Every expense and procedure was scrutinized and the question asked: 'Do we need this to serve the frequent business traveler?' If the answer was no, then it was scrapped, no matter how sacred it might have been. If the answer was yes, then more money was spent to develop it even further.

To meet this aim 147 new projects were launched, costing $12 million a year, in such areas as staff customer service training, punctuality, improving the Copenhagen traffic hub and even putting the olive back in customers' martinis! Unnecessary costs such as the department that promoted tourist trips and another whose function was to improve the image of the airline industry were simply eliminated by closing the departments down.

A new business class was created by dropping first class (never a great revenue generator) and introducing 'Euroclass', which offered noticeably better service for full-fare coach prices. The Euroclass section of the planes was partitioned off, and comfortable lounges with telephones and telexes were provided in airports. Business travelers also got better seats and food and separate, faster check-in facilities. They were allowed to board the plane last and disembark first, and received free drinks, newspapers and magazines.

When business travelers fly, they arrange their business meetings first and then book the airline whose schedule best suits their plans. They don't plan a trip around available flights from one specific airline. SAS therefore concentrated on making its flights more convenient for business travelers by focusing on those destinations that have enough business travelers to support frequent flights, daily and non-stop. This meant that larger aircraft such as Airbuses or 747s were unsuitable. SAS's solution was to mothball the larger aircraft and concentrate on smaller DC-9s, even though a new generation of larger ones was becoming available.

The company's goal had been to increase revenue by $25 million in year 1, $40 million in year 2 and $50 million in year 3. The changes actually generated an increase of $80 million in the first year alone, in a market where other international airlines were suffering combined losses of $2 billion.

FAIRLINES

In direct contrast to the low-cost, no-frills carriers discussed in Chapter 5, Fairlines is an airline that flies the Nice/Paris/Milan triangle and focuses unashamedly on luxury, service and comfort. Founded in 1998 by François Arpels, grandson of the founder of the famous jeweler Van Cleef & Arpels, it caters only to high-paying business travelers.

Its aircraft have 72 seats instead of the normal 140, giving passengers lots of leg room and space for suitcases if they do not wish to wait for luggage at their destination. The seats house screens offering not only TV but also wordprocessing and spreadsheet facilities, and on the ground the airline offers a personal 'groom' to help the passenger. This luxury will not even cost extra, as Fairlines' prices are in line with its main European competition.

Arpels' view is that his company is too small to bother the nationals, believing that like the low-cost carriers he will be left in peace until his company is well established. It is far too early to know whether the airline will be successful, but it has two main problems.

Fairlines has only two aircraft, which chase each other around their triangle of destinations offering three flights per day. Without the frequency of its competitors, business travelers may well be hard to tempt away, however much leg room is offered.

Second, Fairlines is offering much more of a direct threat to the competition by flying popular business routes and targeting their precious, profit-generating business customer. It is actually pursuing a **head-to-head combat** strategy, in that it is aiming at the same customers as its larger competitors, and it is likely that they will retaliate if Fairlines looks like becoming a success. It is therefore a much riskier strategy than that being adopted by the no-frills carriers – easyJet and Debonair were initially left alone because the traditional airlines did not see them as applicable to their market.

BEN SHERMAN

Founded in 1963, the shirt company Ben Sherman Originals took 30 years to build a turnover of £4 million. However, this increased by an astonishing 1100 percent to an estimated £50 million over the following four years after a management buyout and the formation of Ben Sherman Cooper, by following a strategy focusing its products at young working-class men.

The company's shirt was originally an icon of sixties mods and seventies skinheads, but fell out of fashion in the 1980s. After the management buyout, the marketing strategy returned the brand to its roots, using shaven-headed youths in aggressive, 'in-your-face' advertising.

The advertising is irreverent, humorous and tongue in cheek, such as two side-by-side photographs of a bulldog and an aggressive-looking skinhead with the strapline 'Separated at birth'. Under the title 'Washing Instructions', another ad shows a youth dropping his shirt on the floor and saying: 'Mum, clean my shirt.' The advertising concentrates on posters and men's magazines such as *Loaded* and *FHM*.

Ben Sherman is reluctant to expand internationally, given that its heritage is so British (but is carrying out research in the US and the Far East), and has so far expanded into other product sectors. Recognizing that many women were also wearing its shirts, the company launched a range of women's wear in 1997, following a footwear range in 1996 and an extension of its clothing from just shirts to include jeans, fleeces, trousers, leather jackets and belts. However, by appealing to a more mainstream market the company risks alienating its hard core of fans, one of the main problems with a focus strategy.

RISKS OF A FOCUS STRATEGY

The biggest risk of this type of strategy is that the segment itself becomes unattractive through changes in the industry's structure or because demand disappears. Those companies that have not spread themselves across the market as a whole can then find themselves in difficulty.

A second risk is that the segment's differences from the rest of the market diminish, with the result that its needs can now be adequately served by broad-based competitors.

A third is that if the segment is small, the focuser can quickly find itself plateauing in terms of sales volume. When this happens, the temptation is to extend into other segments, by broadening either the product line or the customer base. While this can be done successfully, the inherent danger is the loss of the focus that made the company successful in the first place. Pursuing a focus strategy means consciously bypassing the opportunity for volume if it does not fall within your chosen segment. Companies that do not have the will to do this (and it is difficult to achieve) will never be successful at this type of strategy.

For example, in 1989 Jan Carlzon announced a new strategy for SAS. Instead of being an airline, it would become a 'global travel-services company'. Carlzon said at the time:

> *There are limits to what you can develop in an aircraft cabin in terms of service. So we have to add services on the ground.*

In pursuit of this new strategy, SAS purchased 40 percent of International Hotels Corporation and allied itself with Diners Club Nordic and SAS Service Partner, Scandinavia's biggest tour company. The following year, the airline became unprofitable and eventually accumulated losses of $200 million by 1993, when Carlzon was replaced. His successor, Jan Stenberg, sold off the non-core businesses and brought the company back into profitability by 1994.

The danger of loss of focus is well described by Bernard Marcus, founder and CEO of Home Depot, America's largest DIY warehouse chain:

> *In some cases we have 25,000 to 30,000 people walking through a store a week, 50% of whom are women. We could sell them anything. If we wanted to put panty hose up at the front register, we'd sell a fortune in panty hose. But we don't. We don't want the customer to think we're a discounter, a food store, a toy store, or anything else, because it would confuse her. The perception of the customers always has to be, when they think of a DIY project, they think of Home Depot.*

Rather than expand into additional lines of business within an original geographic area, it is often better for the focuser to expand geographically (perhaps internationally) while maintaining the original focus.

Finally, there is the threat that competitors will focus on even more tightly defined segments and outfocus the focuser. For example, a company specializing purely in video and computer games and accessories (e.g. joysticks) could offer a range even greater than Toys 'R' Us. However, until such a company could match Toys 'R' Us in sales volume, it would be unable to replicate its buying power and therefore its low prices. In order to counter this, it would have to create new points of differentiation, such as staff expertise or helplines to assist with the often difficult process of loading games.

Alternatively, it could adopt a cost focus strategy, aiming to reduce its overheads to a point where the lower margins that would result from competing with Toys 'R' Us on price would be acceptable. It could do this by selling its games purely by mail order or over the telephone, thereby eliminating the costs associated with expensive retail outlets.

Being outfocused is something that can happen to very successful companies. Take one already mentioned above, Home Depot. In 1990, it had approximately $80 million worth of turnover in unfinished wood furniture, but found itself outfocused by companies such as Swedish retailer IKEA. Where Home Depot dedicated between 2000 and 7000 sq ft per store to furniture, IKEA dedicated the majority of its stores' average of 20,000 sq ft, offering customers a bigger choice and generating greater volume and therefore lower prices. Marcus's response was to pull out of furniture altogether and dedicate the space saved to wallpaper and floor tiles.

Self-diagnostic questionnaire

1 Think of the traditional ways of segmenting your market. How many can you come up with?

2 Are any of these segments more attractive than others? For example, are some more profitable, more loyal or easier to do business with?

3 Do the customers in each of these segments have different needs from those in the others? If not, cross them from the list and concentrate on those that do.

4 Are there any ways in which your company could meet those needs better than the competition?

5 Do any of your competitors have a strategy of focusing on one or more of these segments?

6 Discard your original list, identify some potential new ways of segmenting the market and start again.

PART III

COMBAT APPRECIATION:
HOW TO CHOOSE THE
STRATEGY THAT IS
RIGHT FOR YOU

	Head-to-head	Raiding
Combat	Romans/Carthaginians at Cannae Normans/Saxons at Hastings Napoleon in every battle German invasion of France, 1940 Coke vs Pepsi Burger King vs McDonald's Microsoft vs Netscape Barnes & Noble vs Amazon	Parthia vs Rome Vietminh vs France Vietcong vs US England in the 100 Years' War Interski Local specialist shops
Logistics	Russia vs France, 1812 Anglo-Norman conquest of Wales Alexander the Great in Asia Minor Wal-Mart Enterprise Rent-A-Car (later) Canon copiers Honda vs Harley-Davidson	Vietcong vs USA Atlantic U-boat campaign The 'Blitz' Aldi and Netto Enterprise Rent-A-Car (earlier) Amazon

8

THE BASIC STRATEGIC OPTIONS

ART I DEMONSTRATED THE IMPORTANCE OF POSSESSING A SWAT, the power of having a high force:space ratio, and the tactical primacy of the defense. All of these, together with the political objectives of the war or campaign, will determine an army's strategy.

There have been as many political objectives of war as there have been wars themselves, and they will be the first and most important determinant of the type of strategy to be followed. To take the simplest of examples, an objective of annexation or conquest obviously requires an offensive strategy aimed at the seizure and occupation of land, while the immediate objective of survival following such an invasion will usually necessitate a defensive strategy.

Often the choice is slightly more complicated. A defensive strategy following invasion in one theater may be accompanied by an offensive strategy in another, with the aim of diverting enemy resources or seizure of enemy land or resources, which can be exchanged for those lost in the original invasion. Likewise, an initial defense will often be followed by an offensive strategy later in the hostilities as the defending army, having blunted the initial encroachment, counterattacks.

Armies have also often operated on the strategic offensive, while fighting tactically on the defensive. In other words, they have initiated hostilities by invading enemy territory, but then adopted a defensive position that forced the enemy to attack them.

The choice between offense and defense is the simplest and most straightforward, but it is merely the first step. Both of these strategies need to be dissected further, as the choice is made between whether to attack the enemy's forces or its resources. Either can be appropriate, depending on both objectives and circumstances.

OFFENSIVE MILITARY STRATEGIES

The choice between attacking the enemy's forces or its resources means choosing between a combat and a logistics strategy. As its name suggests, a combat strategy is aimed specifically at forcing battle on the enemy. If the objective is the destruction or decisive defeat of the enemy forces (either in order to achieve a quick conquest or because there are other enemies to fight once the first have been disposed of), then the aim of such a strategy will be to force the enemy to engage in a major battle in order to achieve such an end. This is called a head-to-head combat strategy.

If the objective is not conquest or the destruction of the enemy (either because the attacking forces do not have sufficient strength to occupy the territory or because the objectives of the war are to achieve political concessions of some sort rather than territory *per se*), the aim might be to win a series of small victories or occupy part of a territory, which could then be exchanged for those concessions. This is called a raiding combat strategy.

A logistics strategy is aimed not so much at the enemy's forces, but at its resources. If conquest is the objective and cannot be achieved speedily because the enemy refuses to give battle, then the aim of such a strategy would be the gradual conquest of the territory, piece by piece. This would be called a head-to-head logistics strategy, as it gradually deprives the enemy of the land and resources it needs to continue to wage war.

If the objective is something else and the attacker does not have sufficient force to risk everything in a decisive battle, the aim of the strategy will be to raid the enemy's resources in order to capture or destroy them and thus deny the enemy access to them. This can be continued until the enemy tires and agrees to grant whatever political concessions are in dispute. This is called a raiding logistics strategy.

These four basic strategic options are shown schematically in Figure 3.

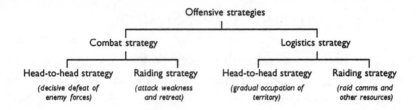

Figure 3 Offensive strategies

Defensive Military Strategies

The defending force's strategy will initially be determined not only by its own objectives but also by the strategy that the attackers have chosen. It has the same four choices of strategy, the only difference being their implementation. When the attackers have a **head-to-head combat** or **logistics** strategy and either seeks a major battle or attempts piecemeal conquest, the most straightforward option for the defensive force is also to adopt a **head-to-head combat** strategy. They attempt to decide things quickly, either by adopting a defensive position and inviting attack or by assuming the tactical offensive and attacking themselves.

Where the defenders do not feel strong enough to do this, a **raiding combat** strategy sees them adopt guerrilla warfare and fight a series of combat raids, constantly harrying the attacking forces but always refusing to engage in a major battle.

Alternatively, a **head-to-head logistics** strategy will involve a 'scorched earth' policy of destroying their own land and resources so that there is nothing left for the enemy, and a **raiding logistics** strategy will consist of guerrilla raids on the attacking force's lines of communications and supply in an attempt to make them retreat.

Where the attackers adopt a raiding strategy of either type, a **head-to-head combat** strategy will see the defenders attempting to pursue the raiders and force them to give battle by cutting off their lines of retreat. Alternatively, one of **raiding combat** will see them use counterraids in an attempt to make the attacking strategy counterproductive and too costly.

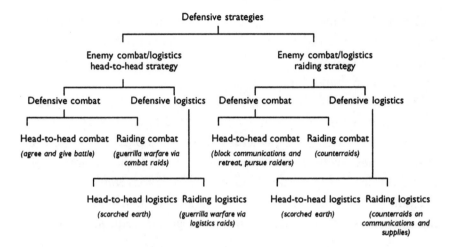

Figure 4 Defensive strategies

A raiding logistics strategy will also involve counterraids, and one of head-to-head logistics will involve a scorched earth policy, denying resources to the invader. These options are shown schematically in Figure 4.

A SUCCESSION OF STRATEGIES: THE CAMPAIGNS OF ALEXANDER THE GREAT

It should not be thought that an attacking or defending force will have one strategy throughout a war and that it will not be abandoned (temporarily or otherwise) if circumstances change. The campaigns of Alexander the Great are perhaps the best example of this, as there we can clearly see examples of a wide range of strategies being first adopted, then put aside, only to be reused later on in different stages of the campaign.

When Alexander invaded modern-day Turkey at the beginning of his campaigns, it would be far-fetched (despite what ancient historians might have claimed) to imagine that he had as his objective the conquest of the entire Persian empire. His stated aim was to avenge the Persian invasion of Greece and the sacrilege of the desecration of Greek temples in the previous century, and as such he probably had a **raiding combat** strategy, i.e. one of engaging in battle first the local *satraps* of Asia Minor and then Darius himself, before returning victorious to Macedonia. The invasion would then have been nothing more than a large-scale raid

The local Persian commanders were advised by their Greek mercenary commander to adopt a **head-to-head logistics** strategy based on a scorched earth policy, whereby they would burn crops and even destroy cities, so that Alexander would 'not be able to stay in the land from lack of provisions'. Such a strategy may well have forced Alexander to return to Macedonia, since the area had only intermittent areas of cultivation and his logistics requirements were huge. However, the Persians balked at the idea of destroying their own property and decided on a **head-to-head combat** strategy, offering battle at the Granicus river.

They were soundly defeated by Alexander, who now faced the problem of advancing onwards to meet Darius himself (who now began to assemble a new army), while leaving his lines of communication with Macedonia exposed. The Persians had a splendid fleet that effectively controlled the sea, and therefore the Macedonian lines of supply.

Alexander temporarily changed his strategy to a **logistics** one, and methodically took the cities and harbors of the Asia Minor coast one by one until that fleet had nowhere to land. Still using a **head-to-head combat** strategy, Darius met Alexander in modern-day Syria and was soundly defeated at the Battle of Issus. He retreated to recruit yet another army, but Alexander refused to pursue him until his own logistics strategy had been completed.

In fact, Alexander did not head east until he had conquered the entire Mediterranean coast under Persian control, including Egypt, by which time most of the fleet had surrendered and come over to his cause (the siege of Tyre alone took seven months to complete). He was now free to revert to his **combat** strategy, but by now ambitions of conquest had taken root in his mind and it had become one of **head-to-head combat** rather than **raiding**.

He met Darius again at the Battle of Gaugamela, in modern-day Iraq, and for the third time annihilated the Persian army due to his possession of a SWAT. Following this he headed eastwards, chasing the defeated Persian king, and after Darius had been murdered by one of his followers kept going, adding province after province to his list of possessions.

However, resistance to his invasion had not ended. Despite the fact that Alexander invariably left the Persian *satraps* in control of their provinces, the by now expected surrender did not apply in the mountainous regions of Bactria and Sogdiana (modern north-western Afghanistan), where the tribes fiercely resisted the invasion.

After Alexander had captured the provinces' major cities, rebels attacked and captured eight of his strongposts almost immediately and massacred one of the relief expeditions sent by him (the only real defeat known of any part of his army during his reign). Using tactics virtually identical to those employed by the Parthians at Carrhae, their light cavalry destroyed the Macedonians from a distance with arrows.

Alexander retook the towns, massacred their inhabitants, and marched to avenge his soldiers' defeat, but could not catch the lightly equipped enemy forces, which simply disappeared into the mountains. The tribesmen then followed a **raiding combat** strategy, avoiding battle and attacking outposts where they could achieve numerical superiority. They attacked and killed isolated detachments and quickly withdrew before reinforcements could arrive.

Again adopting a **head-to-head logistics** strategy, Alexander reacted by building a chain of fortified military posts on the communication routes throughout the country and manned them with quick-response light cavalry so that the rebels 'saw that every place was occupied by the Macedonians with garrisons, and that there was no way of flight open to them'. These both reduced the vulnerability of his own forces to surprise attack and reduced the rebels' movements.

Despite this, he was bogged down in a guerrilla war for two years, lacking enough troops to stop the raids in a large, mountainous country in which the rebels enjoyed popular support. Ultimately he was successful, but only after he resorted to political measures to win over the support of the local population, including marriage to Roxanne, the daughter of Oxyartes, one of the local barons.

Heading east again, he eventually reached the lands of the Indian king Porus, who adopted a **head-to-head combat** strategy in defense of his realm, and was defeated by Alexander at the Battle of the Hydaspes. Shortly after this Alexander's troops mutinied and refused to go any further, and he was forced to head south down the Hydaspes and Indus rivers to return via the coast of the Indian Ocean.

During this trip Alexander was constantly harassed by the locals, who, lacking the strength to confront him directly, employed a **raiding combat** strategy. He in turn reverted to a **head-to-head logistics** strategy, using terror as his main weapon and resorting to massacring whoever held out against him. He finally returned to Babylon where he died of a fever (some say he was poisoned) at the age of 33.

PROGRESSING FROM ONE STRATEGY TO ANOTHER: GUERRILLA WARFARE IN INDOCHINA

Although there have been many examples of guerrilla warfare across the ages – Sun Tzu refers to it, as we saw above Alexander the Great faced it in Bactria and Sogdiana, and the word 'guerrilla' comes from the Spanish meaning 'little war' following the population's resistance to French occupation at the beginning of the nineteenth century – laypeople tend to think of it as a twentieth-century phenomenon due to the proliferation of such wars in the developing countries since 1945.

The most famous theorist of twentieth-century guerrilla warfare was Mao Tse-Tung, who fused traditional raiding tactics with social revolution to make it applicable as an offensive strategy. He recognized that unless the occupying power simply surrendered, guerrilla forces would never be able to force them from power and saw guerrilla warfare as a phase that would eventually be replaced by a move to a more traditional approach. He wrote:

> *The concept that guerrilla warfare is an end in itself and that guerrilla activities can be divorced from those of the regular forces is incorrect.*

Mao taught that there were three phases of a revolutionary war. In phase one, insurgents infiltrated villages and established support among the local population, while guerrilla tactics were used mostly in defensive actions or against small enemy detachments to create 'good PR'.

In phase two, regular units would be created that could be used to attack isolated enemy outposts and lines of communication. As the territory under insurgent control grew, the guerrillas could build up and arm conventional forces. Then in phase three these forces would be unleashed in a general counteroffensive designed to achieve total victory.

One of Mao's most able pupils, Ho Chi Minh, formed the Vietnamese People's Liberation army (VPLA) on 22 December 1944. It consisted of 34 men parading in a jungle clearing. However, it defeated a well-trained, experienced French army within 10 years.

Ho's strategy was vintage Mao, following his teachings of a three-phase struggle, and it is interesting to observe how his forces changed as the phases progressed. In phase one, they consisted of 'Popular Troops', or *dan quan*, which were formed in 50-man, poorly armed platoons. Their role was to act as a home guard of sorts, conducting local patrols, harassing small French detachments, perpetrating acts of sabotage and preparing local defenses (the mines and booby traps that accounted for the majority of French casualties). By 1954 there were about 100,000 of these. Even when confronted by inferior numbers of French troops, they normally withdrew, in line with Mao's teaching:

In every battle concentrate absolutely superior forces – double, treble, quadruple and sometimes five or six times those of the enemy.

In phase two, the strategy of raiding combat/logistics gave way to one of head-to-head logistics, whereby the territory under Vietminh control was steadily expanded. For this, Regional Troops (*dia phing*) were formed in 85-man district companies and 300-man province battalions. Although they still used guerrilla tactics, they were more conventionally organized and better equipped, often with heavy machine guns and mortars.

They were used to attack isolated enemy outposts and bases, forcing the French to withdraw and cede control of the surrounding territory. A favourite tactic was 'assail the fort and strike the rescuers', where they would attack an outpost and then ambush the larger relief force sent to its aid.

In 1950, the VPLA amassed 14 infantry and 3 artillery battalions and began rolling up the French posts on the border between north and south Vietnam. For the first time, well-disciplined regular Vietminh troops took on the French in regular combat and defeated them. Out of some 10,000 troops stationed along the border, the French lost 6000 in addition to enough weapons and ammunition to equip an entire division. The French had been virtually ejected from the northern part of the country.

In 1951, General Giap (the commander of the VPLA) mistakenly thought that the struggle was entering phase three. By now the VPLA had equipped a regular army called the Chu Luc, formed into professional battalions and divisions. This eventually comprised six divisions of 10,000 men each, twenty individual regiments and the same number of independent battalions, supported by artillery, heavy weapons and anti-aircraft units. Each infantry battalion and regiment had a heavy-weapons company, and each division a heavy-weapons battalion.

Finally switching to a strategy of **head-to-head combat**, Giap launched a massive attack on the Red River delta. Although he outnumbered the French by 3:1, the attack was a disaster and he lost over 6000 men in a matter of days.

Being road bound the French were unable to capitalize on their victory by pursuing their retreating enemy, and Giap used his breathing space to strengthen his army still further. Over the next two years he reverted to his previous **head-to-head logistics** strategy of incremental gains of territory, and the tide of the war slowly turned in his favor.

Then in 1954 his troops won a major battle at Dien Bien Phu, when they overran a supposedly impregnable fortified position garrisoned by 12 French battalions and virtually all of the available French artillery. The French hoped that Giap would hurl his army to destruction against it, but after an incredibly fierce fight, the outpost fell. The victory robbed the French of any bargaining strength at Geneva, where diplomats were attempting to work out a peace settlement, and the war, increasingly unpopular in France, drew to a close, dividing Vietnam into two separate countries.

Although the third phase of Mao's revolutionary war never took place successfully, the war in French Indochina shows clearly how one strategy (raiding combat/logistics) can be replaced by another (head-to-head logistics) and finally a third (head-to-head combat), not as a reaction to circumstances and enemy activity but as part of an overall plan.

If the VPLA had engaged the French in head-to-head combat when it had first been formed, it would have been crushed like a gnat. However, by avoiding major battles until it was strong enough, always ensuring that it had overwhelming local superiority when it did fight, and building gradually on its success bit by bit, it was able to take on a well-trained, battle-hardened, better-equipped, professional army of one of the major European powers and win.

COMBAT APPRECIATIONS

A company's decision of which strategy to pursue should follow a detailed *combat appreciation*, which looks in detail at the competitive make-up of a market, including the strategies of each competitor and their strengths and weaknesses.

It is essential that this looks not only at existing, direct competitors in the market, but also at substitutes – those products and services that customers could purchase in place of your own. Coca-Cola, for example, counts tap water as one of its biggest competitors. It also regards tea and coffee as 'the enemy' and has a global objective of increasing what it calls its 'share of throat'. One executive recently stated that the company would like coffee breaks to be renamed 'Coca-Cola breaks' in popular speech.

A combat appreciation must address the following questions as a minimum:

- ❏ Who are your main competitors?
- ❏ What is the market share of each of them in the market overall?
- ❏ Which are growing and which are declining? Why?
- ❏ What is their share in each market segment (geography, customer type etc.)?
- ❏ Are they broad based across the whole market, or do they derive their overall share by domination of one or more segments?
- ❏ Does the share come from one dominant product/service, or a wide range?
- ❏ Which segment does each of them avoid? Why? What is unattractive to them about it?
- ❏ What is the strategy of each?
- ❏ Does any of them have a competitive SWAT?
- ❏ What are their strengths and weaknesses?
- ❏ How could you turn their strengths into weaknesses (see Chapter 9)?
- ❏ Are there any major companies that do not operate in your market but could do so in the near future?
- ❏ What are the main substitutes in your market?
- ❏ Which are growing and which are declining?
- ❏ What are the main companies that provide these substitutes?

Let us take a hypothetical marketplace where various competitors have the following market shares, and look at the options open to company X looking to enter the market for the first time:

A	38%
B	24%
C	18%
D	10%
All others	10%

While the 'others' might look easier targets because of their small size, their business is spread across a variety of sectors and it would not therefore be easy to 'pick them off' without entering the market across the board. Company D, however, has most of its business in one sector of the market, which it dominates, primarily because A, B and C find it unattractive for several reasons. Because of this, D has become complacent.

Company X has identified the sector as an attractive 'beachhead' and has therefore spent time and resources in personalizing its product/service offering to that sector. Its strategy will therefore be one of **head-to-head combat** versus D in that sector.

However, it cannot completely ignore the other companies. Company C sells a different product to customers in that sector, so X will come into contact with it. The strategy will therefore be one of **raiding combat** against C. Because A and B are uninvolved in the sector, it will be one of **raiding logistics** against them.

At the same time as it is attacking D, company X needs to ensure that it is not taken by surprise by A, B or C, who may act in some way to prevent it gaining a foothold in the market (they probably wouldn't, but X cannot afford to take that chance). As Clausewitz wrote:

> *Since we are always open to attack, except when we ourselves are attacking, we must at every instant be on the defensive.*

If we take the market warfare matrix introduced in Chapter 1 and adapt it slightly, we come up with that shown in Figure 5, which shows the various strategies that company X is pursuing simultaneously.

X therefore needs to keep some resources in reserve to be able to fight off such an attack if it comes, and ensure that it ties its newly won customers to it with exit barriers so that it becomes prohibitive for them to switch suppliers. Again, Clausewitz wrote that the keeping of reserves was vital. An important rule was:

> *not to bring all our troops into battle immediately. With such action all wisdom in conducting a battle disappears. It is only with troops*

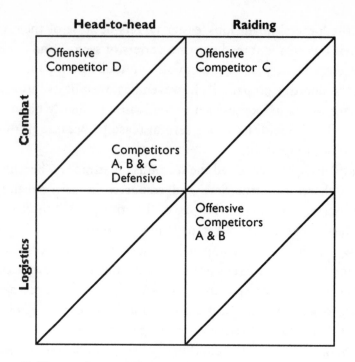

Figure 5 The market warfare matrix

left at our disposal that we can turn the tide of battle ... We can use them either to renew combat at the same point, or carry the fight to other neighboring points.

It is essential that in a combat appreciation the appropriate strategy is identified for all significant competitors in the marketplace.

It is also essential that some resources are kept in reserve: many a battle has been lost for the lack of a reserve at a decisive point. This financial reserve can then be used to strike a decisive blow if the opportunity arises, to construct an improvised defense if an unexpected attack materializes or if an anticipated competitive attack is more successful than was expected.

COMMERCIAL STRATEGIC OPTIONS

The first decision that directors wishing to apply the lessons learnt from the history of warfare to their competitive strategies have to make is which type of warfare they are going to wage – offensive or defensive – as there are different principles for each.

Many companies make the mistake of having one strategy that they apply to all aspects of a brand's activity, regardless of what is happening in different sectors of the market or with different customers. If this is an offensive strategy, it is applied even in parts of the country, or market sectors or individual customers where they are under attack.

A military commander will vary his strategy and tactics depending on whether he is fighting a large or small enemy, and whether he is fighting on flat, open ground or hilly terrain. Likewise, each sector of the market or even each major customer should be looked at as an individual battleground, and the most appropriate tactics and strategy used.

Defensive warfare should only ever be fought voluntarily by a market leader, as it is only the company in a dominant position that can afford to be complacent enough to do so. Even then it is dangerous: commercial history abounds with examples of companies that held dominant market positions and yet succumbed to attack, such as Harley-Davidson, IBM and the 'Big Three' US auto makers.

Only armies that have no offensive objectives of their own, and whose sole aim is the repulsion of an invading army, can have an exclusively defensive strategy. Likewise, only companies that are content with what they have and whose products have plateaued with the onset of brand or market maturity should do the same.

Sometimes owners or managing directors of small to medium-sized companies tell me that they are quite happy with the size they have achieved, and that they have no desire to grow. They say that growth will require expansion and investment; or that they are doing very nicely and do not want to attract the attention of the 'big boys'. Maybe they lack the resources or management time, or simply want an easy life.

While all of these are valid and understandable reasons, the problem with this approach is that it is falling into the trap of 'competitor-free zone' thinking. What happens to an individual company is not just a result of what it chooses to do itself, but also of what its competition decides to do.

Therefore if a company's competition has expansionist plans but it chooses merely to defend itself against their attacks, it is invariably destined to shrink in size. The reason is that it is virtually impossible to defend yourself against all attacks successfully; somewhere along the line, with one major customer or another, the competition will be successful and begin to chip away at the company's business. Unless it is willing to accept a future of long-term decline, the company needs gains in other areas with which to balance the losses.

In addition to strengthening its own position at the top and ensuring that the various offensive strategies of its competitors fail, the market leader also bears the responsibility of creating market growth. Perhaps the best illustration of a company that takes this responsibility seriously is Intel, discussed in Chapter 2.

Companies holding a number two or three position in the marketplace should always be looking to implement an offensive strategy. Their main choice lies between a **head-to-head** or **raiding** strategy.

If the company is large enough, then a **head-to-head combat** strategy is an option, in that it can risk taking the leader on 'toe to toe' across the whole of the market at once, with a good chance of ultimate success if it possesses a SWAT. However, this strategy is practical only if its products' performance are demonstrably superior to those of its competitors. It is normally a realistic option only for a strong number two or three that is not far behind the leader.

For a number three or four, a better option is a **head-to-head logistics** strategy. These companies tend not to be big enough to be able to make a decisive impact on the leaders in a short period of time. Where a strong number two may look to force the leader into a decisive confrontation, numbers three or four need to be patient and follow the example of the Anglo-Normans in their conquest of Wales (see Chapter 9), attacking the larger competition sector by sector and consolidating their hold on each one before moving on to the next. While this strategy by its very nature takes longer than one of **head-to-head combat**, it carries far less risk, is far easier to implement and is much less likely to invite retaliation.

In the majority of markets, however, the remaining companies need to be realistic enough to be aware that their lack of size dictates that the only practical option open to them is to follow a raiding strategy, i.e. to wage guerrilla warfare. For every 100 companies operating in a marketplace, about 95 of them should have raiding strategies.

A **raiding combat** strategy consists of introducing new products and/or services that take advantage of the weaknesses inherent in the leaders' strengths (see Chapter 9), or attacking carefully chosen customers with whom the leader has a weak position. Raiders recognize that their positions may not be defensible if or when the bigger players in the market shore up their defenses by launching their own variants or concentrate their forces to 'recapture' the customer.

A **raiding logistics** strategy consists of concentrating on one sector of the marketplace. Ideally, this sector should be one that is strategically unimportant to the market leaders, either ignored or underserved by them and, most importantly, that is small enough to dominate. Customers who appear unattractive, unprofitable or too small to large companies can be very attractive and profitable to smaller ones with lower overheads, who are more local, or who simply appreciate them better because to them they are large.

Like classic guerrillas, those following a **raiding combat** strategy need to be prepared to abandon a position when a larger, more conventional enemy brings its numerical superiority to bear. This is neither weakness nor cowardice, but common sense. They recognize that there is no glory to be achieved in 'fighting to the last man', and follow the old adage that: 'He who fights and runs away, lives to fight another day.'

PURSUING MORE THAN ONE STRATEGY

Much has been written about the need to pursue one strategy to the exclusion of all others, in order to avoid being 'all things to all men'.

However, two of the main factors determining a company's strategy are its competitors' strategies and the force:space ratio that it possesses, and these will undoubtedly differ in different markets or even market sectors. It therefore follows that a company may well need to pursue several strategies simultaneously, depending on individual market conditions.

As most companies will face more than one competitor within a given marketplace, the question of which of them to attack first needs to be addressed. Some works recommend that the market leader should be the target, because that is where most of the opportunity (i.e. market share) lies.

Some advantages can be obtained by doing this, but it depends on how combat ready the market leader is. A complacent and over-confident market leader may not even notice the loss of business at first, much as a dog might ignore flea bites; or it may notice the loss but not realize that it is all going to one competitor.

Incidentally, I am continually amazed by the number of companies that make no attempt to discover which competing suppliers customers have switched to when they lose them. Whenever a company loses a customer, it must always attempt to discover the reasons (and must not accept 'price' as the answer without attempting to dig deeper; this is the easiest thing for a customer to say), and to which competitor the customer has switched. This is often the earliest warning it will receive of a concerted competitor attack.

Complacent market leaders (e.g. IBM or the 'Big Three' US auto manufacturers – 'these small Japanese cars will never catch on; the American public want huge cars that do 5 miles to the gallon' – may also fail to recognize a serious competitive threat because of the 'not invented here' syndrome. Their internal logic tells them that as they are number one, their way must be the best; and as the competitor's way is different from theirs, it cannot be successful in the long term.

However, any company attacking a market leader without a competitive SWAT must recognize that it is ignoring the most important lesson of war, that of the force:space ratio, and is inviting massive retaliation. If the lessons of war are to be applied to competitive strategy, then head-to-head attacks on a market leader by a small company should be avoided at all costs.

While Clausewitz was of the view that 'a center of gravity is always found where the mass is concentrated most densely', and argued that this was the place where the attack should be aimed, he was talking about battles between armies of similar size. He was never of the view that an attack there would be successful for an army that was numerically inferior.

A small company should look for easy targets or small sectors of the market that are dominated by one small (or equal-sized) competitor. It should be emphasized here that the adjective 'small' is relative; a company is deemed to be small if its competitors are significantly larger than it, or it is number four or lower in the market. Rolls-Royce and BMW are both tiny when looked at in the context of the global auto industry.

Here the smaller company is not restricted to a raiding strategy, as this competitor can then be attacked with overwhelming force using a head-to-head combat strategy, preferably facilitated by the use of a competitive SWAT.

Clausewitz wrote in *The Principles of War*:

> ... *a maxim which should take first place among all causes of victory in the modern art of war [is] 'Pursue one great decisive aim with force and determination'.*

In other words, the most effective use of a company's resources is to concentrate them on defeating one competitor at a time, rather than on the more common practice of spreading them thinly across the marketplace as a whole.

As this strategy becomes successful and domination is achieved in the chosen market sector, the company can gradually move on to another sector (changing its strategy to one of head-to-head logistics) and repeat the process, again choosing one competitor to attack wherever possible.

This step-by-step approach ensures that the company does not bite off more than it can chew, and that it only picks fights it has a good chance of winning. No competitor is attacked in any significant way until the gap between it and the attacking company has narrowed to the point where it can be crossed with a sustained effort; again, it must be stressed that this will be much easier and far cheaper if the company possesses a sustainable and competitive SWAT.

Finally, the attacking company may achieve a size where it is able to challenge the number one for market leadership. This is almost an exact replica of the Mao Tse Tung 'three-phase' approach, and should be taken as a blueprint for small companies with expansionist ambitions or even large companies entering a new market for the first time.

The difference is that whereas Mao or Ho Chi Minh could concentrate solely on one enemy, you may not have this luxury. At the same time as you are planning to attack one competitor in a sector of the marketplace, you will also have to defend your position against attack from other competitors in the market.

Self-diagnostic questionnaire

1 Identify your current position in each of your markets: are you the market leader, a strong no. 2 or 3, a weak no. 2 or 3, or a smaller player? If any of these markets have strong regional biases in terms of sales, repeat the exercise for each region.

2. Do you have clearly set objectives for each market or region? Is your objective to defend what you already have, or to increase your share of the market, i.e. is your strategy defensive or offensive?

3 Does that strategy need to be revised? Remember that unless you are a dominant market leader, a defensive strategy should only ever be a short-term expedient.

4 Do you have a sufficient force:space ratio (i.e. do you have sufficient resources and the will to use/risk them) to adopt a head-to-head combat strategy and take on the leader across the market as a whole?

5 If not, do you want to take the leader on directly in one segment of the market at a time, using a head-to-head logistics strategy, or would you prefer to adopt a raiding strategy?

9

HEAD-TO-HEAD STRATEGIES

A s outlined in the previous chapter, head-to-head strategies can be subdivided into two: combat and logistics.

HEAD-TO-HEAD COMBAT STRATEGIES

For **head-to-head combat strategies** to be successful when used offensively, the attacking army needs one (preferably more) of the following:

❏ numerical superiority or a high force:space ratio in relation to its opponents
❏ a SWAT
❏ the opportunity to fight tactically on the defensive.

This is because a **head-to-head** strategy is concerned with the decisive defeat of the enemy's forces or the swift occupation of territory, i.e. conquest.

Some commanders, such as Napoleon, nearly always adopted this strategy. The battle itself was central to Napoleon's way of fighting. He was uninterested in occupying an enemy's towns or cities while its army remained intact elsewhere. One of his own principles of war was: 'There is nothing better than to march on to the enemy's capital after a decisive victory; before it, no!' In fact, on one of the few occasions when he ignored his own advice and occupied Vienna in 1809, leaving the Austrian army unmolested, the result was the Battle of Aspern in which he suffered his first defeat.

As an ardent admirer of Napoleon (although he spent the best years of his professional life fighting him, even transferring at great personal cost from the Austrian to the Russian army in 1812 to be able to do so), Clausewitz consistently held the view that the head-to-head annihilation of the enemy must always be the overriding objective.

He is at his most passionate when discussing *die Schlacht* (a German term that can be translated as 'the slaughter' as well as 'the battle'). In his book *Clausewitz*, Michael Howard makes the memorable observation that the emotional quality of his writing suggests that 'he regarded a campaign that culminated in such an encounter as somehow morally superior to one that did not'.

HEAD-TO-HEAD COMBAT STRATEGY: THE GERMAN INVASION OF FRANCE, 1940

Following his army's successful invasion of Poland in 1939 and the subsequent declaration of war by France and Britain, Hitler ordered the preparation of an offensive in the west. He had written in *Mein Kampf* about 'one last, decisive' battle against France, and the Allies both steeled themselves for the expected attack.

They were expecting a rerun of the 1914 invasion, and the French had built the heavily fortified Maginot Line, manned by 50 divisions, along the Franco-German border. This long, intricate fortification was thought to be impregnable; after all, the experiences of 1914–18 had demonstrated the tactical superiority of the defense. It was thought to be literally impossible for Germany to break this line.

To the west of the Maginot Line lay the Ardennes, densely forested hills through which it would also be impossible to move troops of any size. Everyone knew they were impassable; there was even a detailed study from the First World War that proved it. The only possible strategy that was left to the Germans was therefore a repeat of the 1914 Schlieffen plan, i.e. an invasion through the lowlands of Belgium.

Accordingly, the Allies deployed four French armies and the British Expeditionary Force (BEF) northwards, planning to move into Belgium and join 14 Belgian divisions once an invasion had jolted the country out of neutrality. The French Second Army was positioned at Sedan to form a link between these forces and the Maginot Line.

The German General Staff had intended to invade through Belgium, but when the plans for the attack fell into French hands, this plan was replaced by something much more unpredictable. Instead of the obvious, Hitler now planned to do the impossible; to move heavily armored troops *en masse* through the supposedly impassable Ardennes, and take the Allies totally by surprise.

Both sides had roughly the same manpower, with 136 divisions each, and the allies had a decided superiority in tanks, with about 3000 to Germany's 2600. As they were fighting on the defensive, the odds were clearly on their side. However, in its highly mechanized army Germany had a SWAT.

Steeped in 1920s doctrine, the Allies had their tanks spread out along the entire front, some parceled out to support the infantry. The Germans, on the other hand, had concentrated 75 percent of theirs in a Panzer corps as part of Army Group B and planned to use it to deliver a concentrated, unstoppable blow.

On 10 May the Germans attacked Allied airfields and bombed and dropped paratroops on the Netherlands. The allies moved predictably into Belgium and, while they did so, German Army Group A with 45 divisions moved through the supposedly impassable Ardennes.

The French had expected some movement through the Ardennes, but thought that it would comprise a relatively small body of infantry and thus sent only lightly equipped troops to stop it. The heavily armored Germans swept this resistance aside, and on 13 May they emerged into French territory unannounced, delivering a blow to France that was as much psychological as it was military.

Thinking that the Germans planned to roll up the Maginot Line from the north, the French Second Army moved south, widening the gap between it and the forces in Belgium still further. The German General Guderian lunged through this gap on 15 May and by the end of the day the French First Armored Division had been destroyed and the Ninth Army mauled.

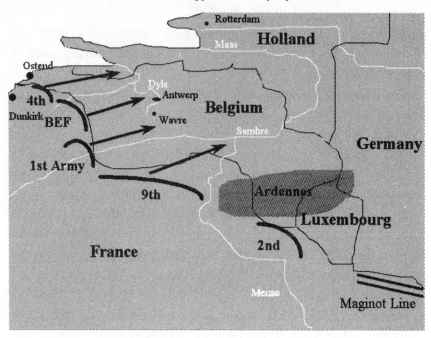

Most of the Belgian army withdrew to the north, leaving the way clear for the Germans, and on 16 May the allies in Belgium began to withdraw, under repeated and morale-sapping air attacks from the Luftwaffe. By 18 May it was obvious that Guderian was heading not for Paris but for the Channel. The allies had no strategic reserve and no way of stopping him, although a counterattack northwards by the French and southwards by the BEF did halt him momentarily.

By 20 May the German advance guard had reached the Channel, but instead of trying to cut the Panzers off from the following infantry, the Allies wasted time in a series of unproductive and vacillating conferences, allowing the German infantry to secure the corridor that had been carved by their tanks.

By 24 May the corridor was fully secured and the campaign was all but over. All that was left to be decided was the size of the German victory. Fortunately for the BEF, Hitler halted his tanks for reasons that have never been fully explained (among the possible ones are concern over heavy tank losses, a desire to maintain a mobile reserve for use elsewhere in France and fear of an Allied counterattack) and this, along with a spirited defense of the Channel

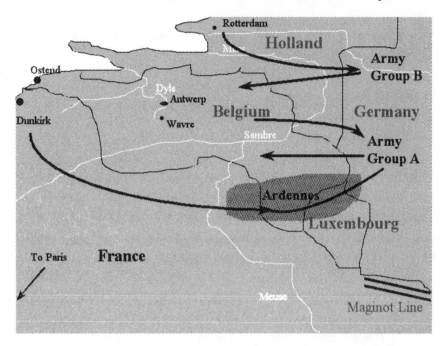

ports, gave it time to evacuate most of its troops via Dunkirk.

On 14 June the Germans took Paris and on 28 June, once Marshal Pétain had replaced the French Premier, who resigned, an armistice was signed. It was signed in the Forest of Compiègne, scene of the 1919 armistice, and left all of France north of a line from the Swiss frontier at Geneva to St Jean-de-Port under German occupation.

HEAD-TO-HEAD COMBAT STRATEGIES IN BUSINESS

A **head-to-head combat** strategy in commerce consists of direct confrontation, with two or more companies 'slugging it out'. Famous examples would be the 'burger war' between McDonald's and Burger King and the 'cola war' between Coke and Pepsi.

Although the companies involved would probably disagree, none of the four companies mentioned above has a SWAT at its disposal. The 'wars' they are engaged in are reminiscent of the trench warfare of the First World War, complete with static positions, frontal charges, heavy casualties (in terms of expenditure wasted) and gains measured in yards not miles, which are soon balanced by an enemy gain elsewhere. This strategy should only be a realistic option for three categories of company:

❏ market leaders
❏ strong number twos or threes
❏ those with a competitive SWAT.

Despite this it tends to be the most commonly selected option, if only because it is the simplest and most obvious and requires least imagination and mental effort. However, for any company not in one of the above three categories it is usually commercial suicide because of the advantages possessed by larger competitors.

Sometimes almost an entire industry engages in this type of strategy. An example would be travel agents in the UK, where competitive advantages are conspicuous by their absence (can you tell me the difference between one travel agent and another?) and all companies, big and small, appear obsessed with the use of one type of weapon: price. Most markets characterized by customers having an 'unhealthy' obsession with price (e.g. car or house insurance) are those where the main players have no competitive advantage.

However, a strategy of deliberately taking on the competition head-to-head can be successful when a company does have a competitive SWAT. Dyson vacuum cleaners (see Chapter 3) is a good illustration of how a company can enter a marketplace – and win – with such a strategy without any numerical advantage if its SWAT is demonstrably superior.

Microsoft adopted a **head-to-head combat** strategy when attacking Netscape. Possessing both numerical superiority and a competitive SWAT, any other strategy would not have made sense. Its browser was probably inferior to Netscape's, but it had an unbeatable distribution system in Windows 95 that it could use to provide its own browser free of charge. Microsoft's objective was therefore to force a decisive battle on Netscape by creating widespread awareness of its product and giving customers a definitive choice of one or the other. How it fared was explained in more detail in Chapter 2.

SELECTIVE USE OF TERRAIN

When adopting a head-to-head combat strategy against a numerically superior enemy, one method of negating this advantage is to use ground so that it is unable to use its numerical superiority. The main proviso to Lanchester's N-square law, outlined in Chapter 2, is that it applies only where all troops are able to participate. The study of the Battle of Issus in Chapter 5 shows how Alexander the Great chose a narrow coastal plain as a battleground so that the Persian king, Darius, would not be able to use his huge numerical advantage. The battleground, flanked by mountains on one side and the sea on the other, was so narrow that most of his troops were forced to wait aimlessly in the rear without participating.

Chapter 6 showed that the main strength of the Macedonian system was the phalanx, and its biggest weakness its inability to fight effectively on broken ground because the phalanx could not maintain formation. The Romans' victory over the Macedonians in 197 BC was due to their being able to lure Philip IV (one of Alexander's successors) into battle on such terrain where they were able to exploit this weakness.

Likewise, the strength of the French army in the fourteenth century lay in having the best (and the most) heavy cavalry in Europe. The weakness inherent in this was the fact that the army had no tactics other than the frontal charge, and was so arrogant and over-confident that it disdained any force not similarly composed. Thus at Crecy, Edward III was able to take up a strong defensive position on ground unsuitable for heavy cavalry, confident in the knowledge that the French knights would repeatedly charge his archers head on and be massacred.

Therefore it is possible to counterbalance a larger opponent's numerical superiority by fighting it so that it is unable to *use* those numbers. At the Battle of Shiloh (1862) during the American Civil War, the Confederate General Albert Johnston told a member of staff who was advising caution because of the number of troops opposing them:

I would fight them if they were a million. They can present no greater front between these two creeks than we can, and the more men they crowd in there, the worse we can make it for them.

BATTLE OF CANNAE, 216 BC

Perhaps the best example of selective use of terrain is the Battle of Cannae in 216 BC, the worst military defeat ever suffered by Rome and one of the most complete defeats for any army in military history.

Following his famous crossing of the Alps in 218 BC, Hannibal won two victories over separate Roman armies at Trebbia and Lake Trasimene, and set about conquering Italy. His forces comprised 40,000 infantry and 10,000 cavalry from Gaul, Spain and North Africa, fighting very much in the traditional Macedonian manner (see Chapters 5 and 6 for a comparison of the Macedonian and Roman tactical systems).

Both sides were pursuing head-to-head combat strategies and several battles had already taken place (all won by Hannibal). Rome's existing forces had been annihilated at Trasimene, so this time it did

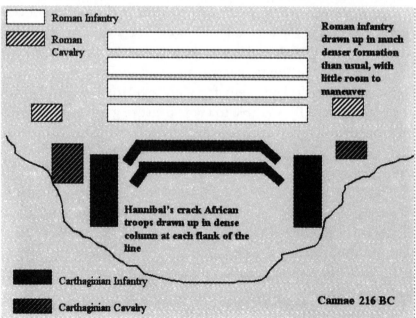

Roman Infantry

Roman Cavalry

Roman infantry drawn up in much denser formation than usual, with little room to maneuver

Hannibal's crack African troops drawn up in dense column at each flank of the line

Carthaginian Infantry

Carthaginian Cavalry

Cannae 216 BC

not underestimate its opponent – 80,000 infantry and 6000 cavalry were sent to meet Hannibal under the joint command of the two consuls Varro and Paulus. Unfortunately, neither was very experienced at commanding large armies in battle, and the brilliant Hannibal was able to lure them into a trap.

While his army was superior to that of the Romans in cavalry (in skill as well as numbers), he knew that he was outnumbered in infantry by about 2:1, and therefore needed a battle plan that would prevent the Romans from using this advantage.

Hannibal drew his troops up across a loop in the river Aufidus, thus guarding his flanks, and placed his cavalry on the wings with the infantry in the center, as was usual for the period. His brother Hasdrubal commanded 8000 Spanish cavalry on the left and 2000 Numidians were stationed on the right. His Gauls and Spanish infantry were placed in lines in the center in a slightly advanced position, and his crack north African veterans were positioned on their flanks in columns.

The strength of the Roman military machine lay in its linear formation, its flexibility and its ability to maneuver against its much more rigid foes (see Chapter 6), but Hannibal's choice of ground

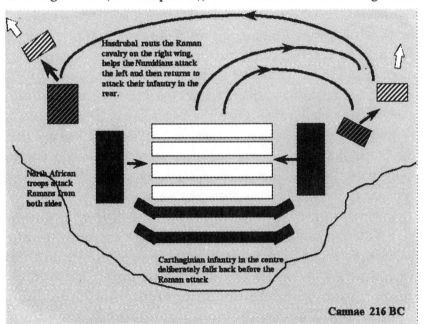

Hasdrubal routs the Roman cavalry on the right wing, helps the Numidians attack the left and then returns to attack their infantry in the rear.

North African troops attack Romans from both sides

Carthaginian infantry in the centre deliberately falls back before the Roman attack

Cannae 216 BC

meant that they did not have enough room to deploy in their usual manner.

The consuls took turns to command the army, and it was Varro's turn on the day of the battle. Paulus cautioned him against fighting, but he thought that his colleague merely wanted to fight on a day when he was in command and thus gain the glory of defeating Hannibal, and therefore ignored his advice. So instead of declining battle, the inexperienced Varro saw only that Hannibal had positioned himself with his back to the river and thought that it was the Carthaginians who were trapped. He therefore offered battle and drew his army up in a much denser, phalanx-like formation than was usual. This gave him depth, but little flexibility.

Hasdrubal's superior horsemen soon routed the Roman cavalry on the right, and rode completely around the back of the Roman infantry to attack the cavalry on their left wing from the rear. Already sore pressed by the Numidians, they were smashed and driven from the field.

The Romans now had no cavalry left, but with their massive superiority in infantry numbers (and skill) were still confident of victory. The legions pressed forward against the deliberately thinned Carthaginian center, and were jubilant when it fell back in apparent terror. They pressed forward, eager to finish the job, oblivious to the fact that the Carthaginian columns to their right and left remained motionless and facing to their front.

In their eagerness to achieve victory the Romans became a disorganized mess, and at that point the Carthaginian flanks turned to their left and right and attacked them in the flanks. At the same time the Carthaginian cavalry attacked their rear, preventing any retreat. Only those on the outside could fight, and even they were so hemmed in they could hardly use their weapons.

Unable to fight back, the Romans were butchered like cattle, their superior numbers suddenly turned from an advantage to a liability. Varro managed to escape with about 3000 men, but over 70,000 were killed where they stood and a further 10,000 taken prisoner. Hannibal's total casualties were fewer than 7000.

USING TERRAIN TO NEGATE A BUSINESS ENEMY'S SIZE

Just as it is possible to fight a bigger enemy in war by using the terrain against it, it is also possible do so in business. The best way to fight a larger competitor is to possess a competitive SWAT, and the second best is to fight defensively. However, unlike in warfare, in commerce the choice of whether to fight defensively or not does not always lie with you.

The commercial equivalent of using ground to work for you is selecting a market or niche of a market where your competitor's strength is less important, or even becomes a weakness.

Companies facing a larger, stronger competitor should therefore examine it closely in order to identify the weaknesses that are inherent in that strength. It should be noted that this is different from identifying your competition's weaknesses. *All companies have weaknesses, but what we are after here are those that stem from their strengths.*

Let's take a situation where company A has a competitor, B, whose strength lies in its extremely low pricing. In addition to looking for ways to cut its own prices, A needs to identify what it is that enables B to charge those low prices. Is it simply a willingness on its part to accept low margins, or is it due to the way it is structured? If it is due to having a low-cost manufacturing system relying on high-volume runs of standard product, plenty of advance notification of changes and economies of scale, then the weakness inherent in that strength is the company's inability to customize product and respond quickly to changes in orders. In any market there will be customers who would like customized product and who would prefer to use a supplier that can respond quickly to last-minute orders or to changes once orders have been placed.

Such customers are the terrain on which B's strength cannot be brought to bear, because if A positions itself to them as the flexible alternative, B cannot respond without going against the very competencies that have made it strong.

McDonald's, Beamish Stout and Avis

A simple example would be the ongoing 'burger war' between Burger King and McDonald's, in which Burger King is the challenger. What weaknesses are inherent in McDonald's strength? One of its strengths is the fact that wherever you are in a given country, you get the same burger, every time, in every outlet. This conformity to laid-down specifications and the resulting confidence this gives consumers – you know exactly what you are going to get when you order a Big Mac – is one of the reasons behind its success. The weakness inherent in this is the lack of choice (other than being able to order it 'plain'). One of Burger King's campaigns ran with the slogan 'It's Your Burger', offering consumers burgers the way they wanted them, not the way McDonald's had decided they should have them. It would be difficult for McDonald's to compete with this approach without completely reversing its operational procedures.

Another good example is Beamish stout. A few years ago, this product was launched in the UK in direct competition with Guinness. If companies were able to choose their competition, very few would deliberately choose a giant like Guinness, given its strengths. It is a global brand sold all over the world with massive promotional and advertising funds supporting it. It 'owns' its category, by which I mean that it is the first brand people think about when they hear the words 'Irish stout'. It has massive distribution in pubs, clubs, bars, off-licenses and grocers, and prompted percentage recall with the public that is probably in the high 90s.

All in all, it is a formidable competitor. But if you make an alternative Irish stout, you cannot escape the fact that your main competitor is going to be Guinness, so what are the weaknesses inherent in these strengths? Beamish decided that Guinness's Achilles' heel was the fact that because it was a global brand, it had actually lost its Irish roots. Guinness drank in England is brewed not in Dublin but in London; any product that is mostly water is very expensive to transport around the world, so Guinness has local breweries in any country where it has significant sales.

Beamish therefore ran a poster campaign using clever puns that highlighted the fact that while Guinness was brewed in England, Beamish was 'the real thing,' still brewed in Ireland. The posters carried bylines such as 'Brewed over Eire, not over 'ere' and 'Importers, not imposters'.

A more famous example would be Avis's use of the slogan 'Our Queues Are Shorter'. The strength of its traditional competitor Hertz was the fact that everyone knew it was number 1, and therefore used it because of the tendency to think: 'There's got to be a reason why they're the biggest.' The weakness accompanying this, however, was that whenever travelers got off a plane and headed for the Hertz desk in the airport, there was usually a long queue as everyone else did the same thing.

SEGA VS NINTENDO

An especially attractive **head-to-head combat** strategy for a number two to adopt is to launch a new product or service which, if the market leader reacted to it, would decimate its existing business. However, it is important for the challenger deliberately not to pose too great a threat in the beginning, in order to prevent the established and larger competitor from reacting with all the force at its disposal.

Assuming that the new product or service has some added value/ benefits when compared to the existing one (and let's face it, unless it is to be launched on a price platform, it cannot hope to succeed if it doesn't), it is important that the challenger pitches its prices sufficiently higher than the incumbent's. While the temptation might be to offer added benefits at the same (or even lower) prices, such action would be guaranteed to bring the full weight of retaliation down on the challenger's head. If prices are high enough that they avoid eating too far into sales of the incumbent's existing product, it is possible to be given a 'breathing space' until it really starts to hurt. This gives the challenger the time to build its defensive fortifications around the customers that it has managed to gain in the meantime.

By 1990, games console manufacturer Nintendo was riding the crest of a wave and it seemed that nothing could stop its 8-bit machines becoming ubiquitous across the US. However, a relatively small rival called Sega was soon to usurp it, by turning its strength into a weakness.

In 1988, Sega launched its own 16-bit Mega Drive computer game system. Based on the arcade games for which the company was famous, this had a number of advantages over Nintendo's 8-bit system, including better sound, more colors and the ability to display multi-layered images. However, the ability to sell computer games hardware is dependent to a great extent on the number of games available and, hampered by a lack of software developers to design games for its system, Sega only managed to sell 200,000 units in its first year.

In 1990, it renamed the system Genesis and reduced its price in the US by $50, to $150. Sega's best software, Sonic the Hedgehog, was included free of charge, and the whole package was aggressively advertised with the slogan: 'Genesis does what Nintendon't.' Sales finally took off, and software developers flocked to develop games for it.

Nintendo had had its own 16-bit system on the shelf for several years, but was in no hurry to bring it to market. Its view was that the market could still be enlarged using the old 8-bit system, and that all of these customers would then eventually switch to the 16-bit when it was launched. It felt that it could sell an 8-bit system and a 16-bit system to the same customers, if it bided its time. It also feared that the software developers and retailers might abandon its successful 8-bit system if the 16-bit was launched too soon. Why risk killing the goose that was laying the golden egg?

The new system (called Super Nintendo Entertainment System, or SNES) was eventually launched in 1991 at a price of $200, two years after Sega's; competition between the two was fierce. Prices dropped, software was given away free of charge, and the two companies raced to see who could develop the biggest range of games. However, in this Sega had a huge head start. By the end of 1991, Genesis had 125 games while SNES had only 25.

Then in May 1992 SNES was reduced in price to match Genesis's price of $150, and both companies launched stripped-down versions for less than $100. Nintendo's fears came true. As 16-bit prices fell, there was less reason for consumers to buy 8-bit systems. The price of 8-bit games dropped to $20, and in 1991 games manufacturers developed less than half the usual number of games. The 8-bit market started to go into terminal decline.

Both companies claimed 16-bit market leadership (at one point both claimed to have over 60 percent!), but it took until September 1994 for Nintendo to be able to prove undisputed leadership.

While Sega had a monopoly on 16-bit systems, Nintendo knew that it would have an incentive to keep prices high, and the effect on its existing 8-bit system would at least be limited. It also knew that as soon as it entered the market itself, price competition would become fierce.

Nintendo was willing to grant Sega a three-year monopoly of the 16-bit market, as long as it did not pitch its new system in direct competition with its own existing one. Nintendo felt that to delay the launch of its own new system was the lesser of two evils.

HEAD-TO-HEAD LOGISTICS STRATEGIES

As much of the study of warfare concentrates on famous battles, the inexperienced amateur military historian might be forgiven for thinking that head-to-head combat strategies have been the most common; they have not.

Even Clausewitz was forced to recognize and admit that history produces numerous examples of campaigns where neither side sought a decisive battle:

> *The history of war, in every age and country, shows not only that most campaigns are of this type, but that the majority is so overwhelming as to make all other campaigns seem more like exceptions to the rule.*

Victories of annihilation – such as those enjoyed by Alexander over Darius, Hannibal or the Parthians over Rome, the Prussians over the French in 1870 or the Germans over virtually everybody in 1940 –

have been a rarity, enjoyed only by those who possessed a SWAT. Usually, commanders following a **head-to-head** strategy have had to be content with the gradual, piecemeal conquest of territory rather than the absolute destruction of enemy forces.

An offensive **head-to-head logistics** strategy aims not at the destruction of the enemy in one decisive battle, but at the piecemeal conquest of territory, thereby denying the defending enemy the land, resources and population that it needs to sustain the war effort.

Later, in the Second World War, lacking the force:space ratio that had enabled them to defeat France in 1940, the Germans attempted to defeat Russia with a **head-to-head logistics** strategy by trying to capture the Russian oilfields in 1942. The fact that they failed did not make this the wrong strategy, since if they did not have sufficient manpower to hold large swathes of territory they could not have had the ability to destroy the Russian army via a **head-to-head combat** strategy.

During the Second Boer War, the British overcame the regular Boer armies in about six months, but for nearly two years faced guerrilla warfare where the surviving Boers adopted a **raiding combat** and **logistics** strategy. Using hit-and-run attacks by commandos (i.e. groups under command, but not formal discipline), they broke British railway lines 250 times in 12 months and on one occasion held the waterworks of the major city of Bloemfontein for 27 days, forcing the British troops to resort to polluted wells, which doubled the death rate from typhoid.

Unable to bring these 'bitter enders', as they were called, to battle, the British responded by building thousands of lines of barbed wire across the country, guarded by blockhouses placed close enough to keep the wire under rifle fire. Ultimately they had 9000 blockhouses covering 5000 miles of barbed wire, and the countryside was subdivided into small compartments. The movement of the raiders was severely inhibited, and using mobile columns the British were eventually able to hound them down and end resistance.

The Spaniards in Cuba followed a similar strategy, dividing the island into three segments using two lines of forts and blockhouses. They then followed this with a concentration in each segment to achieve the force:space ratio necessary to defeat the guerrillas.

*USING A HEAD-TO-HEAD LOGISTICS STRATEGY DEFENSIVELY:
NAPOLEON'S INVASION OF RUSSIA, 1812*

In 1812 Napoleon invaded Russia with about 675,000 men, less than half of whom were French. As usual, Napoleon followed a head-to-head combat strategy, the aim of which was to defeat the Russian army decisively in battle.

The Russians had about 218,000 men split into three armies, and Napoleon's plan was to advance on a relatively narrow front, splitting the middle one under Bagration from the northern one under Barclay, and at the same time cutting their communications with the capital, St Petersburg.

Not knowing Napoleon's intentions once he had crossed the border, the Russians had no option but to leave large gaps between their three armies, aiming to identify his main thrust and fall back before it until they could regroup somewhere in the rear. Their strategy at the time was also one of head-to-head combat, in that they intended (and wanted) to give battle; the withdrawal was a temporary activity until they could find an appropriate point at which to do so.

They eventually united under Barclay at Smolensk, where the first battle of the campaign took place on 17 August. Its outcome was inconclusive, but the Russians feared Napoleon would use his infamous mobility and surprise them from the rear, and they again withdrew in the direction of Moscow.

Napoleon was now faced with his first dilemma: whether to stay at Smolensk for the winter and recommence hostilities in the spring, or follow the retreating Russians towards Moscow. Although in later years at St Helena he said that moving from Smolensk was the biggest error he had ever made, at the time the argument for doing so seemed unanswerable.

The Russian army was undefeated and its main forces had not even been engaged. During the winter Tsar Alexander would have the opportunity to recruit and train thousands of new troops and also to bring his armies from other parts of his empire to Moscow. The city was only 270 miles away and once there Napoleon could quarter his men for the winter in much greater comfort than in Smolensk.

If he stayed put, Austria and Prussia might see the prolongation of the campaign as a sign of weakness and rebel, and Alexander would surely feel less inclined to agree terms with a conqueror who had stopped two-thirds of the way. Despite the entreaties of some of his generals, he decided to follow and to bring the Russians to battle once again.

Disgusted by Barclay's withdrawal, Tsar Alexander appointed the 67-year-old Prince Michael Kutuzov as Commander-in-Chief of the Russian armies; 200 miles to the east of Smolensk, the second battle of the campaign was fought at Borodino, 70 miles west of Moscow. Approximately 100,000 more men fought at this battle than at Waterloo, and the two armies were fairly evenly matched. The battle lasted all day and was again inconclusive, with both sides claiming victory. As dusk fell, the French had possession of the battlefield, but the Russians had withdrawn only half a mile to a new position.

The Russians had lost about 44,000 men (about one in three of their number) and the French 35,000 (including 43 generals). While Napoleon could claim that he held the battlefield, in his experience victory meant the complete destruction of the enemy forces, the capture of thousands and the imposition of an armistice or surrender, and the fact that this had not happened meant his claim had a hollow ring to it, if only in his own ears.

By this time the French army was only a shadow of its former self. It had actually encountered logistical difficulties very soon after crossing the Russian border. The four days' rations issued to each man had more or less been consumed on the first day through indiscipline, and within days men were falling by the wayside in huge numbers. Food was scarce, diarrhea was rampant and what wells were found had been polluted with dead horses by the Russians. After the initial contacts, the retreating Russians pursued a 'scorched earth' policy, destroying everything behind them so that the invaders found only a wasteland.

At first torrential rains turned the roads into muddy quagmires that were virtually impassable for carts, and there was almost no shelter during the short nights. Then after the rains came stifling heat (alternated with hail storms at night), and the dust was so thick that drummers had to be stationed at the head of columns so that men would know in which direction to march.

By mid-July the horses were in a terrible state, always short of fodder, sweating unbearably during the day and in pain from the cold during the night. Over 10,000 died before the army reached Smolensk.

Everybody had wanted Borodino to be the decisive victory, and when it was apparent that it was not, morale plummeted still more. Kutuzov withdrew further to the east and deliberately set Moscow alight in order to show Napoleon his determination not to surrender. For the French, knowledge of the fact that they would not be returning home as soon as they had expected was now worsened by this destruction of their expected winter quarters.

Napoleon tried to reach terms with Alexander, who dismissed the attempt with the frightening words: 'Peace? But as yet we have not made war. My campaign is only just beginning.'

The French soon exhausted what meager supplies remained in Moscow, and they were unable to venture far without being attacked by Russian Cossacks or even peasants, who murdered any Frenchman who fell into their grasp. Communications with Smolensk and beyond were also cut by the Cossacks, and supplies arrived only as a trickle.

Napoleon now faced several equally unattractive options. First, he could march on the capital St Petersburg, but that would take six weeks and the troops were in no fit state. Second, he could advance eastwards into central Russia and try to defeat the Russians in a third battle. Third, he could retreat, but this was unthinkable as the world would take it as an admission of defeat and his hold on 'allies' such as Prussia and Austria would be weakened, perhaps irrevocably. Fourth, he could winter in Moscow and renew hostilities in the spring.

This last option was the most tempting, but was rejected for two reasons. The supply situation was becoming perilous and there was no certainty that the army could have survived the winter. In addition, reinforcements were pouring into the Russian camp and

Kutuzov would have an overwhelming superiority after winter was over. He decided to defeat Kutuzov once again in battle and then withdraw to winter quarters further west, using the victory as a mask for what would, in effect, be a retreat.

Just over a month after they had entered Moscow, the French set off. Encumbered with loot and baggage, they were a slow, cumbersome convoy rather than the light mobile force that was needed. At Maloyaroslavets the two armies fought yet another indecisive action, after which the Russians withdrew (yet again) into an almost impregnable position protected by impassable swamps.

The game was finally up for Napoleon. By now it was too late for glory; it was a question of trying to save the army. The next day the retreat began.

From the beginning, the French were continually harassed by the Cossacks and partisans who showed no mercy to any who were captured. There was little they could do in return, as there were no inhabited villages that could be held to ransom, as the Germans would do in occupied territories during the Second World War in the face of such attacks.

The horses died in their thousands by the road, leaving the French guns to be taken as trophies by the pursuing Russians. The men themselves were by now dressed in rags or motley collections of clothes looted in Moscow, and their boots soon rotted from their feet.

But the decisive element was the weather. The first snow fell on 5 November and soon it was so thick that visibility was reduced to less than 50 yards. Men's breath froze on their beards, their lips cracked, their noses turned blue and literally dropped off. Many turned in desperation to cannibalism, and the wounded were left to die by the doctors, embarrassed by their inability to give them any assistance.

By the time it reached Smolensk the army, once half a million strong, had been reduced to 41,000 men. As the Russian armies gathered and threatened to cut them off completely, Napoleon decided not to stay in the city, as had been his original intention, but to head for home.

The Russians attacked in force while the army was crossing the Beresina and nearly captured it *en masse*, but 30,000 managed to escape, due more to a lack of Russian coordination than anything else. A week later, only 13,000 were left. Reduced in some cases to drinking their own blood or eating their own severed, frostbitten fingers, the last soldiers crossed the border on 14 December.

Kutuzov stopped at the border and made no attempt to follow them. Rather than seek to defeat Napoleon, he allowed him to escape, using his armies 'less as converging jaws to trap (him) than as thumb and forefinger on a tube to extrude him'.

Despite invading with the largest army he had ever commanded, Napoleon quite simply never had a sufficiently high force:space ratio to impose his will on the Russians. His forces had no more effect on Russia than those of Edward III did on France during the Hundred Years' War. Tsar Alexander's adoption of a **head-to-head logistics** strategy completely negated Napoleon's **head-to-head combat**, and he never achieved anything more than a raid on a giant scale.

USING A HEAD-TO-HEAD LOGISTICS STRATEGY OFFENSIVELY: THE ENGLISH CONQUEST OF WALES

Although the whole of England was conquered quickly by the Normans following the Battle of Hastings, it took over 200 years for the conquest of Wales to be completed. The lowlands of southern Wales were conquered within a couple of decades of the battle, but attempts to conquer the rest were thwarted by the Welsh use of a defensive **raiding** strategy, which consisted of avoiding pitched battles and escaping into the barren and rugged Welsh mountainside until the English faced supply problems and returned home. Heavily forested terrain and a damp climate literally bogged down the invading forces, and it was also difficult for them to find supplies in a largely pastoral economy; the Welsh simply took their flocks and herds with them as they retreated. The terrain was also better suited to infantry, of which the Welsh had a preponderance, than to heavily armored cavalry.

After several dismal attempts, the Anglo-Normans realized the futility of their **head-to-head combat** strategy, and substituted in its place a head-to-head logistics one, which did not depend on the actual defeat of the Welsh army, but was aimed at the piecemeal conquest and occupation of territory.

Once a region had been invaded and the Welsh forces had predictably withdrawn, the English simply built a castle there to dominate the area. By doing this they utilized the power of the defense in its strongest form, and threw the burden of the offensive back on to the Welsh if they were to prevent the permanent loss of the occupied territory. By the middle of the eleventh century, the English had an average of one major castle for every 100 square miles of conquered territory.

This pattern of small, intermittent conquests allowed the English to permanently raise the force:space ratio, and as they consolidated their power in each new territory they were able to use its revenues and manpower for the conquest of the next (most of the manpower used in the conquest of Wales by the English was, in fact, Welsh; their disunity and a predisposition to fight among themselves were major advantages to the English).

This strategy rendered useless the advantages of the Welsh raiding combat strategy. The Welsh avoidance of battle and their dependence on retreat simply played into English hands. By giving up territory, the Welsh yielded up their base area to the enemy, who now simply converted it to their own ends and used its resources.

The English would not have required two centuries to complete the conquest had they used more of their own country's resources or pursued it continuously rather than intermittently. However, this strategy took time, not only in building the necessary castles but also because the English needed to reconcile the defeated gradually to their rule, until governing the area needed less force and resources could be freed up for the invasion of the next. The growth of towns around the castles and the cultivation of the soil also accelerated the process of establishing English culture, institutions and language.

HEAD-TO-HEAD LOGISTICS STRATEGIES IN BUSINESS

If we take the Anglo-Norman conquest of Wales as a perfect example of a **head-to-head logistics** strategy being used offensively, it is clear that it had four elements:

❏ It selected and concentrated on a specific piece of undefended geography, such as a valley and its surrounding area, and dominated it with a high force:space ratio by clearing it of Welsh forces and then building a castle to consolidate English rule.
❏ It linked the new area with territory already conquered via roads, improved communications and commercial ties.
❏ Because additional territory was only conquered once the last gains had become acclimatized to English rule, the overall force:space ratio required lessened, as manpower previously needed for garrison duty could be freed up. Therefore the cost per square mile conquered reduced as more and more territory was annexed; this was further offset by the collection of new revenues.
❏ It used the manpower and resources from each territory for the conquest and domination of the next.

The commercial application of such a strategy uses a similar model. Companies following a **head-to-head logistics** strategy need to do the following:

❏ Identify sectors of the marketplace that are currently underserved or ignored by the competition, perhaps by defining them in different and creative ways or by creating new sectors entirely, and dominate them both quantitatively in terms of market share and qualitatively in terms of satisfying customer needs for such things as service, and also by providing such complete solutions for customers that they are encouraged not to look elsewhere. In extreme cases, customers can virtually reorient their own lives or methods of operation around a company. The aim is to have a 100 percent share of several small sectors rather than a smaller share of the larger overall market. This domination makes these sectors unattractive to competitors, who would have to incur very high costs to persuade customers to switch, and they are therefore motivated to look elsewhere for 'easier pickings'. These sectors should also, if possible, have identifiable boundaries, such as barriers to entry and customers' unwillingness to go outside them.

❑ Link these sectors together by identifying and concentrating on the elements that they have in common.

❑ Create economies of scale in terms of process, organization, design, manufacturing, sales, marketing and distribution in order to lower overall unit costs.

❑ Use these economies of scale to lower prices continually and provide unbeatable value to customers, giving them a further disincentive to look elsewhere and reinforcing the initial domination of the sectors.

The beauty of such a model is that it can be used by small companies as well as large, new as well as established. The Wal-Mart example below describes how a company with no real advantages over its competition was eventually able to dominate its marketplace.

WAL-MART

Today Wal-Mart is the largest discounter in the US, having reached sales of over $100 billion in 1996 with over 2000 stores of different formats spread across the country and abroad (314 of which are in Canada, Argentina, Brazil, Indonesia, China, Mexico and Puerto Rico), linked by one of the most sophisticated information networks in the world. However, Wal-Mart has not always been the market leader.

In the 1950s, a combination of post-war affluence and car ownership led to a revolution in US retailing when many retailers began to move from small stores in the high street to much larger ones in the suburbs, where lower costs and economies of scale enabled them to charge significantly lower prices. By 1960 the total revenues of discount stores were over $1 billion, but no one chain dominated the market.

The nearest thing to a market leader was K-Mart, which grew out of the SS Kresge discounting chain. K-Mart strategically positioned its large stores with ample parking space near existing malls and towns with more than 50,000 people, and by the mid-1960s it was a multibillion-dollar business with 1000 branches.

At the same time, however, a new business was growing in Arkansas, founded by Sam Walton, who unashamedly borrowed from the K-Mart model. However, Wal-Mart differed from K-Mart in one significant way: while K-Mart located its stores in urban districts with considerable spending power, Wal-Mart decided to concentrate on clearly defined rural and small-town areas bounded by natural geography consisting of about 5000 people. In these areas there was often little decent competition, as existing stores served their customers quite poorly in terms of range, quality, price and service, and it was relatively easy for Wal-Mart to dominate them as the best-stocked, best-value, biggest store in town.

While Wal-Mart in later days was criticized for putting small-town retailers out of business, this was a result of its success, not the cause of it. Quite simply, the company had stores that were clean, bright, well stocked and merchandised and attractive, offering products at great prices. In these small towns, it played the role that department stores such as Bloomingdale's and Nordstrom play in the suburbs of a large city.

Used to dealing with local stores, the customers in these areas also had a natural reluctance to drive more than 10 miles to a general merchandise store, and this meant that Wal-Mart could saturate demand within that radius. Wal-Mart markets were therefore small enough for it to dominate and too small to attract major competition. The customer population of these areas just wasn't big enough to sustain two major discounters. K-Mart, on the other hand, stimulated demand in its markets and attracted competition from other discounters such as Target and Venture, and later on from 'category killers' like Toys 'R' Us and Home Depot.

Once the chain was up and running in the South and Midwest, Wal-Mart management concentrated on building systems and organizational capabilities that would enable it to replicate its success rapidly. This included the company's famous hub-and-spoke distribution system, with warehouses serving constellations of stores all located within a day's drive, and its renowned IT systems (today, only the US government buys more computers than Wal-Mart). As more and more stores opened, the company achieved vast economies of scale by using this infrastructure more efficiently.

As it grew to be more and more successful, Wal-Mart resisted the temptation to raise prices and margins, and continued to view each individual store catchment area as 'contestable', fearing that rivals might be attracted if the company ceased offering the maximum possible value to its customers. The cost savings resulting from its economies of scale were ploughed back into providing excellent value, and its system of 'everyday low prices' where there is no need for special promotions is now famous throughout the retail industry.

The company grew from having 32 stores in 1970 to 195 in 1978, and to 553 in 1983, when it actually launched its own satellite at the center of a communications network that could keep its management in touch with the farthest reaches of its fast-growing empire. Sales hit $1 billion in 1979, growing to $100 billion by 1997, and the company is forecast to achieve $200 billion by 2002.

Starting in the 1980s, Wal-Mart began to move into other areas, using its huge buying power and economies of scale to open stores in more competitive markets. In 1983 it entered the membership discount market with Sam's Club, which by 1997 had 436 stores. In 1990 it purchased the McLane Company, which services about 30,000 convenience outlets across the US, and in 1992 it acquired 6000 7-Eleven branches as a result of the purchase of Southland Corporation.

After some early problems, Wal-Mart is now replacing some of its smaller stores with 170–200,000 sq ft hypermarkets that also sell food, and the company has swiftly become the US's second-largest grocer. In 1999 alone 150 more hypermarkets are being built and it plans to overtake the leader, Kroger, by 2002.

Wal-Mart's current virtually unassailable position was reached by a brilliant execution of a **head-to-head logistics** strategy:

❑ It chose small-town, rural locations for its branches that were ignored by its major competitors, which preferred larger catchment areas.
❑ It picked areas that were small enough for it to dominate, thus preventing the later arrival of the competition.
❑ It linked the branches together with its famous 'hub-and-spoke' distribution system and satellite communications.
❑ It ploughed the economies of scale achieved into even lower prices, further cementing its dominant position.

Self-diagnostic questionnaire

1 Do you have a sufficient force:space ratio to adopt one of the two types of head-to-head strategy?
2 If you are a strong no. 2 or 3, and intend to adopt a head-to-head combat strategy by attacking the market leader directly across the market as a whole, why should a large proportion of customers take you seriously as a realistic alternative to the leader when they don't do so at the moment? What is the SWAT that will enable your attack to succeed?
3 Which segments of the market are currently underserved or ignored by the leader? Are any of these more attractive than others (e.g. more profitable, easier to service, better cultural 'fit' etc.)?
4 How can you dominate these sectors? What can you offer them that the competition cannot? Once you have dominated a segment, how will you erect barriers to entry to prevent the competition from recapturing them?
5 What are the similarities between customers in these segments that would enable you to create links and build economies of scale?

10

RAIDING STRATEGIES

RAIDS HAVE BEEN A FEATURE OF WARFARE SINCE ANCIENT TIMES, and have often had objectives that were not purely military. Some, like the Viking raids that terrorized much of western Europe and the English 'invasions' of France during the Hundred Years' War (see below), had as one of their goals the winning of booty. Some have had the objective of destroying enemy resources and others that of seizing such resources or territory with the express intention of exchanging it for what were viewed as more important political concessions.

Such a strategy was also often used when the attacking force felt that it would be unable to force the defending one to give battle on terms that it was willing to accept. Often the defenders, especially if inferior in strength, would refuse to give battle and 'sit it out' behind fortified city or castle walls, or simply retreat before the numerically stronger attacking enemy.

The ancient Greeks, for example, usually had very limited political objectives in their wars with each other, rarely seeking the overthrow of their enemy. Once an army had invaded enemy territory, it would destroy whatever crops it could find, giving its enemy the choice of accepting the destruction of its scarce agricultural resources or coming out from behind its city walls and fighting. Once the battle was over and the desired political objectives achieved, the attacking force would usually return to its own territory of its own free will.

USING A RAIDING COMBAT STRATEGY OFFENSIVELY: ENGLAND IN THE HUNDRED YEARS' WAR

The Hundred Years' War, a 'David vs Goliath' conflict between England and the much larger and more powerful France, is a good example of a raiding strategy being used offensively. The English and French monarchies were locked in conflict over the question of who had the right to rule France, but in this the French royal house had a distinct advantage: it lived there! For this reason, the burden of responsibility for commencing military operations usually lay with the English.

The problem faced by successive English kings was that England was a small country with a low population and little economic surplus that could be devoted to the pursuit of war. After the battle of Crecy in 1346 (see Chapter 7), it was apparent to both sides that the English system of fighting defensively by dismounting their cavalry as heavy infantry and supporting them with archers was superior to the French one, and the French were loath to give open battle on terms that suited their foes.

France was too large to occupy, and even if the English had had enough manpower (which they didn't), to do so would have taken years of protracted sieges. The thousands of square miles and millions of people of France simply swallowed up the largest English armies of between 10,000 and 20,000 men. The English kings had no alternative but to rely on a guerrilla strategy with three main aims:

❏ to make the continuance of the war so costly to France that its monarch would sue for peace, granting England the political concessions that it sought
❏ to force the French to give open battle, which the English were confident of winning, by causing great devastation
❏ to gain enough booty to pay for the war itself.

Nine years after Crecy, Edward III once again invaded France with the aim of making the new king, John II, give battle. This John refused to do and he stayed in the fortified city of Amiens, confining his efforts to ravaging the country in front of the English. This cost him little because he knew that the English would destroy it themselves in any case.

At the same time Edward III's son, the 'Black Prince', embarked on an even greater raid eastwards from Guyenne, territory held by England in the southwest of France. He marched from the Atlantic to the Mediterranean over two-and-a-half months destroying everything in his path, but he too was ignored by the French armies.

The following year (1356) he set off again, this time northwards towards Paris, and now John II was determined to stop him. A huge French army overtook the much smaller, booty-laden English one near Poitiers. The Black Prince used the same tactics as his father at Crecy, and although this time the French cavalry dismounted and attacked on foot, the result was identical. The French lost over 2000 cavalry and the king himself was taken prisoner. Eventually a truce was signed between Edward III and John II's son that gave England valuable concessions, including the important port of Calais, adjacent territory in northwest France and more in the southwest.

The war, however, was quickly resumed, and year after year the English raided French territory, with the new king Charles V deliberately avoiding battle, strengthening the fortifications of any towns on the English route of march and attacking isolated English-held towns in Guyenne. The largest of the English raids went from Calais to Bordeaux, and involved an army devastating 1000 miles of French countryside without battle being joined.

Although this was embarrassing to the French, they avoided battle, instead only attacking stragglers, foragers and looters, and over a five-month period the English lost half of their army without any major successes. After a decade of renewed war, the French had won back not only the territory in the southwest that they had been forced to concede but also some in Guyenne, which had been English for 200 years.

Exhausted by both war and the plague, peace followed but war was resumed in 1415. France was divided internally and ruled by a madman. Following the battle of Agincourt, one of the most famous and celebrated victories in English military history, the English king Henry V conquered most of northern France (including Paris). However, inspired by Joan of Arc, the French counterattacked and gradually won back the lost territory.

This counteroffensive avoided pitched battles (by now the French had learnt their lesson) and involved a process of sieges and attacking the English in camp, on the march or when they could not protect their flanks.

Throughout the whole of the Hundred Years' War, England lacked sufficient force to do much more than offer to give battle and then resort to destructive raids if the challenge was not accepted. Given the disparity in size and resources between the two armies, it could not really have done otherwise while the French population remained loyal to their monarch and institutions. Such a raiding strategy was the only sensible one it could have followed.

USING A RAIDING COMBAT STRATEGY DEFENSIVELY: PERSIA VS ROME

In 359 the Persian king Shapur II attacked imperial territory in Asia Minor, and the new Emperor Julian assembled a vast army of 65,000 men and set out for Mesopotamia to teach him the folly of messing about with Rome.

The logistical problems of supplying an army that size were enormous and are perhaps best illustrated by an anecdote that tells us more about what was required than any statistics. At one point cavalry grooms were collecting fodder from a huge depot where it had been stacked high, and as they took what they needed from the bottom of the pile rather than the top, it collapsed and killed 50 men in the process.

Julian's strategy was one of **head-to-head combat,** and he sought a decisive battle in which he could defeat Shapur and occupy his capital, Ctesiphon. He divided his army into two, leaving 30,000 men in Mesopotamia with instructions to guard the rear of the main army as it proceeded down the Euphrates. By doing this, he could catch Shapur in a pincer movement if he tried to move against Julian's advancing column. He expected Shapur also to adopt a **head-to-head combat** strategy and to fight him somewhere along the way.

However, while the Persians harassed the advancing Roman army, they refused to give battle and Julian was forced to stop when he got to within a mile of Ctesiphon's walls. He could not afford to become engaged in a prolonged siege of the city while the Persians were at large in his rear. His only option was to move on, but the Euphrates route had been stripped of supplies, so the thousand ships that had supported him were destroyed in order to prevent them falling into the hands of the Persians. Julian then marched up the Tigris, aiming for eastern Persia, where he hoped to find Shapur and force him to give battle.

At this point, the Persians adopted a **head-to-head logistics** strategy using 'scorched earth' tactics and burning everything in the Romans' path. Finally the Persian army arrived, but again refused to give battle, while continually harassing the increasingly demoralized Roman army. Battle was eventually joined at Maranga, but although the Romans won, the Persian army was not destroyed and Julian found himself adrift in a foreign land, having lost the initiative and at the mercy of the Persians. He was eventually killed in a minor skirmish, and the new emperor Jovian was forced to negotiate a humiliating settlement with Shapur, conceding the northern part of Mesopotamia.

RAIDING STRATEGIES IN BUSINESS

Raiding strategies should be the preferred option for most companies, given that most lack not only numerical superiority (or even parity) but also a competitive SWAT.

Companies pursuing these strategies use their small size to their advantage by seeking weak spots or niche markets that are unattractive to larger companies. Those following a **raiding combat** strategy look for weak spots in two areas.

First, they can identify products or services that are not being provided either properly or even at all by the market leaders. Second, they can identify individual customers who for some reason are not being serviced to their satisfaction.

This may be because they have been let down by one of the leaders and the relationship has suffered accordingly; such customers are extremely vulnerable and likely to switch. It may be because the leader's product is of a higher quality than they need and is correspondingly too expensive. It may be because they need some type of customization that the leaders are not interested in providing because it would interfere with their high-volume production runs.

Whether combat raiders concentrate on products or customers, they have to accept that their gains may be short lived. If larger competitors react by bringing out their own version of the raider's product or taking action to 'recapture' the customers they have lost, the raiders' position may become untenable. They may have to beat a tactical retreat, only to resurface and harass the competitor elsewhere.

A **logistics** strategy in warfare (either **raiding** or **head to head**) seeks to deprive the enemy of vital resources, and in business it does exactly the same. The one vital resource that a company needs to thrive is customers, as without them it cannot even exist.

While a **head-to-head logistics** strategy looks for temporary possession of customers whose needs are not being met, one of **raiding logistics** looks for *permanent* possession. It does this by identifying not individual customers, but an entire sector of the market whose needs are unmet. By satisfying those unmet needs, the logistics raider can 'remove' the customers in that sector from the marketplace, depriving the competition of its custom on a long-term basis.

It therefore segments the market by customer type (rather than by product/service), looking for customers who are unattractive to larger competitors for some reason and who share a special need that cannot be satisfied by the less focused competition. This segment should be large enough to be attractive while still being too small to attract larger companies.

Like practitioners of a **head-to-head logistics** strategy, these companies then seek to saturate demand in their chosen sector and erect barriers to entry so that they are seen to 'own' it and thus deter new entrants.

The advice to adopt one of these two strategies is unwelcome to most small/medium-sized businesses, because many of them do not want to limit themselves or place 'handcuffs' on themselves (their words) by doing this. They want to have a stab at any business that might be up for grabs. To deliberately forgo any business because it did not fall into their area of specialization would be unthinkable.

However, while most companies might think there is no harm in saying 'Our main concentration will still be on *x*, but it won't do any harm also to do this piece of business over here', there are significant dangers in this. To divert your resources once is often the thin end of the wedge. If it has been done once it can be done again, and then a third time. Before long, the focus is lost and the company is trying to service the whole market.

INTERSKI

Interski is a UK company based in Nottingham specializing in providing ski holidays. The skiing holiday market is a very competitive one, with dozens of companies operating in it.

Some of these competitors are the major holiday tour operators, which completely dwarf Interski in both size and resource. If Interski was to operate across a variety of European destinations (France, Germany, Austria, Switzerland, Italy etc.) it would come into direct contact with the 'giants' in the industry such as Thomsons, and this would be the equivalent of following a **head-to-head combat** strategy.

However, this strategy would be doomed to failure, as the major operators' buying power would mean that Interski would be severely disadvantaged on costs and therefore on price. Instead, it has opted for a **raiding** strategy, whereby it concentrates on one small part of the market, organized school trips.

Schools obviously have very specialized needs, such as additional safety and security, extra instructional facilities, organized transport and appropriate evening activities, and Interski has structured itself to provide these better than anyone else in the marketplace.

However, these things do not make the company unique, as there are other companies that specialize in schools. It has therefore segmented its market still further, by focusing on one small geographic patch, two resorts in the Aosta valley in northern Italy.

Interski does not offer holidays anywhere else, and as a result is the largest ski operator in the valley. This concentration of force at one point gives it two main advantages.

First, it is the biggest spender in these resorts, which gives it buying power out of all proportion to its actual size and enables it to keep costs down. Second, it is able to 'blanket' the resorts with Interski personnel, so that it is impossible to spend a day without seeing and meeting dozens of them. It currently has upwards of 40 personnel in the valley, compared to a handful from the major tour operators. This high ratio of staff to customers enables it to offer an extremely high level of service.

The results of this strategy have been amazing, with the company experiencing growth rates year on year that would be the envy of most others in the travel industry.

TELCO VS AT&T

AT&T has dominated the long-distance telephone market in the US for some time. It is a true giant, the tenth biggest company in the country in terms of revenue in 1998 ($53.6 billion). However, its share of the market has been falling steadily, and much of it has been going to tiny (in relative terms) competitors following raiding logistics strategies.

Until recently, to qualify for AT&T's discount schemes, customers had to be frequent users of long-distance calls, meaning that millions of Americans who were infrequent users were being ignored by it and the other large competitors in the market. These were people such as immigrants or the elderly, who are often price sensitive and would usually shop around for bargains, but for whom it was just not worth the effort to switch long-distance carriers for the occasional call.

Recognizing that the market leaders were not really interested in this sector of the market because of its low volume, a set of fast-growing companies emerged known as 'dial-arounds', the largest of which is Telco Communications Group. They buy long-distance calls in bulk from AT&T and then act as a wholesaler, reselling the calls on to consumers at reduced rates. It was estimated that during 1997/98 the size of the dial-around market would have grown by 120 percent, and in 1996 (the last year for which data is available) Telco grew sales by *99 percent* to $429 million!

In addition to radio and press advertising, Telco blankets US homes with almost 300 million pieces of junk mail per year, and has arrangements with other companies whereby its stickers are placed on their products (e.g. bananas). These stickers inform the consumer that they will be eligible for massive savings simply by dialing a seven-digit code before the number they are calling. The stickers then find themselves attached to millions of individual telephones as 'reminders' to their users.

Learning lessons from fmcg marketing, Telco has a whole variety of brands separated by only nominal differences. For example, one scheme might be targeted at students from a particular university, while the same scheme will be marketed under a different name to students of another. Various brands also target different nationalities.

For years AT&T watched passively while its share fell, as its traditional way of monitoring customer attrition didn't identify when customers used dial-arounds. If a customer switched to (for example) Sprint or MCI, that permanent loss would be registered. But Telco customers still use the AT&T network, which made it harder for the company to identify what was happening.

Eventually recognizing the threat, AT&T reduced its own rates, and offered residential customers a maximum rate of 15 cents per minute, anywhere, any time. This failed to do the trick with dial-arounds offering calls at prices as low as 9.5 cents.

Finally in 1998 AT&T started the Lucky Dog company, offering rates of 10 cents per minute plus a 10 cents connection fee, backed by automatic entry into sweepstakes for cash and holiday prizes. Undoubtedly this will create a certain amount of cannibalization from its existing customers, but it is better for AT&T to cannibalize itself than to allow others to do it. The company has launched the service without using the AT&T brand (the first time it has ever done so) in an attempt to minimize such cannibalization.

It is too early to say what effect this will have on the market. Not knowing that Lucky Dog is from AT&T, many customers will not see any particular reason to use it rather than Telco or one of the other dial-around companies, and it may be a case of 'too little, too late'. However, Telco is taking the threat seriously; in addition to fighting back it has moved into the commercial sector selling to small and mid-sized companies, and is now looking at providing a similar service to consumers by wholesaling cheap electricity.

MAXIM INTEGRATED PRODUCTS

While most Silicon valley chipmakers have had to ride a profits rollercoaster over the last decade, Maxim Integrated Products has consistently reported amazing gains in both sales and profitability. The surprise is that it has done so by concentrating on analog integrated circuits, a technology that the rest of the industry abandoned as obsolete in the mid-1980s.

Most of the competition assumed that the digital revolution would eliminate the need for the older technology, but in fact the growth of high-performance digital products has actually fueled demand for high-performance analog ones, which interact better with the 'real' world.

Analog circuits do this because its varying physical properties are better measured by the wide range of analog waves than by digital chips. In many electronic products, analog chips analyse real-world physical properties such as temperature, pressure and voltage on to the digital 'brains' of the product, which then calculates a response. Analog chips are also crucial to handheld devices such as laptop and palmtop computers, because voltage is a primary function of anything powered by a battery.

The high-performance end of the analog chip market is worth over $8 billion a year, and Maxim is achieving comfortable growth of about 30 percent per annum. The only serious obstacle to further growth is a lack of chip designers trained in analog technology, as most engineering schools have replaced classes on analog technology with ones on digital. However, even this can be seen as a blessing in disguise, as it also acts as a significant barrier to entry for start-ups.

Maxim has erected another entry barrier in its product proliferation. It offers a wide range of analog circuits with relatively low volumes and a relatively low selling price. The resulting fragmentation means that any new entrant would immediately have to equal this range to be viable.

This is a perfect example of a **raiding logistics** strategy where a company focuses on a sector of the market that appears unattractive to the larger players and then dominates it to the point of ownership.

ENTERPRISE RENT-A-CAR

Another good example of a company pursuing a **raiding logistics** strategy by concentrating on one specific sector of a market that was unattractive to the main players is Enterprise Rent-A-Car in the US. Enterprise is the second biggest car-rental company in the country, with sales not far behind those of Hertz (1997 sales were $3.7 billion vs Hertz with $3.8 billion) and more cars and offices. Yet it is virtually unknown outside the US.

Started in the early 1960s, Jack Taylor's fledgling company was too small to take the likes of Hertz and Avis head on in airport rentals with a **combat** strategy, and thus had to search for a different sector of the rentals market where it stood more of a chance.

In the early 1970s, the law courts decided that casualty insurance companies were liable for an insured motorist's economic loss from being without a car, and insurers began providing low-priced rental cars. Taylor therefore decided to focus on the insurance-replacement market, and more than 67 percent of the company's sales come from people who have had their cars stolen or wrecked.

Recognizing that when a customer's car has been towed away from a collision he or she is probably not in the mood to 'shop around' for a replacement, and that the repair shop's recommendation will carry a lot of weight, Enterprise has always had a policy of developing close relationships with the repairers. On most Wednesdays, right across the country, Enterprise employees will visit garages and take gifts such as donuts and pizza to maintain that relationship.

Enterprise has also taken advantage of the growing trend for auto dealers to offer free or cheap replacements when a customer's car is being serviced, and now has agreements with many major dealers. With large dealers, it even has an office on the premises!

Taylor started with one office in St Louis and opened a second in Atlanta. Florida and Texas soon beckoned, and the company now has offices nationwide. Every time a branch grows to about 150 vehicles, the company opens another a few miles away, and the staff fan out to develop close relationships with any dealer or body shop in the vicinity. It now boasts that 90 percent of the population lives within 15 minutes of a company branch.

By opening new branches so close to existing ones it is true that the company suffers from some cannibalization, but in doing so it is pursuing a raiding logistics strategy whereby it aims to dominate a given area, leaving no 'gaps' between offices that could then be exploited by direct competition. If the existing office loses some sales to the new one because it is nearer, then the staff just have to go out and replace them.

As insurance companies expect to pay 'bottom dollar' for rental cars, Enterprise has had to adopt a different approach to costs than its bigger competition. It eschews the expensive sites at airports favoured by Hertz and Avis, and instead concentrates on inexpensive sites on shopping strips. It also keeps its cars for two or three years instead of three to six months as airport rental organizations do. In doing so it pursues a low-cost strategy, which enables it to offer rates up to 30 percent lower than its competitors.

Both Hertz and Avis entered the replacement car market in the mid-1980s, but quickly retreated as they discovered that the rates the insurance companies were prepared to pay would generate insufficient margin to cover their higher cost base.

HOLIDAY AUTOS

Holiday Autos, a UK car-rental company, took a different route, although there are many similarities between it and Enterprise. Like Enterprise, competing directly with the major multinationals was a non-starter and the company adopted a raiding logistics strategy aimed at one specific segment of the market – the provision of rental vehicles to UK holidaymakers going abroad.

Founded by Clive Jacobs in 1997, Holiday Autos recognized that many were either finding it difficult to organize rental for a holiday in, for example, Spain before leaving the UK (because travel agents were not encouraged to sell such packages, which provided little commission), or were being taken advantage of by local rental companies when they got there.

It therefore decided to offer a simple, all-inclusive service and arrange everything in advance for customers so that all they have to do on arrival at the airport is pick up the car. Allied to this is a price guarantee, which says that the company will undercut the best alternative by £5.

This low-price strategy is achieved through the simultaneous pursuit of a low-cost one. The company's luxury offices in south London are virtually its only assets. First, it does not own its vehicles, but rents them *en bloc* from local rental operators at the holiday destinations, who are happy to offer reduced prices because of the volume of business on offer.

Second, although it does have a telephone salesforce that sells direct to the public, it relies heavily on travel agents to sell its services when the holiday is booked. The benefit to them is that they can sell their customers peace of mind at much lower rates than those of the larger companies.

The approach appealed to the major travel agent chains and also to the car-rental companies which were attracted by the prospects of mass bookings. After a year turnover hit £1 million and by 1989 the company was the market leader in holiday rentals in the UK. Once it had achieved domination of its original market segment, the question of how to achieve further growth was addressed. Less strategic companies might have been tempted by hubris to try to take the major competitors on head-to-head, but Jacobs decided to change the company strategy to one of **head-to-head logistics** rather than **combat**.

Rather than remain concentrated in the UK and dilute its focus by expanding into other sectors of the rental market, it chose to remain focused on holiday rentals and expand internationally. It quickly opened offices in a number of other countries, and now more than half the company's sales are outside the UK. With over 4000 international locations, it operates in 50 countries, and in 1999 expects to achieve sales of $180 million.

From zero to $180 million, all within 12 years! And this was in an industry dominated by huge multinationals such as Hertz, Avis and Budget with their massive buying power, huge fleets and offices around the world. Holiday Autos (like Enterprise) is a perfect example of how a carefully planned raiding strategy can enable small companies to succeed even when the competition is daunting.

RAIDING LOGISTICS VS HEAD-TO-HEAD COMBAT STRATEGIES IN THE MICROPROCESSOR MARKET

Chapter 2 explained how Intel has managed to achieve a virtual monopoly in the advanced microprocessor market, with its product used in about 80–90 percent of new PCs. Until recently, its position seemed unassailable.

Its competitors have been forced into a position where their only option has been to compete on price, but as they don't possess Intel's economies of scale, this invariably means lower profit margins and border-line profitability.

Take Cyrix, for example. Until recently it had no manufacturing facilities (it was what the trade calls a 'fabless' company) and paid IBM to make its chips. This cost it two to three times as much as Intel's manufacturing, and as it could only charge half the price, lower profitability was inevitable.

However, Cyrix recognized the inescapable mathematics of the above equation and that it just didn't have the clout to compete directly with Intel. Its purchase in 1997 by National Semiconductor gave it access to first-class manufacturing capacity and its deal with IBM has been ended. From now on Cyrix will make its own chips, which will reduce costs significantly.

It has also replaced its old **head-to-head combat** strategy, where it tried unsuccessfully to compete directly with Intel, with one of **raiding logistics**, whereby it is now concentrating on one small (but growing) sector of the PC market, i.e. the sub-$1000 sector.

Concentrating on this sector has become a practical option for the first time because Intel's business model of driving demand for new, exciting PCs by producing ever more powerful chips is showing the first signs of faltering.

The traditional pricing model in the electronics industry has been an annual reduction in price of around 30 percent. This has happened with calculators, electronic watches, VCRs, radios, pocket games etc., but never with PCs. Models have come on to the market at about $2500 and have stayed until prices hit the $1500 mark, at which point they have simply disappeared, replaced by the latest fancy model.

However, many consumers simply don't need or want any more power, as their PCs already have more than they can use. The choice facing them is something along the lines of: 'Shall I pay $1000 for a PC that is 10 times as powerful as I actually need, or $1500 for one that is 20 times as powerful?'

Many industry observers are viewing growth in the lower end of the market as a major trend that won't go away. Compaq has launched an inexpensive PC containing a Cyrix microprocessor, and has also negotiated agreements with a number of 'second-tier' Taiwan-based manufacturers which industry observers are soon expecting to introduce sub-$500 PCs.

From Cyrix's point of view, the best thing about the sector is that Intel is not really interested in it. To concentrate on it would be to divert from where Intel really wants to be, at the top end of the market, driving demand for ever more power-hungry applications. It is therefore unlikely to react unless the sector experiences growth beyond anyone's expectations.

In other words, for Cyrix this is a perfect raiding logistics strategy. Whether it can make money out of it, however, is another matter.

Intel's other main competitor, Advanced Micro Devices, has continued with a head-to-head combat strategy. It has repeatedly tried to reduce the time lag between Intel introducing a new generation of microprocessors and AMD introducing its own version, but has consistently failed to do so successfully.

In 1996 it launched the K5, its equivalent to the Pentium. It negotiated a major agreement with Compaq, only to finally deliver the product months late, seriously damaging relations with the customer (who had annoyed Intel by signing the agreement). AMD missed its announced sales target by $400 million, and suffered three fiscal quarters of losses.

The following year it introduced the K6, its version of the Pentium II, again with grandiose designs of gaining 25–30 percent of the market by the end of the decade. In addition to being cheaper, the product actually had some advantages over the Pentium II in that it was simpler and cheaper for PC manufacturers to install.

This appeared to be AMD's best chance of taking Intel on, and the company claimed that 10 of the top 20 manufacturers would use the K6. However, once again manufacturing problems prevented a successful launch. AMD planned to produce 15 million K6s in 1997 but managed only 1.5 million! Those microprocessors that were despatched went to only a couple of major customers, once again leaving many others disgruntled.

Operating in what is largely a fixed-cost business, AMD needs high volumes to make the K6 profitable. But even if it can overcome its current difficulties and produce that volume, therein lies the problem. For unlike Cyrix, it is competing in an area that is of significant strategic interest to Intel, and if it manages to achieve the high volumes it needs, it will automatically invite that company's wrath. And we have already seen what happens when the market leader decides 'enough is enough'.

AMD currently makes little or no money from its microprocessor activities, but it does from various other revenue streams. There are many on Wall Street who wish that the company would pull out of microprocessor production altogether, but it is held there by pride and jealousy of the money being made by Intel. It is pride that is probably going to come before a fall.

Of the two strategies, Cyrix's makes far more sense and it has a good chance of carving a profitable niche for itself without incurring Intel's retaliation.

Self-diagnostic questionnaire

1 Ask your customers about their unserved needs, i.e. those that are not currently being met at the moment. Are there any opportunities that are too small to attract the interest of the larger companies, or that they cannot meet (for any reason)?

2 What products or services could you introduce to meet these needs that could sit safely (and unthreateningly) alongside those of the larger players in the market, even with the same customers?

3 Are there any customer segments that are unattractive to the large companies operating in your markets (ones that are too small, that order infrequently, have special needs or are uneconomic)?

4 Could you turn them into a profitable opportunity if you changed your current methods of operation in some way?

5 As with a head-to-head logistics strategy, how could you dominate these sectors and erect barriers to entry to deter others from directly competing?

11

CONCLUSION

PICK UP ALMOST ANY NEWSPAPER AND MAGAZINE TODAY AND you will read about the latest takeover or merger, each threatening to eclipse anything before it in size, and each offering even more theoretical strategic advantages and potential cost savings than the last.

1998 was the biggest year in history for mergers and acquisitions (M&A), with eight of the ten biggest deals of all time taking place during the year. According to Securities Data Company, mergers worth $2.4 trillion took place, a 50 percent increase on 1997. Just consider a few of these:

Companies	Value
Exxon and Mobil	$86 billion
Travelers Group and Citicorp	$73 billion
SBC Comms and Ameritech	$72 billion
Bell Atlantic and GTE	$71 billion
AT&T and Tele-Communications	$70 billion
BP and Amoco	$55 billion
Daimler-Benz and Chrysler	$40 billion

'Merger mania' looks likely to remain for some time. January 1999 alone saw deals worth $131.5 billion, compared with $88.7 billion in 1998. Vodafone announced that it was to purchase AirTouch for $55 billion, British Aerospace announced it was to buy Marconi, Ford announced its intention to purchase Volvo. The newly merged BP Amoco is now about to purchase the Alaskan oil company Arco, which would leapfrog the group ahead of Shell to the number two position in the oil industry.

Renault has gained operating control of Nissan by buying a 35 percent stake in the company for $4 billion, and Glaxo is rumored to be plotting the takeover of Bristol Myers Squibb to produce a company that would be not only the biggest in the pharmaceutical industry, but would be twice as big as Novartis and Merck, which currently jointly occupy the top slot.

Even the rest of Europe is beginning to jump on the M&A bandwagon, primarily in the banking sector. In Spain, Santander is merging with Banco Centro Hispano; in the Netherlands, ABN has merged with Amro; in Belgium, Fortis is purchasing Banque de Generale; in France, BNP is bidding for a newly merged Paribas/Société Générale to create the world's biggest bank; in Italy, UniCredito Italiano is merging with Banca Commerciale Italiana and San Paulo-IMI with Banca di Roma.

All of this M&A activity is invariably announced as being 'strategic' and an attempt to achieve 'critical mass' in an increasingly global economy, or as an opportunity to achieve significant cost reductions and economies of scale.

However, reality normally falls far short of expectation. Successive studies have shown that about 66 percent of deals fail to achieve their objectives, for a number of reasons.

First, expected synergies often prove to be illusory, such as Citibank's expectation of being able to sell its credit-card services to Travelers' insurance customers and vice versa, and Renault's desire to use Nissan's distribution networks in Asia and the US.

Second, anticipated cost savings do not always materialize; one study in the US showed that merged banks actually had a poorer record on cost cutting than non-merged competitors, and their charges to their customers also tended to be higher.

Third, competitors don't stand still and wait for the new organization to get its act together. Many mergers are followed by a suspension of marketing activity while things settle down, and provide an opportunity for competitors that are fleet enough of foot.

In the 1980s, Imperial Tobacco (the number one company in the UK tobacco market) was bought by the British conglomerate Hanson. Following the latter's usual practice after an acquisition, a complete freeze on everything but basic expenditure was imposed while its accountants went through the books with a fine-toothed comb. This included halting all advertising and promotional activity; recognizing the opportunity, a multifunctional project team was formed at Gallaher (the strong number two in the market) with the remit to take advantage of the breathing space. Following a Gallaher marketing 'blitz', the challenger achieved market leadership within six months while the Imperial managers sat powerless to retaliate.

To give three other examples:

❑ Quaker's acquisition of Snapple (purchased for $1.7 billion in 1994, sold for $300 million in 1997) was a disaster because the company did not anticipate how quickly Coke and Pepsi would react with Fruitopia and Lemon Iced Tea.

❑ Nationsbank and Barnett Bank in the US rapidly lost market share after their merger to fast-moving Florida competitors who refused to wait for them to settle down.

❑ In 1998, Boeing wrote off $4 billion and reported its first loss in 50 years following its merger with McDonnell Douglas. While its attention was distracted by implementation of the merger, the Airbus consortium took the opportunity not only to overtake it in terms of sales, but also to win a prestigious £3 billion contract with British Airways – the first time BA had placed a big order with anyone but Boeing.

The only guaranteed winners tend to be the shareholders of the company being purchased, who usually make windfall profits due to the premium paid for their shares. As a not particularly high example, Exxon paid £19.8 billion more than the market thought Mobil was worth before its bid, representing a 34 percent premium (and prior to the bid, Mobil's share price had already stood at an all-time high).

Exxon needs to achieve a return on capital on its 'investment' in Mobil of 17.6 percent by the year 2003. However, Mobil's highest annual return since 1993 has been only 12.2 percent. Can Exxon really achieve this?

Such purchases are, in a way, akin to a ceasefire. Just as a cease-fire can often lead to a truce in which hostilities cease permanently without either side claiming outright victory, M&A is often an admission that the trench warfare being fought between the two companies involved has produced a stalemate. In such a situation, the easiest option becomes the removal of the competition that caused the conflict in the first place. US tycoon John D Rockefeller realized that one surefire way of dealing with competitors was to buy them, thus removing their threat at a stroke.

Likewise in the 1920s, when the growing auto industry in the US was having trouble selling cars in cities because of the availability of cheap, easy travel via electric trolleys, General Motors, Standard Oil, Phillips Petroleum, Firestone Tires and Mack trucks employed the Rapid Transit Company to travel around the country, buying up small trolley franchisees and closing them down. The competition was removed at a stroke.

Something similar is happening with many of today's mergers. Some of the deals, such as Vodafone's takeover of AirTouch and AOL's purchase of Netscape, are offensive in nature in growing markets where size will be important when the inevitable shakeout arrives.

However others (and this includes Exxon/Mobil, BP/Amoco, Chrysler/Daimler, Ford/Volvo, Renault/Nissan, BAe/Marconi, Citicorp/Travelers and the European bank mergers) have taken place in industries that are declining and/or are bloated with over-capacity. Consider the following:

❑ There will be fewer defense companies in the twenty-first century than at present as defense spending continues its decline since the end of the Cold War.
❑ Excess capacity and ever-decreasing oil prices mean that there will be fewer oil companies. Mobil's sales declined from £43 billion in 1996 to £33 billion two years later.
❑ The global car industry has about 30 percent overcapacity, which means that plant closures and staff layoffs on a massive scale are inevitable at some point. Western Europe alone has capacity for 20

million cars, but only sells 13 million; even at the peak of an industry cycle, most plants struggle to achieve 70 percent utilization.

❑ A variety of new entrants to the financial markets means that traditional financial service companies are struggling to hold on to customers who are deserting to these lower-cost alternatives.

The creation of the euro has in theory turned the participating countries into one large, single banking market, making high-cost national banks vulnerable to lower-cost international competitors. However, the wave of M&A activity that is taking place is all happening within national borders rather than across them, and as such appears to be deeply conservative in nature and a shameless attempt to secure local monopolies rather than inject competition into the sector.

Is it a coincidence that Glaxo's plans to merge with Bristol Myers Squibb come after a year in which its sales growth was a disappointing 1 percent, because of the loss of its patent on one of its top-selling products, and the sales growth of its target was 11 percent? John D Rockefeller would certainly have approved.

Such activity is in one very real sense an admission by the companies concerned that they are bankrupt in terms of ideas on how to compete effectively. For many chairmen, CEOs and managing directors, M&A activity is quite simply the easiest 'strategic' option and one that panders to their egos and gets their photographs in the newspapers. If you think that egos do not play a major part in M&A, you only have to look at the proposed merger in 1998 between Glaxo and SmithKline Beecham, which collapsed in acrimony after the two companies could not agree on who should get the top jobs (not much concentration on shareholder value there!).

However, long-term profitability does not come from factory closures, staff layoffs, capacity reduction and other cost-cutting exercises. Long-term growth does not come from buying up the competition to increase a company's size artificially.

Both result in short-term improvements, but what happens in the following year? Does the company continue to swallow up the competition until it becomes a bloated monolith, prevented from becoming a monopoly only by government legislation?

Size can be crucial, as has been clearly demonstrated in Chapter 2, but this is only the case if a company can use that size (and the resources it generates) to stay at the top. Size for the sake of it is simply not a viable long-term strategy. Many of the companies reported in the financial press in recent months as stagnating or having financial difficulties are huge in their respective markets (e.g. Marks & Spencer, J Sainsbury, Shell, Boeing, British Airways). For all the reasons explained in Chapter 2, big companies tend to become slow moving, bureaucratic, myopic and resistant to change, confident that their sheer size will protect them from changes in the marketplace.

The only real way for a company to succeed over the long term is to defeat its rivals in open competition, by possessing a SWAT and adding value in the eyes of its customers better (or faster, or cheaper, or all three) than its competitors can.

This necessitates a return to basics for many companies, and a complete re-evaluation of the platforms on which they compete. For many, what worked in the 1980s and the 1990s will not work in the twenty-first century.

❑ The traditional value chains of PC manufacturers will not be able to compete with that of Dell Computer without radical surgery.

❑ British Airways' cost-heavy structures will make it difficult for it to compete with lean, hungry competitors such as easyJet and Debonair for anyone other than business travel passengers, and its bureaucracy will make it slow in dealing with the likes of Virgin Atlantic.

❑ Traditional high-street banks such as Barclays and NatWest will continue to lose customers to the likes of First Direct and new market entrants such as the grocery multiples, and the banking industry will face dramatic restructuring. A recent report by Deloitte Consulting forecasts that as many as 3600 of their 11,000 existing branches will be closed by 2005.

❑ Major companies from all sectors of the British retail industry will have to reinvent themselves completely when Wal-Mart continues its European expansion into the UK.

❑ All retailers will need to reinvent themselves as a result of the coming electronic commercial revolution, as consumers increasingly buy via the Internet.

❑ Washing machine manufacturers will have to do the same when James Dyson launches his new product, which will do to them what the cyclonic vacuum cleaner did to its competitors.

Once this realization sets in, these companies (and thousands of others) will have to face the unpalatable fact that their financial health, and perhaps even their survival, will depend on their declaring 'war' and actually taking the battle to their competition.

No doubt for most this will entail a direct, unimaginative strategy based around price competition (after all, experience has taught them that their customers are only interested in price, so why not?). For most this will also entail defeat, though not until they have experienced a series of poor annual financial results culminating in their being purchased as part of the next wave of M&A.

The companies that not only survive the battle but also emerge from the battlefield victorious will be those that follow the lessons outlined in this book. The most successful will be those that employ several lessons at once, combining them in a cohesive competitive strategy.

Dell Computer is an excellent example of a company that clearly demonstrates a number of strategic lessons. When Michael Dell first founded the company in his college dorm in 1984, it was a minnow selling computer components. Selling direct via advertisements in PC magazines, he eliminated the 10–15 percent mark-up usually earned by traditional channels, and soon graduated to selling complete PCs.

To have tried to compete directly with the existing PC manufacturers for the same customers would have been the equivalent of a **head-to-head combat** strategy, and would also have represented commercial suicide.

His product did not complement theirs in any way; it was a direct competitor. A raiding combat strategy, aimed at selling to the same customers, would also have been doomed to failure. He therefore chose a raiding logistics strategy, whereby he concentrated initially on a sector of the market that was ignored by the major manufacturers, i.e. non-brand-conscious customers who would buy a PC with an unknown name if it was cheap enough.

Dell's policy of eliminating the middleman also meant that he did not need to manufacture a machine until he had an order for it, so his finished stocks were virtually non-existent, keeping costs down and enhancing his ability to be price competitive.

By 1986 the company had sales of $60 million, and Dell changed its focus. Now the targeted market segment became large corporate customers, backed by an uncompromising level of service that enabled the company to personalize its PCs to the requirements of each individual customer, again made possible by the fact that the PCs were made to order. Dell had now achieved the difficult task of combining all three methods of achieving a competitive SWAT: low cost, differentiation and focus!

However, the strategy had to change. By aiming at large corporate customers, it was no longer operating in a segment of the market that the competition was happy to ignore. It was now adopting a raiding combat strategy, where it was in direct head-to-head competition with the larger computer manufacturers for part of the same customers' business, by using a competitive SWAT that enabled it to add value for the customer in both service and price. For the next seven years the company went from strength to strength.

The road to victory seldom runs smooth, and the company became obsessed with maintaining its amazing growth. In 1993 it temporarily succumbed to its competitors' propaganda (i.e. that direct sales would never be more than a niche) and branched out to sell to consumers via mass-market retailers such as Wal-Mart and CompUSA. Sales hit $2.8 billion in 1994, but the company lost $36 million.

The main problem lay with Dell's desire to lower prices continually, using the benefits of its strategy of low-cost leadership. Through having very little parts inventory, it was used to being able to pass on reductions in component costs to customers very quickly, but in the retail trade it had to follow the industry's common practice of compensating dealers for any reduction in the selling price of a PC.

Realizing that it had made a major mistake and was in danger of becoming another run-of-the-mill PC manufacturer, the company made the brave decision to withdraw from retail, and both competitors and industry 'experts' claimed that it had plateaued. However, now focused with laser-like intensity on its direct sales/low-cost model, it defied their pessimism and continued to grow.

Dell's attempts to enter the consumer and small business market had finally brought it into direct confrontation with the rest of the industry with a **head-to-head combat** strategy. This was retained, but the target in this sector now became second- or third-time purchasers who knew what they wanted, and the method of getting to them became the Internet.

Dell has now grown to a size where it competes directly across the board in the PC market for large and small businesses, consumers and government contracts.

One would think that having witnessed the company's meteoric rise, other PC manufacturers would have adopted a similar model. However, what has made Dell's strategy virtually competitor proof is the fact that it has fought its battles on terrain that did not suit the competition.

Companies such as HP, Compaq and Digital could not imitate its direct sales, low-cost model without alienating the very people on whom they depended for their existing sales, i.e. their dealers. The only way in which they could have done this would have been to establish completely new organizations (as British Airways did with Go) or to buy one that already operated in that way, such as Gateway, a relatively small PC manufacturer with a similar model to Dell.

In conclusion, Dell has managed to combine all three routes to achieving a competitive SWAT. It used terrain that negated its larger competitors' size, initially adopted a clearly defined **raiding logistics** strategy that was appropriate to its own size, and has moved to a head-to-head combat strategy now that its success has given it the resources to do so. With such a structured approach mirroring the advice given in this book, is it any wonder that the company has been so successful?

By drawing an analogy between commercial competition and warfare, this book has concentrated on the factor common to both – the aim of defeating an opponent before it can defeat you. Many companies may not like this approach and prefer to take a less harsh view of the commercial world, but a large percentage of those that have been forced into bankruptcy or been merged/purchased would certainly have benefited had they adopted it.

To give the closing words to the Swiss Antoine-Henri Jomini, a Napoleonic officer who in some people's minds rivals Clausewitz for the title of 'father' of western military thought:

> *It is true that theories cannot teach men with mathematical precision what they should do in every possible case; but it is also certain that they will always point out the errors which should be avoided ... for these rules become, in the hands of skilful generals ... means of almost certain success.*

BIBLIOGRAPHY

BUSINESS

Carlzon, Jan (1989) *Moments of Truth*, HarperCollins.

Clark, Jim (1999) *Netscape Time: The Making of the Billion Dollar Start-Up that Took on Microsoft*, St Martin's Press.

Daffy, Chris (1999) *Once a Customer, Always a Customer*, Oak Tree Press.

De Kare-Silver, Michael (1998) *e-shock: the Electronic Shopping Revolution*, Macmillan.

Dell, Michael (1999) *Direct from Dell*, HarperCollins Business.

Dyson, James (1998) *Against the Odds*, Orion Business.

Freiberg, Kevin & Freiberg, Jacquelin (1997) *Nuts! Southwest Airline's Crazy Recipe for Success*, Orion Business.

Gale, Bradley T (1994) *Managing Customer Value: Creating Quality and Service that Customers Can See*, Free Press.

Gates, Bill (1996) *The Road Ahead*, Penguin.

Gilmore, Fiona (1999) *Brand Warriors: Corporate Leaders Share Their Winning Strategies*, HarperCollins Business.

Grove, Andrew (1998) *Only the Paranoid Survive*, HarperCollins.

Hamel, Gary & Prahalad, CK (1996) *Competing for the Future*, Harvard Business School Press.

Hamel, Gary & Heene, Amie (1994) *Competence-Based Competition*, John Wiley.

Huguet, Jim (1999) *Great Companies, Great Returns: the Breakthrough Investing Strategy that Produces Great Returns over the Long-term Cycle of Bull and Bear Markets*, Broadway.

Jackson, Tim (1998) *Inside Intel*, HarperCollins.

Nalebuff, Barry J & Brandenburger, Adam M (1997) *Co-opetition*, HarperCollins.

Naumann, Earl (1994) *Creating Customer Value*, Van Nostrand Reinhold.

Porter, Michael E (1998) *Competitive Advantage: Creating and Sustaining Superior Performance*, Free Press.

Porter, Michael E (1998) *Competitive Strategy: Techniques for Analyzing Industries and Competitors*, Free Press.

Reid, Peter C (1989) *Well Made in America: Lessons from Harley-Davidson on Being the Best*, McGraw-Hill.

Ries, Al (1997) *Focus*, HarperCollins.

Saunders, Rebecca (1999) *Business the Amazon.com Way: Secrets of the World's Most Astonishing Web Business*, Capstone.

Stringer Vance, Sandra & Scott, Roy V (1994) *Wal-Mart: a History of Sam Walton's Retail Phenomenon*, Twayne.

Walton, Sam (1994) *Made in America*, Bantam.

Womack, James P, Jones, Daniel T & Roos, Daniel (1990) *The Machine that Changed the World*, Simon & Schuster.

MILITARY

Anderson, Duncan & Holmes, Richard (1998) *Hutchinson Atlas of Battle Plans: Before and After*, Helicon.

Bradford, Ernle (1993) *Thermopylae: the Battle for the West*, Da Capo.

Burn, Alfred H (1999) *The Crecy War*, Wordsworth Editions.

Chandler, David (1989) *Marlborough as Military Commander*, Spellmount.

Clausewitz, Carl von (1997) *On War, Vols I–III*, Wordsworth Editions.

Davis, William C (1991) *The Battlefields of the Civil War*, Salamander.

Delaney, John (1996) *The Blitzkrieg Campaigns*, Cassell Military.

Fuller, JFC (1998) *The Generalship of Alexander the Great*, Wordsworth Editions.

Healy, Mark (1994) *Cannae: 216BC*, Osprey.

Howard, Michael (1983) *Clausewitz*, Oxford Paperbacks.

Keegan, John (1998) *The First World War*, Hutchinson.

Lane Fox, Robert (1986) *Alexander the Great*, Penguin.

MacDonald, John (1992) *Great Battles of the Civil War*, Collier.

Mallett, M (1999) *The Italian Wars, 1494–1559*, Addison Wesley Longman.

Morris, JE & Prestwich, Michael (1998) *The Welsh Wars Of Edward I*, Sutton.

Nosworthy, Brent (1996) *Battle Tactics of Napoleon and his Enemies*, Constable.

Oman, Sir Charles (1998) *A History of the Art of War in the Middle Ages, Vol II: 1278–1485AD*, Greenhill.

Regan, Geoffrey (1991) *The Guinness Book of Military Blunders*, Guinness World Records.

Schwartzkopf, Norman (1993) *It Doesn't Take a Hero*, Bantam.

Sumption, Jonathan (1999) *The Hundred Years War, Vol I: Trial by Battle*, Faber & Faber.

Tzu, Sun (1981) *The Art of War*, Shambhala.

Wilson, Sir Robert (1996) *French Invasion of Russia*, First Empire.

Windrow, Martin & Chappell, Mike (1998) *The Indochina War, 1946–1954*, Osprey.

INDEX

CORPORATE COMBAT™: THE MONTHLY ELECTRONIC NEWSLETTER

Corporate Combat™ is a monthly electronic newsletter written by Nick Skellon for executives and entrepreneurs operating in competitive markets who recognize that business is 'war with the gloves off' and who want the opportunity to learn more about the concepts outlined in this book. Over time, *Corporate Combat*™ will become a participative forum that will enable like-minded people to share views as well as keep abreast of what is happening at the cutting edge of competitive strategy

Corporate Combat™ is published direct to your e-mail address. Each issue contains a wealth of information on how companies from Europe and the USA are pursuing the strategies outlined in this book, and the lessons you can learn from their successes (and failures). Why try to reinvent the wheel when you can learn from the experiences of others? In addition, it will also give you the opportunity to share your views with other subscribers on what is happening in the real competitive world in which you operate.

Among other features, forthcoming issues will contain the following:

✓ Examples of how successful armies from history developed and used SWATs that enabled them to defeat their enemies, from the Norman 'combined-arms army' at the battle of Hastings, to the 'thin red line' employed by Wellington in the Peninsular War, to the Gulf War.
✓ Case studies of how companies such as GEC and Ford are 'inventing the future before it arrives' and restructuring themselves in order to deal with the challenges of the future.
✓ How armies have successfully used terrain to defeat larger opponents and how some companies are using the same tactic today.
✓ Stories of how successful companies are achieving meteoric growth via a competitive SWAT based on differentiation: what they are doing and how they are doing it.
✓ Information on how others have structured themselves in a way that avoids the ungainly cost structure of their competitors, undercutting them as a result, and how you can follow the same route to success.
✓ How fighting defensively has enabled small armies to defeat much larger ones, and how small/medium-sized companies are doing the same against bigger competitors.
✓ Why an increasing number of well-established companies such as British Airways, Boeing and Marks & Spencer are heading for box 4 on the Competitive SWAT Matrix: what they did wrong, how they are trying to turn things around and the lessons you can learn from them.
✓ Examples of companies that have chosen combat strategies, and others that are implementing one of logistics, and whether they are implementing them in head-to-head or raiding fashion.
✓ Subscribers' letters and views on any aspect of competitive strategy, including their own experiences and practical advice.

No-Quibble Money-Back Guarantee
If at any time you feel that (for whatever reason) you no longer wish to receive *Corporate Combat*™, simply inform us in writing or by e-mail and we will immediately refund the unused part of your subscription.

Get your first trial issue absolutely FREE of charge!
The first issue is published in January 1999 and a year's subscription costs only £50, or less than £1 per week! You can get the first issue absolutely FREE without further obligation by e-mailing us at the following address:
     nickskellon@compuserve.com

Subscribe now for less than 80p per week
Alternatively, if you subscribe now, before 31 December 1999, you can get 15 months' subscription for the price of 12, equating to less than 80p per week. Just fill in the details below and send the completed subscription form together with a sterling cheque made out to 'NP Skellon' to the following address:
     Corporate Combat, 21a Elbow Lane, Formby, Merseyside L37 4AB, UK.

You will receive your first issue within one week of our receiving your cheque and details. We will not bank your cheque until you have received your first issue. Your details will not be passed on to any third party. (NB: PLEASE COMPLETE IN BLOCK CAPITALS.)

Surname: ....….......... Initials: ....
Title: Mr/Mrs/Miss/Ms Other: ....
Address:...
....
Town/City: .... County/State: ....
Post/Zip Code: ....…......... Country: ....
Tel: .... Fax: ....
e-mail address:...
(NB: Please ensure that your e-mail address is correct. *Corporate Combat*™ is an electronic newsletter and as such is only published via the Internet. Readers cannot subscribe without an e-mail address.)

I enclose a cheque for £50 made out to NP Skellon. If the date below is 31 December 1999 or earlier, this entitles me to 15 months' subscription to *Corporate Combat*™, otherwise it will be for 12 months. I understand that the unused portion of this subscription is refundable to me at any time if I inform you in writing or by e-mail that I no longer wish to subscribe for any reason at all.

Signature: ....…..................
Date (dd/mm/yy) : ....
NB: Please tick this box if you require an invoice.   ❏